They Eat That?

They Eat That?

A CULTURAL ENCYCLOPEDIA OF WEIRD AND EXOTIC FOOD FROM AROUND THE WORLD

Jonathan Deutsch, Editor with Natalya Murakhver, Contributing Editor

ABC-CLIO

Santa Barbara, California • Denver, Colorado • Oxford, England

Library of Congress Cataloging-in-Publication Data

They eat that? : a cultural encyclopedia of weird and exotic food from around the world / Jonathan Deutsch, editor and Natalya Murakhver, contributing editor
     p. cm.
  Includes index.
  ISBN 978-0-313-38058-7 (hardback) —
  ISBN 978-0-313-38059-4 (ebook)
1. Food habits—Miscellanea—Encyclopedias. 2. Cooking—Miscellanea—Encyclopedias. I. Deutsch, Jonathan. II. Murakhver, Natalya.
  GT2850.T44 2012
  394.1'2003—dc23   2011032630

ISBN: 978-0-313-38058-7
EISBN: 978-0-313-38059-4

16 15 14 13 12   1 2 3 4 5

This book is also available on the World Wide Web as an eBook.
Visit www.abc-clio.com for details.

ABC-CLIO, LLC
130 Cremona Drive, P.O. Box 1911
Santa Barbara, California 93116-1911

This book is printed on acid-free paper ∞

Manufactured in the United States of America

The publisher has done its best to make sure the instructions and/or recipes in this book are correct. However, users should apply judgment and experience when preparing recipes, especially parents and teachers working with young people. The publisher accepts no responsibility for the outcome of any recipe included in this volume and assumes no liability for, and is released by readers from, any injury or damage resulting from the strict adherence to, or deviation from, the directions and/or recipes herein. The publisher is not responsible for any reader's specific health or allergy needs that may require medical supervision, nor for any adverse reactions to the recipes contained in this book. All yields are approximations.

Contents

List of Entries

Preface

Eating is the most intimate act one commits. Internalizing food as nourishment and pleasure is a great commonality across time and space. Yet it is striking how the content of what is considered palatable or draws disgust varies among people. This notion is what inspired us to develop *They Eat That?*, an homage to the myriad cuisines and dishes one encounters as one travels around the planet, and often, just across the street, as food shrinks the distance between populations.

As adventurous food lovers ourselves, we challenged chefs and food writers, food studies students, and scholars to dish up their most bizarre or curious entrees; though to those who eat them, they may just be dinner.

From 1,000-year-old eggs to camel to casu marzu, this collection tries not to shock readers (though some entries may be particularly shocking), but rather hook them by introducing fascinating food habits that may be in one's own backyard or on the other side of the world. Some, like the entry on insects, take an item found everywhere and consider how it is consumed as food by various people, from chocolate-covered ants to roasted grasshoppers to the shellac used in making jelly beans. Others, like Vieux Bologne, a particularly potent cheese, are specific foods from particular regions.

The list of entries came through surveying our colleagues on food studies list-servs: "What are some foods that a typical U.S. or Canadian student would find weird?" was the framing question. Those responses that were mentioned multiple times, or those of particular interest, became entries in this volume. These responses ranged from everyday foods that we might take for granted (for example, bone marrow, found inside bones, steaks, and chops), unusual cultural preparations like hákarl (fermented shark), foods common worldwide but with somewhat of a gross-out factor to many (eel), and some foods that most would not consider foods (urine, earth).

The wonderful thing about the study of food (or the frustrating thing, depending on your perspective) is that it never ends. There will always be a food of which you have never heard, and just when you feel you have mastery of a topic, more and more new products are introduced to the market. The study of food is a commitment to a lifetime of learning. Similarly, this volume is not intended to be comprehensive but rather reflective of the diversity and complexity of the foods we eat. This book could easily be 10 times larger and still omit important foods.

We aim to establish the cultural identity of each entry. Who eats it and how? Foods have individual meanings, and this was our opportunity to examine them. What is this dish's significance? Is it a food with health associations? What is the historical significance—how did it come to be? When is the dish generally eaten— is it an everyday item or a ceremonial food? Our hope is that you use these teaser entries to become fascinated by the study of food and culture and keep exploring. To that end, each entry has suggestions for further reading.

For those who want to taste these foods, we have included adapted or original recipes where possible. Many of the ingredients may be challenging to find (and certainly not at your local grocery store) but we hope you will not let that deter you!

There are a few ways to use this book—it can be read cover-to-cover; it can serve as a reference for projects and papers; it is great to browse for ideas; and you can even challenge yourself to expand your palate by trying a new food every week (though please skip the human entry if you are taking this approach).

Finally, the strength of this volume is in its contributors, people thinking, writing, and eating food all over the world, who took time to share their passion for these foods of their own culture or the cultures they love. Our deepest appreciation for their hard work.

Bon appetit and let the journey begin!

Introduction

When I teach cooking and food studies courses, I often have students meet one another on the first day of class by conducting a food interview. There is only one rule that students have to observe: every question of the interview must be about food. So a question like, "Where do you live?" would be out of bounds, but "What are your favorite foods?" "What did you have for breakfast today?" or "If you were stranded on a desert island and could only have one food for the rest of your life, what would it be?" are all fair game.

The answers are illuminating. Students connect with each other instantly and meaningfully in a way not possible with standard introduction questions like "Where did you go to high school?" or "What's your major?" Food is a potent medium that opens up so many other issues. Starting with food, students launch into stories about their ethnic heritage, their childhood and family dynamics, gender roles and division of labor at home, their neighborhood structure and urban planning, their schedules at school and work, their deep-seated likes and dislikes, health conditions, allergies, nutrition concerns and weight loss goals, finances, budgets and career goals, and so much more. The French gastronome Brillat-Savarin quipped, in 1825, "Tell me what you eat, and I will tell you what you are" (often misquoted as "You are what you eat"). He understood the social and cultural power of food well.

By far the most fascinating question that comes up in this exercise, though, is, "What are some things you do *not* eat?" If asking about what we eat can reveal something about ourselves, asking what we do not eat and why we avoid it introduces even more deeply held opinions, passions, ideas, and emotions. Religion, culture, nutrition, upbringing, childhood memory, sensory perception, morals, taboo, status, and more are wrapped up in these simple responses to what one would not eat. Who knew that a grasshopper, fermented beans, or a barbecued rib could be so fraught! Further fascinating is that, inevitably, food that is the grossest thing imaginable for one student (perhaps pork for a Muslim student), is the desert island food for another.

These foods, familiar to some, strange to others, but ultimately eaten by someone somewhere, never fail to fascinate and are the subject of this encyclopedia. Beyond the shock value, however, of eating a cheese covered in maggots, for example (see casu marzu, p. 44), it is our hope that you as a reader ask some key questions:

Why?
How did this food come to be eaten?
What is the cultural significance?
And most important, where can I try some?

Because in reading this book, an open mind is the difference between a voyeuristic and ethnocentric approach ("Eww, they eat that? Gross!") and an educational touristic one ("They eat that? Interesting. I want to learn more about the food, the people, and the culture").

Why Food?

The need for food and drink is our most powerful biological drive. Quite simply, without it, we die. But food is much more than nutrients allowing us to thrive. The foods we eat—how they are grown, how they come to market, how we procure them, cook them (or buy them cooked), and eat them, including when and with whom—together form our *foodways* or ways with food.

These foodways are shaped by numerous factors. Consider something as simple as what you ate during your last meal. What considerations went into determining why you ate what you did? To name a few: the region of the world in which you live and what foods are available in that region and at what cost; what are the food traditions of that region and are you following them, bucking them, or adapting them; were you home or on the go; were you dining alone or with others; if dining with others, were these peers, colleagues, or family members; who paid for the meal; who prepared it; did the flavors and preparation methods come from your cultural tradition(s) or others; were you trying to reach any health goals; did you have health conditions or food allergies of concern; how were you feeling at the time—adventurous, seeking comfort, happy, sad, celebratory, blasé? Was it a holiday or an ordinary day?

Food is a simple substance necessary for life but also extraordinarily complex and an important signifier of individual or group identity. The foods you eat or avoid communicate with what food scholar Annie Hauck-Lawson calls the *food voice*. If I invite you over for dinner and offer you oysters, champagne, and filet mignon, what is the food saying differently than if I offered you spaghetti and meatballs? And how would the food voice change if the spaghetti were homemade?

In this encyclopedia, the challenge is to go beyond the mere description of the foods to listen to the food voice—what does eating this food say about the people who are eating it? And what does avoiding this food say? Flip through the book now, and choose a food on which to try asking those questions.

What Is Weird?

Some foods, like human flesh (see human, p. 104), are almost universally rejected and considered weird, gross, deplorable, depraved. Others, like lutefisk (p. 139), are considered culturally important to some and strange and unappealing to others. And, of course, many foods beloved by you, the reader, whether it is a peanut butter sandwich for lunch or a breakfast of congee with 1,000-year-old egg (p. 1) may seem weird to others who do not share your personal, family, or cultural tradition.

Often foods we take for granted as normal are, in fact, unusual or even off-putting when you think about them critically. Imagine eating insect vomit. Any volunteers? When you realize that our beloved honey, made from honeybees that eat pollen and then process it through regurgitation is so made, you may look at it differently. The sweet taste and seductive aroma certainly masks its provenance. Or how about a dish made from sour, moldy milk? It may be more familiar as cheese. Put this way it becomes easier to understand why someone from one culture may find a bleu cheese dressing as deplorable as another finds stinky fermented tofu (p. 186).

It becomes critical then to remember throughout this encyclopedia that while weird can be fascinating, it is also relative—weird to you may be snack to me. And vice versa.

Weirdness

Despite the relativity of weirdness, we can, nevertheless, categorize unusual food—beloved by some, hated by others, and totally ridiculous to more—into a few categories. These are arbitrary for sure but most of the weird foods we consider are:

- Animals. People are picky about their meat. In the United States, for example, Americans eat fish and seafood, chicken, beef, pork, veal, lamb, and turkey, and almost nothing else. But there is a host of edible animals eaten throughout the world: insects, snake, lizard, frog, armadillo, rabbit, bear, squirrel, turtle, horse, dog, sea cucumber, seal, camel, and even human. All (and more) are explored in this book.
- Fermented. Fermentation is a process where yeast or bacteria eat the sugar in food and produce alcohol, heat, and carbon dioxide. The thought of bacteria in your food may be off-putting at first, but many of the staples of diets around the world—bread, beer, wine, pickles, yogurt, cheese, sausages, soy sauce, ham, and even chocolate are fermented. Fermentation can yield a variety of

flavors, as illustrated by the list above. The same process can also yield some strongly flavored—often dubbed "weird" foods like kombucha, natto, stinky tofu, poi, hákarl, and fermented walrus flipper.

- Manufactured. Sometimes weird foods are not long-standing culinary traditions but products introduced by creative manufacturers or commercial versions of traditional foods. Canna Cola, Spam, Vegemite, and Salmiakki come to mind.
- Slimy. Often the sensory properties of the food make it seem weird or inapproachable to those unfamiliar with it. Words like slimy and gooey are used for foods like lutefisk, natto, fish eyes, octopus, squid, frog, snake, hákarl, and blood. The image, texture, and mouthfeel of these foods go a long way to putting them high on the weirdness scale.
- Creepy/Crawly. Anthropologist Mary Douglas theorized that taboo foods in the Bible are those that do not confirm to standard categories—for example shellfish are sea creatures but do not swim. Foods like squid, octopus, eel, insects, honey ants, rat, and snake fit into this category. Many people don't quite know what to do with creepy crawly things and eating them may not come to mind right away.
- Body parts. Many people relish the opportunity to eat part of an animal (a ham, for example), but other parts nearby (such as the pig's testicles a few inches from the ham) are weird or gross. Placenta, sex organs, liver, bile, ink, blood, eyes, and air bladder are examples in this encyclopedia.

Invitation

When I was in high school, I hated history and social studies. We spent time learning about wars, politicians, museums, and monuments. The only day I liked was each year we would bring in a food from a culture we were studying. Later, in graduate school, I discovered the field of food studies. Starting with the food—what is being eaten here, how did this come to be, what is the significance, and what does it taste like—introduced what was, to me, a much more meaningful way to learn about history, society, and culture. Why is salt cod eaten in the Caribbean where there is an abundance of fresh fish but not a live cod to be found? How did Spam come to be a culturally significant dish in the State of Hawaii? How did cardamom come to be a standard ingredient in Swedish desserts? How did bagels and lox become such an important Jewish food? Why do women do most of the cooking in the United States, but male chefs dominate the food TV show schedule? Answering these food studies questions necessarily invokes the history and politics that I shied away from in my secondary education, but in a way that makes sense to me.

We invite you to take a similar food studies journey in this encyclopedia, getting hooked first by the *wow* factor—*They Eat That?* And next, by the thoughtful questioning of how things came to be that way, and what it means.

This encyclopedia can be used in a number of ways. We made an effort to recruit not only smart food scholars but scholars who are engaging and entertaining writers. We've read this book cover-to-cover a couple times while putting it together, and it's actually fun! We encourage you to do the same. Of course, as an encyclopedia this book is primarily a reference work and the alphabetical organization allows it to be a helpful aide in working on projects or papers on various cultural food traditions or, we have found, getting ideas about foods and food traditions you may not have known existed. Finally, you may find this book, as we do, a great bedside, travel, or waiting room companion. Flip through, and when your eyebrows raise and you ask yourself, "They *eat* that?" stop and learn more.

A

Ackee

Ackee, sometimes spelled akee, is a bright red tropical fruit. It has three main parts, the exterior pod, and the seeds and the arils (seed coverings) on the inside. During its eight-week maturation process, the ackee pod changes from green to red; when ripe, the fruit blooms exposing shiny black seeds and the edible cream-colored arils. Native to western Africa, the ackee plant arrived in the Caribbean in the 18th century on slave ships, purportedly to feed the captives. In 1793, ackee received its scientific name, *Blighia sapida,* to honor Captain William Bligh, who brought the fruit to England.

Though found in most Caribbean countries, ackee is most commonly associated with Jamaican cooking and further, with the Jamaican Vomiting Sickness (JVS) ackee can induce. Also called Toxic Hypoglycemic Syndrome, JVS only occurs when unripe ackee is consumed. If the aril is eaten before the fruit is ready, it can cause violent vomiting, hypoglycemia, drowsiness, convulsions, coma, and, potentially, death. The cause for this illness was not discovered until 1955 when the toxic amino acid called hypoglycin A could be isolated. The immature green fruit contains the acid at a rate of 10,000 times greater than that in ripe ackee. This acid produces hypoglycemic effects, hence the name; meaning there would be a lower-than-normal amount of glucose in the body. Treating people with JVS, therefore, includes giving them sugary foods to eat as well as easing their other symptoms such as vomiting and dizziness.

Despite its aggressive nature, this fruit has been used for constructive medicinal purposes. In Cuba, the ripe arils are eaten mixed with cinnamon and sugar to help reduce fever and treat dysentery. The extract of the seeds is used in Brazil to expel parasites. In its native region, the Ivory Coast of Africa, the bark of the ackee plant is made into an ointment to relieve back pain, and its leaves are combined with salt to eliminate ulcers. Nutritionally, 100 grams of ripe aril provide about 9 grams of protein and almost 19 grams of fat.

Much food culture surrounds the ackee fruit, especially in Jamaica where it comprises half the national dish of Ackee and Saltfish. The arils are generally boiled about 15 minutes and then scrambled with the fish, chili, onions, and tomatoes. Because it is considered toxic, ackee is subject to import laws, and it is difficult or impossible to find fresh ackee outside the Caribbean; however, the canned fruit is available in West African and Latino specialty stores.

Ackee and Saltfish

Ingredients

1 lb. boneless salt cod, soaked in fresh
   water 1 hour
1 tbsp vegetable oil

Why Saltfish?

Though the Caribbean historically has had an abundance of fresh fish, saltfish, especially salt cod, has become a staple and a delicious complement to ackee. Eating salt cod in the Caribbean is a relic of the triangle trade, when sugar grown on Caribbean island plantations by slaves would be shipped to New England for distillation into rum. In New England, there was an active cod fishery, so cod, preserved by air drying and salting, served as a low-cost nutritious export to Europe and back to the Caribbean.

---

1 scotch bonnet chili, seeded and thinly sliced
2 scallions, thinly sliced
1 tomato, diced
1 19-oz. can ackee
Salt and pepper to taste

1. In a large pot, cover the salt cod with 1 quart of cold water. Bring to a boil and drain. Remove and flake fish.
2. Drain ackee and reserve.
3. In a separate pan, heat the oil over medium heat. Add the chili, scallions, tomato, and onion. Sauté until the onion is translucent, 3 to 4 minutes.
4. Add ackee to the pan along with the fish. Reduce heat to low; cover and cook for about 5 minutes, or until all the flavors are blended. Season with salt and pepper.

Further Reading

Department of Chemistry. "Jamaican Ackee." University of the West Indies. http://www chem.uwimona.edu.jm/.

Goldson, Andrea. "The Ackee Fruit (*Blighia Sapida*) and Its Associated Toxic Effects." *Science Creative Quarterly* (2011). http://www.scq.ubc.ca/the-ackee-fruit-blighia-sapida-and-its-associated-toxic-effects/

Houston, Lynn Marie. *Food Culture in the Caribbean*. Food Culture around the World. New York: Greenwood Press, 2005.

Morton, Julia Frances. *Fruits of Warm Climates*. Miami, FL: J. F. Morton, distributed by Creative Resources Systems, 1987. Horticulture and Landscape Architecture. Purdue University. http://www.hort.purdue.edu/newcrop/morton/akee.html.

Willinsky, Helen. *Jerk from Jamaica Barbecue Caribbean Style*. New York: Ten Speed Press, 2007.

Eleanor Barczak

Ankimo

Ankimo is monkfish liver. A common food throughout Japan, the word *ankimo* is the shortened name of *ankou* (monkfish), *no* (of), and *kimo* (liver). Still a relatively new ingredient in the United States, ankimo is often described by westerners as comparable to foie gras, because it too is liver and when cooked has a silky texture similar to pâté, but the flavor is distinct, more like rich shellfish. It is customarily steamed, then chilled, rather than served raw, and it is typically served as an appetizer, or in the case of *izakayas* (casual drinking establishments), an accompaniment to sake, like tapas. A serving usually consists of one to three medallion-shaped slices about 1 inch in diameter, a ½ inch thick, in a dish with ponzu (a citrus) sauce and chopped scallions.

Monkfish (*Lophius piscatorius*, also called goosefish, anglerfish, and ankoh) is a toothy bottom-feeding fish. It is caught wild off the shores of Japan as well as in the Atlantic Ocean. With a wide mouth and tentacles, the monkfish, which grows up to four feet long, is not a pretty catch, which is why its head is usually removed before it reaches the market. Additionally, most of the meat is in the tail of the fish. Firm and white, the tail has been referred to as a poor man's lobster. A monkfish's liver is relatively large for the size of the fish. Freshness is important when selecting monkfish liver. It should be firm, not wobbly, and pink in color with its thin membrane intact. One liver yields about one serving of ankimo.

Curing imparts additional flavor to the ankimo. After being rinsed in water, they are packed in salt for about one hour, then rinsed again and soaked in sake for another hour—ridding it of much of the fishy aroma. The livers are then packed or rolled into a cylinder of tin foil, forming the livers into a compact and sliceable cake. The whole roll is then steamed for 10 to 15 minutes. Once cooled, it can be kept for a day or two and sliced to serve. The ankimo flakes apart with an effortless pinch of the chopsticks.

If one is lucky enough to catch a whole monkfish, making ankimo is a delicious way to utilize offal, but livers on their own can be difficult to obtain. For this reason, because the livers are very perishable, and because it is somewhat labor intensive, ankimo is consumed in restaurants more so than at home.

Ankimo contains vitamins A and B12 but is slightly higher in calories and fat than monkfish filet. Gaining mainstream acceptance in the United States as an eating fish, monkfish is now on the Seafood Watchlist for overfishing. Also, harvested with bottom trawls, weighted nets have been found to damage seafloor habitats, making fishing monkfish and eating ankimo on a regular basis not a sustainable option.

Ankimo

This dish should be served as an appetizer or accompaniment to sake. Ankimo can be made one day in advance and stored

---

Monkfish, Anglerfish, Goosefish: What's in a Name?

According to the Oxford English Dictionary (OED), the origin of the term *monkfish* comes from "the supposed resemblance of the head of the fish to that of a cowled monk." *Anglerfish*, on the other hand, a term used to describe the same species, refers to the way the fish catches prey—by dangling its luminescent appendage in front of its mouth to lure smaller fish, not unlike an angler (fisherman) with a lure. As for goosefish, yet another name by which monkfish is known, the OED gives little guidance. The editors leave that to the reader.

*in the refrigerator. Once cooked and
chilled simply slice and serve with a
drizzle of ponzu and scallions.*

Ingredients

1 lb. fresh monkfish livers
1 cup salt
2 cups sake (for cooking)
6 oz. ponzu sauce
3 chopped scallions

1. Clean the livers by rinsing under cold,
   running water. Pat dry.
2. Sprinkle the livers with salt until
   completely coated, and let sit for
   1 hour to cure.
3. Rinse again in cold water, and pat dry.
4. Place the livers in a medium-size bowl
   and pour the sake on top. The sake
   should cover all of the livers. Let marinate in the sake for 1 hour. This step
   takes away any fishiness and mildly
   flavors the livers.
5. The livers must now be formed into
   a cylinder, which makes them easy to
   slice, the way you would a pate. To do
   this, place the livers on a sheet of tinfoil lined with plastic wrap. Roll them
   up in the tinfoil tightly, to a diameter
   of about 2 inches. It will be about 10
   inches long (looking similar in shape
   to a salami). This mold is now the
   shape your ankimo will conform to
   once it is steamed.
6. Place your ankimo mold in a steamer
   and allow to cook for 15 to 20 minutes. When steaming is complete, let
   the mold cool and refrigerate until it is
   time to eat.
7. To serve, remove your ankimo mold
   from the refrigerator and peel back the

tinfoil and plastic. Cut three ½-inch
slices per serving. Plate and drizzle
each one with 2 tbsp ponzu and
chopped scallions.

Further Reading

Burros, Marian. "And Now, Will America
Take to the 'Other Foie Gras'?" *New York
Times,* February 11, 1998. http://www.
nytimes.com/1998/02/11/dining/and-now-
will-america-take-to-the-other-foie-gras.
html.

Monterey Bay Aquarium Seafood Watch.
http://www.montereybayaquarium.org/cr/
seafoodwatch.aspx.

Sadie Flateman

Armadillo

Armadillos are mammals that began their
journey to the plate in South America. The
name means "little armored one" in Spanish, and it belongs to the order Cingulata
and the family Dasypodidae. They are not
rodents or reptiles, and their shell is actually
bone. There are 20 varieties of armadillo,
but only 2 outside of South America. The
nine-banded armadillo (*Dasypus novem-
cinctus*) is the only one found beyond the
southernmost part of Mexico. Other varieties are eaten throughout South America,
but some are increasingly scarce. Armadillo is also consumed by some Asian cultures as high-priced imported exotic fare
or embraced by immigrant communities in
the United States. Frozen armadillo meat
can be found in the Manhattan and San
Francisco Chinatowns.

Beneath the infamous armor, the armadillo's meat has a light, almost pork-like
hue and tastes similar to a rich and oily

version of that meat and also a bit like rodent or reptile. It has a musty and gamey aroma that is influenced by its diet of plants in addition to ants, beetles, and grubs. Despite its smell, the armadillo has a subtle flavor.

During the Great Depression, the armadillo was referred to as a Hoover hog when many had to resort to eating armadillo meat. The animal's similar behavior and comparable gamey taste to rodent obviously spawned its other glorified moniker of possum on the half shell. Though the phrase Hoover hog was pejorative toward then president Herbert Hoover's failed promise of a chicken in every pot, the armadillo has become an iconic meat, finding its way into chili and barbecue at festivals in Texas and through the southeastern United States. In the Louisiana Cajun country, it would likely be prepared with a sauce piquante containing an aggressive amount of cayenne, black, and crushed pepper. The nine-banded armadillo consumed in this area is approximately 2½ feet long and weighs 12 to 17 pounds. The armadillo was only introduced to the United States in the 1850s, but its population has thrived and has spread beyond the southern states, though it remains to be seen if it has become food in the new areas. All said and done, once its bony exterior is done away with, it is ready for various preparations, and can be treated similarly to pork.

In the Yucatan state of Mexico, it is considered a delicacy and is prepared *pibil* style, which is traditionally a pork dish. It is rubbed with achiote (annatto seed), spices, and sour orange juice and roasted in an underground pit with banana leaves or braised with the same ingredients. In the states of Guerrero and Veracruz the meat is seasoned with *hoja santa*, a leaf with an anise-like quality, and in Oaxaca it is roasted in a guajillo chili marinade. Slow roasting on sticks over open fire is a fine way to treat armadillo and is how they prepare it in Colombia. It can be found simply boiled in its shell, then hacked into pieces before being coated in flour and flash fried in the Amazon basin of Bolivia. Due to a great deal of fat between the muscles, the armadillo can be prepared successfully in many different ways.

It is worth noting that the armadillo does carry some bacteria and is a known carrier of leprosy. Though this might dissuade the squeamish, as long as the meat is cooked thoroughly, there isn't much concern.

Armadillo Pibil

In the Yucatan, the armadillo is known as huech. Pork is the most common preparation of this recipe, but prior to the Spanish introduction of pigs, armadillo and other game were used. The armadillo is now considered a delicacy and eaten only rarely, but its rich and oily meat is a perfect match for tart and typical Yucatan dish.

Ingredients

1 armadillo, shelled and butchered into
  2-inch chunks
1 cup achiote paste
Head of garlic, roasted
2 red onions, 1 halved and sliced, 1 diced
1 medium green cabbage, chopped
16 Seville oranges, juiced, about 4 cups
4 large banana leaves
Salt and pepper to taste

1. Mix achiote with 2 cups of orange juice, onion, salt, and pepper. Then marinate armadillo for 4 hours or overnight.
2. Preheat oven to 300°F. Line baking dish with 2 banana leaves, then add armadillo and head of roasted garlic and additional cup of orange juice. Cover with 2 more banana leaves and foil. Put in oven and roast for 2 to 2½ hours until tender.
3. In separate bowls, mix diced red onion with ¼ cup orange juice, and cabbage with the remaining ¾ cup of orange juice. Season with salt, toss, and let sit at room temperature.
4. Serve armadillo with black beans, warm tortillas, pickled cabbage, and onions.

Further Reading

Kalmbach, E. *The Armadillo: Its Relation to Agriculture and Game*. U.S. Fish and Wildlife Service, 1943.

Pembleton, Seliesa. *The Armadillo*. Minneapolis, MN: Dillon Press, 1992.

Alex Yellan

Aroids

Aroids, or taro, are ornamental, edible, and medical plants and belong to the Arum family of plants in botany known as Araceae. The main centers of origin and diversity are tropical Asia and tropical America. There are approximately 3,200 aroid species known, and each has its own botanical distinction and features. Aroids are popular ornamental plants, but at the same time are used as food, medicine, and animal fodder.

Although most aroids are edible, the most popular species cultivated for food are varieties of *L. colocasia esculenta, alocasia, cyrtosperma,* and *xanthosoma* spp. Aroids are consumed by between 400 million and 600 million people in and from the tropics.

Apart from the scientific names in literature, various languages, and oral tradition, names for aroids many times overlap and tend to be very confusing. As ornamental plants, aroid is the general accepted term used in botanical circles. If referred to as a food plant, commonly the generic Austronesian, the term *taro* is applied. *Colocasia* and *xanthosoma* varieties are the most important taro food crops, and both are known by many overlapping and different names.

Colocasia taro common names are taro, dasheen, eddo(e), elephant ear malanga, tayoba, and cocoyam. *Xanthosoma* taro common names include tannia, tannier, yautía, malanga, tayoba, and (new) cocoyam.

The beginnings of Araceae are in the Cretaceous period when early aroids formed colonies in swampy areas of tropical regions. Ever since the Cretaceous period, which started almost 140 million years ago and lasted 65 million years, aroids have remained predominantly a tropical rainforest plant. As its domestication and cultivation had already occurred when rice and wheat were just weeds, taro is probably the oldest cultivated crop.

Colocasia, alocasia, and *cyrtosperma* taro are believed to originate in Asia, from where they spread eastward to other regions with homogeneous equatorial climates. From Southeast and eastern Asia and the Pacific Islands, it probably diffused west to Madagascar and Africa, where it expanded to the Mediterranean, the Caribbean, and the Americas. Archeological evidence suggests that *colocasia* taro was already in use on the Solomon Islands approximately 28,000 years ago. The first European navigators reported cultivated taro as far as Japan and New Zealand. Captain Cook and his companions noticed taro on Maori plantations in 1769. Especially in traditional dishes from the Pacific Islands, taro remains a popular ingredient. In ancient China, taro cultivation dates back to 8000 BCE or before, and apart from a staple for the commoner, taro is listed among foodstuffs acceptable for people of noble and imperial standing. In later times, wheat and rice became the more important staples.

Xanthosoma is the only aroid that originates in tropical America. Its domestication and dispersal throughout the Americas took place long before 1492. Before the Columbian Exchange, the bulk of the diet of many indigenous Amerindian societies consisted of starchy roots and tubers. *Xanthosoma* was among the important crop plants cultivated in home gardens located in or at the edges of tropical rainforests. As a result of the colonization of Latin America and the African Diaspora, *xanthosoma* migrated from the Americas to West Africa. In the following centuries, the root spread across the African continent, where nowadays it is successfully cultivated, and together with *colocasia* taro a prominent staple, and perceived as a traditional food in the diets of numerous indigenous communities.

At present *colocasia* and *xanthosoma* taro are cultivated in approximately 70 countries in tropical regions. They can be found in African countries such as Cameroon, Ghana, Kenya, and Nigeria. In the Americas, they are cultivated by small native farmers, such as in Brazil, Cuba, Costa Rica, Puerto Rico, Surinam, and Venezuela. They are also cultivated in large fields throughout the world, such as in Costa Rica, Cuba, Florida, Massachusetts, Texas, Bangladesh, Indonesia, Japan and Taiwan, and Australasia.

During the post-war period, the growing demand for low-skilled labor in the Western world resulted in a massive global south to north migration. Together with migrants from tropical regions *colocasia* and *xanthosoma* taro arrived in the Western world, and at present are available in so-called ethnic stores and tropical markets, where the leaves are sold fresh, and the corms and cormels are available fresh, frozen, fermented, and as flour. In tropical regions they are either homegrown, bought at markets, and/or in supermarkets (where they are available fresh and peeled).

Taro contains oxalic acid, and the acridity of the corm, cormels, and leaves are known to cause irritations of the skin and mouth. Common and ancient techniques to make the calcium oxalate crystals deposited in taro digestible and denature toxins are cooking (baking, roasting, and boiling), drying, and fermentation.

When thoroughly cooked, not only the corms and cormels but also the leaves, stalks, and even the petioles are edible. In most subtropical regions and societies, not all plant parts of taro are used and/or seen fit for human consumption; it is the corms, cormels, and leaves that are most frequently eaten.

Although all plant parts are edible, taro is particularly grown as a root crop. The starchy corms and cormels provide for carbohydrates, and have a food value similar to potatoes. The protein content of taro is higher than in sweet potatoes and cassava; furthermore, taro contains minerals, vitamins C, B1, B2, and niacin. The leaves are rich in protein, and similar to spinach, considered an excellent source of vitamins A and C, and calcium, potassium, phosphorus, and iron.

In the Caribbean, the leaves traditionally serve as an ingredient for the one-pot dish *callaloo,* also known as *calalu,* which throughout the region is a popular soup and/or stew. In Puerto Rico both at home and as a street food, *alcapurrias,* fritters or pancakes of *xanthosoma* and plantain are very popular. Traditionally consumed boiled in soup, mixed with other vegetables and pork, chicken, fish, or beef, in Nicaragua the cormels of *xanthosoma* are also peeled, boiled, and pounded to a pulp with butter, milk, spices, and salt. In Dominica, together with coconut, sugar, eggs, and spices, it is an ingredient for pudding. Cubans consider the *xanthosoma* the queen of the stew vegetables, and use it as a common ingredient in the popular multiethnic stew *ajiaco.* The national dish of Suriname is *pom,* an oven dish with chicken and the grated corm of *xanthosoma.* A typical Costa Rican dish is *olla de carne* a thick stew-like soup with chunks of beef, chayote (*L. sechium edule*), and starchy vegetables such as potato, cassava, *colocasia,* and *canthosoma* taro.

Both taros are a prominent staple in the diets of numerous indigenous African communities where starchy tubers and roots—alone or in combination—are used for the preparation of the traditional staple dish *fufu* or *futu,* a porridge or pudding.

Other common preparation methods for the corms and/or cormels include boiling whole in the skin, pounding, roasting, fermenting, and baking.

In Cameroon, various ethnic groups prepare the *xanthosoma* taro. Cormels are peeled, boiled, and eaten with a vegetable sauce. Together with palm oil, crayfish, salt, and pepper, the grated and peeled corm, and young leaves, the dish *ekwam* is regarded as a delicacy. This is also the case with *akwacoco,* a traditional staple for the Bakweri people from the Southwest province. *Belbach* is a thick sauce prepared from young, tender, unopened leaves and petioles. Young leaves are also used as a vegetable in *nyeh* (bell soup). *Kohki* or *koki* (referred to as cake or bread) from ground cowpeas, ground corn, or *xanthosma,* so-called Kohki beans are eaten with boiled cormels or plantain. In the colonial period, *cocoyam koki* or endeley bread was the school snack of children.

In the Pacific region, taro is an important supplement and staple food with a high social status. The leaves are boiled in water or coconut cream. Peeling and boiling the corm is most common, but all over the region, most popular are cooked, mashed, or fermented pastes and puddings commonly known as poi. In Asia (e.g., China, Vietnam, Cambodia, Indonesia) the stalks are often thinly sliced and used in soups. The petioles are sometimes eaten raw and the Chinese are known to deep-fry grated tuber strips. In traditional Japanese cuisine, boiling taro in water is most common, the dishes are referred to as *nimono* (boiled materials or stews). Boiled taro is used in miso soups (miso is a fermented soybean paste), eaten as a side dish with rice, and also mashed. The leaves and petioles (zuiki) are used as a vegetable. In Cyprus, there are at least nine different ways to prepare taro which are referred to as skhara, vrasto, souppa, skourdalia, tiganites, kappamas, yiakhni, psito, and moussakas.

Surinamese Pom—Jewish Style

Pom is a festive dish from Suriname, a small South American country with a highly diverse population. The oven dish is commonly served on holidays and festivals. Various residents of Suriname add their own touch: Hindus add piccalilli relish; Javanese add soy sauce; Jews use oil instead of butter; and Chinese add ginger or lychees. Leftover pom is often consumed on a bread roll. In recent years both pom and broodje pom (on a bread roll) started to appear on the Dutch menu, and nowadays can even be ordered in Dutch take aways and home-delivery restaurants.

Ingredients

2 lb. chicken, cut in pieces
Juice of 2 lemons
2 lb. *xanthosoma* corm, peeled and grated
1 small onion, chopped
2 tomatoes, chopped
1 bunch celery leaves, finely chopped
Juice of 2 bitter (Seville) oranges
1 tbsp kosher salt
½ tsp black pepper
¼ tsp nutmeg
½ cup sunflower oil
2 tbsp vinegar

1. Preheat the oven to 375°F.
2. Wash the chicken pieces with lemon juice; sauté the pieces in oil (if the chicken is fat, use little oil); remove the chicken from the pot.
3. Sauté the chopped onion, tomatoes, and finely chopped celery in the pot for approximately 5 minutes. Stir occasionally.
4. Put the grated *xanthosoma* in a separate bowl, mix with the juice of bitter oranges, salt, and vinegar. Mix the sautéed onion, tomato sauce, and the *xanthosoma* mixture. Add salt, pepper, and nutmeg to taste. Sauté the mixture for a few minutes in the pot.
5. Put oil in a high-rimmed, round, enamel oven dish. Put half of the *xanthosoma* mixture in the dish. Place the chicken pieces on top, and cover the chicken with the rest of the mixture.
6. Bake the pom for 1 hour in the oven (approx. 375°F/175°C). The pom is done when the inside is yellow, and the crust is golden brown.

Further Reading

Bown, Deni. *Aroids: Plants of the Arum Family.* 2nd ed. Portland, OR: Timber Press, 2000.

Flach, M., and F. Rumawas, eds. *Plant Resources of South-East Asia 9: Plants Yielding Non-Seed Carbohydrates.* Leiden: Backhuys Publishers, 1996.

Vaneker, Karin. "Cooking Pom." In *Petits Propos Culinaires,* edited by Tom Jaine, 30–48. Totnes, Devon, Great Britain: Prospect Books, 2007.

Vaneker, Karin. *Pomtajer: Exploring the Potential of an Under-Utilised Species in Domestic Cuisine and Gastronomy.* Rome, Italy: Global Facilitation Unit for Underutilized Species, Electronic document. http://www.underutilized-species.org/features/Pomtajer/august2008_pomtajer.html.

Karin Vaneker

B

Balut (Fertilized Egg)

Balut is the Filipino term for fertilized duck (or chicken) eggs that contain a nearly developed embryo. They are a common food and are eaten as a snack and prepared similarly to hard boiled eggs, served with salt. They are most popular in the Philippines but are eaten throughout Southeast Asia and parts of China. Other terms used to refer to this food include *Khai Luk* (Laos), *Phog tea Khon* (Cambodia), *moadan* (China), and *Trung vit lon* or *Hot vit lon* (Vietnam). Balut is considered particularly unpalatable to westerners and has been featured on the NBC television program *Fear Factor* as one of the stunts for contestants of the show.

Balut eggs range from 14 to 21 days old and come from a variety of ducks and chickens, though the latter is less common. The older the egg, the larger the embryo or chick found inside will be. Mallard ducks are the most common breed for producing balut in the Philippines, but it is suggested that Muscovy ducks produce the best balut. Balut is typically sold ready-to-eat by street vendors and is usually consumed in the evenings as a snack. Venders keep them in buckets of sand to maintain warmth and accompany them with packets of salt. Balut is usually served with a pinch of salt, lemon juice, and sometimes ground pepper. To eat balut one must tap the large end of the egg to make a little hole. At this point the liquid is sipped out of the egg. The eater continues to break away the shell to expose the yolk, embryo, and albumen. At this point it can be eaten right from the shell or the parts separated on a plate and seasoned.

Balut is widely believed to be an aphrodisiac in the Philippines and is mainly consumed by men for this quality. It is also known as an energizer food, which is the reason many women give for eating balut. However, it is also viewed as a high-protein, hearty snack. The nutritional profile for balut per serving includes 188 calories, 14 grams of fat, 116 milligrams of calcium, 176 milligrams of phosphorous, 2 milligrams of iron, and 14 grams of protein. It also contains retinol, B-carotene, thiamine, riboflavin, niacin, and ascorbic acid. It is considered a super food by some in the Philippines, and is sometimes consumed instead of vitamin supplements for this reason. Balut is a very inexpensive source or protein and calcium, which may also contribute to its popularity.

In the Philippines, the preferred age of duck embryos for balut is 17 to 18 days old and is referred to as balut sa puti. However, in Vietnam, older embryos are preferred and the balut there is aged 19 to 21 days, when the chick is old enough to be considered a baby duck. While it is most common to purchase ready-to-eat balut from vendors, it can also be prepared by the home cook. The raw embryonic egg is placed in boiling water and cooked for 20 to 30 minutes, similar to preparing a standard hard-boiled egg in the West (though with a longer cooking time). It is always eaten warm—never cold.

Further Reading

Fernandez, Doreen. *Tikim: Essays on Philippine Food and Culture.* Manila: Anvil Publishing, 1994.

Magat, Margaret. "Balut: Fertilized Duck Eggs and Their Role in Filipino Culture." *Western Folklore* 61, no. 1 (Spring 2002): 63–94.

Mydans, Seth. "The Snacks Are Here: Duck!" *New York Times,* January 26, 1997.

Christine Caruso

Bats

People have been eating bats for hundreds of years in parts of the tropics. But they are a delicacy that comes with a risk.

There are more than 4,000 mammal species found in the world, and bats belong in the order Chiroptera. Within the order, there are two major sub-orders, the Microchiroptera and the Megachiroptera. Microchiroptera, also known as the true bats, possess a highly developed sense of echolocation, and when combined with their superior flying skills, are successful nocturnal hunters. While most members of Microchiroptera eat insects, some indulge in additional food sources such as fish, amphibians, small mammals, blood, fruit, and flowers. The Megachiroptera consist of a single family, the Pteropdidae, which are referred to as the Old World fruit bats or flying foxes. This family is found in the tropical areas of Africa, the eastern Mediterranean, Madagascar, the western Indian Ocean islands, across southeastern Asia, and in the Indo-Australia part of the world. Members of this family do not possess the same sophisticated echolocation as those of Microchiroptera, however, they do have a well-developed sense of smell, large eyes, and night vision capabilities that are ideal for locating their preferred food—fruit and flowers. They suck on the flowers or fruit, swallowing the nectar or juice, and spitting out the remaining pulp. In the process, bats assist in the pollination and seed dispersal for a variety of foods. As a result of this diet, they often feed in trees and in areas where they are unable to perform graceful landings post-flight, so one could call their hunting style crash and snatch.

Bats have captured the imagination of humans for generations. When they are not connected to vampire lore and utilized as a symbol of horror, the root of much European vocabulary refers to bats as being mice with fluttering wings or a butterfly mouse. Ancient Chinese and Persian mythologies use bats to symbolize longevity and happiness. It wasn't until post-Christian Europe that the flying nocturnal creatures were first linked to the Devil; in fact Western European painters began to depict the Devil with bat wings during the Middle Ages. This difference of perspective regarding bats is best illustrated in the response to a bat entering one's home. In Europe this was considered to be a forewarning of a death in the house while in China is was considered to be a sign of good fortune. North American Indian culture links bats with various death rituals, and in Africa, bats are highly regarded for their intelligence (due to echolocation and the ability to fly in the dark without hitting anything). In shamanism, the bat is a symbol for both death and rebirth, but also serves as a guide to those experiencing dark times in their lives.

In many tropical areas, eating the flying fox is considered to be a delicacy, and this traditional dish is regularly featured at weddings, fiestas, and feasts. Early hunters used a number of uniquely crafted tools to lure, flush, and capture these animals, some of whom can have a wingspan as wide as five feet. Aborigines in Australia would camp beneath fruit trees heavy with bats and light campfires, allowing the smoke to stupefy the bats before using boomerangs to knock the animals to the ground. But this changed after World War II, when the islands in the Pacific and Indian Oceans became strategically important to military endeavors. Small bases began to emerge, and, as a result, the numbers of soldiers and guns increased in these native communities. As guns became more accessible, the days of spears and nets lessened as natives began to hunt the flying fox with more mechanical proficiency. The use of guns lead to the extinction and near extinction of many species of bats, but the traditional taste for bat remained strong.

Once the bats are captured, they are traditionally roasted over hot coals creating a crispy, skinned wing for nibbling. The rest of the animal is then butchered and cooked in soups before being served to excited diners who have grown up with this traditional food. Another preparation involves boiling the animal in milk and then eating the entire animal—fur, flesh, organs, and brain. This dish was also featured on the 16th season of the CBS-TV show *Survivor Micronesia: Fans vs Favorites* where one contestant likened it to juicy rabbit.

But the enjoyment of eating bat for one group, the Chamorro people of Guam, has had serious consequences. When scientists decided to examine why there was such a high rate of a unique neurological disease, they discovered a link between the Chamorro and the bats. Guam is home to a primitive, fern-like tree called the cycads, which produce a brightly colored fruit that contains neurotoxin. While the Chamorro enjoyed the seeds, they were aware that they must wash the seeds thoroughly to eat them safely. The bats, who also enjoyed the cycads, did not practice the same precautions as the humans, and as a result, the neurotoxins accumulated within the cycad-eating bats' flesh. When the tribal members ate enough of the flesh and had enough neurotoxin accumulated in their own systems, they started showing symptoms of ALS-PDC—a syndrome with Alzheimer's-like dementia, ALS-like slow paralysis, and Parkinson's-like shaking. Eventually this became the predominant cause of death among the adult Chamorro population during the 1970s, and even 30 years later some cases still exist amongst the elder members of the tribe. But this didn't diminish the culinary craving for flying fox.

Due to the advent of gun-hunting, the species that had sparked the outbreak of ALS-PDC were hunted to near extinction. As a result of the demand for this food, a new species was imported from Samoa to assuage the demand—a great caveat was the absence of cycads in Samoa which meant there was no neurotoxin danger for those safely eating the Samoan fruit bats.

For those still interested in partaking of flying fox, it is highly recommended that one consume the fruit-only eating species, preferably from non-cycad growing areas. As a result, younger members of the Chamorro have been able to indulge their craving for flying fox without displaying the effects of ALS-PDC.

Bats pose another risk to humans. They are carriers of viruses such as Ebola, Hendra, Neepa, and SARS. During the day, as they huddle together with members of their colonies composed of camps, which have eight females to every one male for warmth, they sneeze and cough on one another exchanging germs. At night, they spread out for miles, carrying the diseases far and wide. While the bats might not get sick, the close physiological similarity to primates and humans makes it quite easy to for humans to become ill as they enjoy eating a dangerous delicacy.

However, the number of bats available for consumption has begun to lessen. Many species are threatened or considered near extinct. While some of this is due to their culinary appeal, some bat conservation groups cite the affects of the agricultural clearing of forests and programs that allow the culling of these animals on crops or herds of livestock by farmers. But bats, like humans, are unable to make vitamin C, and as a result, they must consume fruit to obtain that necessary nutrient. Bats face challenges in obtaining fruit when monoculture farming takes place on land that used to offer vegetative diversity. Bats have also suffered as a result of man's pesticide-fueled war against insects. Bats have a high sensitivity to DDT and to the chlorinated hydrocarbons used to protect wood. As more people become aware of the important role bats play in natural insect management and in pollination, greater pro-bat legislation and policy has been put into action. Currently, all European countries have bat protection laws, and conservationists continue to seek an expansion of pro-bat policies.

Further Reading

Altringham, J. D. *Bats: Biology and Behaviour.* Oxford: Oxford University Press, 1996.

Hall, L. S., and G. C. Richards. *Flying Foxes: Fruit and Blossom Bats.* Sydney: University of New South Wales Press, 2000.

Hill, J. E., and J. D. Smith. *Bats: A Natural History.* London: British Museum (Natural History), 1984.

Leroy, M., B. Kumulungui, X. Pourrut, P. Rouquet, A. Hassanin, P. Yaba, A. Délicat, T. Paweska, J. P. Gonzalez, and R. Swanepoel. "Fruit Bats as Reservoirs of Ebola Virus." *Nature* 438, no. 7068 (2005): 575–576. doi: 10.1038/438575a. ISSN 0028-0836. PMID 16319873.

Monson, Clark. "Eating Bats Linked to Neurological Disease." Society for Conservation Biology. www.conbio.org/SCB/Services/Tips/2003-6-June.cfm#A2.

Neuweiler, G. *The Biology of Bats.* New York: Oxford University Press, 2000.

Alexa Johnson

Bear

Bears have been hunted and consumed by humans for millennia, as is evidenced by numerous archeological sites containing bear remains. In many societies, bears have not only been a food source but revered as deities. Large piles of carefully arranged polar bear skulls found in Siberia suggest that bears were considered ancestral spirits who needed to be placated. Similar ideas are held by the Inuit throughout the Arctic Circle, who are still legally allowed to hunt polar bears, which form a traditional and essential part of their diet. Black and brown bears played an important role in Native American mythology and were also regularly hunted and eaten. In Russia, the bear, though practically a national symbol, is nonetheless enjoyed as an elegant food, as it is in Finland, where the brown bear is the national animal.

Until recently, bear meat would not have been considered strange or unusual as food in the range of their natural habitat, which stretches across most of the northern hemisphere with concentrations in mountainous and forested regions such the Appalachians and Sierras in America, the Caucasus and Alps in Europe, as well as several species in Siberia. The major challenge for modern consumers has been dwindling bear populations, inaccessibility of hunting grounds, and ultimately ethical concern over eating an intelligent and attractive animal whose physiognomy seems to bear a distinct relation to our own, especially when skinned. For these reasons, bear is normally eaten as a regular part of the diet only in remote mountainous regions by those who hunt. This was not, however, always the case. Early settlers in North America happily consumed bears, using the fat for cooking as well as fuel, and the meat as steaks and roasts. Though it had ceased to be a common food by the mid-19th century in the United States in all but the frontier and mountain regions, bear remained in cookbooks well into the 20th century, and it was probably only the ban on selling wild game that caused

the disappearance of bear meat from butchers shops and restaurants. The only way to taste bear today is to hunt it yourself or to be given it by someone who hunts. This rarity alone seems to account for the revulsion that many westerners feel toward eating bears. Although, arguably, teddy bears and Winnie the Pooh have played some role in our feelings of empathy for bears.

The taste of bear meat is not unlike beef, though darker in color and in certain seasons significantly more fatty. This makes the flesh remarkably sweet and juicy, and the fat itself is accounted by connoisseurs among the most delicious of any animal, especially when the bear has been feeding on berries. But with a diet heavy in salmon, the flavor of the meat can be much less pleasant if not rank. It should also be noted that the majority of cases of parasitic trichinosis come not, as many people think from pork, but from bear. So special care must be taken to cook the meat fully to an internal temperature of about 145 degrees.

Bear fat has a very low melting point and is suitable for cooking. In his 19th-century compendia called the *Curiosities of Food*, Peter Lund Simmons recounts a story from a century earlier about the taste for bear fat. "The fat is as white as snow, and extremely sweet and wholesome, for if a man drinks a quart of it at a time, when melted, it will never rise on his stomach!" Depending on the cut, bear meat is best roasted, though tougher shoulder, chuck, and brisket portions are best stewed or slowly braised. Any part may be ground and made into bear burgers or sausages. Bear also makes an excellent jerky.

Examples of eating bear meat around the world abound, but a few examples should suffice to show that it has been a common practice wherever there are bears.

There is a very important ceremony called *iomante* among the Ainu of northern Japan. It involves taking a young bear cub from a cave while it is still hibernating, bringing it back to the village, and raising it almost as if a child. The bear is fed well and revered as a god. At two years old, the bear is readied for sacrifice by thanking it and explaining that it is about to be sent back to its parents. The bear is tied to a post, shot with arrows, and eventually killed with a final shot to the heart. The blood is drunk, and the meat is distributed to the villagers. Lastly, the bear's fur is re-wrapped around its skull, at which point it is sent off to live with the gods.

Bear was also consumed in Europe. The great 16th-century chef to the popes, Bartolomeo Scappi, offers a bear recipe in his *Opera* (Works), explaining that while an unusual meat, he has roasted the legs with excellent results. Scappi came from the far north of what is today Italy, Dumenza, where bear populations still existed in his time. Farther south they would have been extraordinarily rare. The once abundant bear populations of the Alps are very slowly recovering today through conservation efforts and occasionally one finds bear meat on a menu.

In Vietnam and China, moon bears, so called for the white crescent on their chests, are kept confined in small cages for the extraction of bile from their gallbladders, which plays a role in traditional medicine. They are also eaten, eventually, their paws being considered a delicacy, especially in Canton. Keeping confined bears has become one of the targets of animal rights groups, not only for the cruelty to the animal, but because the Asian black bear is considered endangered.

In North America, bear is among those animals regularly hunted for its meat. In most states, there are strict controls on the season and number of bears that can be taken, but many butchers will happily process a bear brought in after a hunt. In the end, what might appear to be a strange and exotic food turns out to be quite ordinary, though nonetheless delicious if prepared properly and countless recipes can be found easily. Estelle Woods Wilcox in the *Buckeye Cookbook of 1890* puts it best: "Bear meat, especially the flesh of young bear, nearly resembles a good quality of beef, and may be fried, boiled, roasted, or cooked like beef in any way preferred."

Ingredients

1 bear
2⅜ tbsp salt

1. Preheat oven to 400°F.
2. Take your room-temperature bear, or preferably a piece therefrom, and season it well with salt.
3. Place it in a roasting pan on a rack and bake in the oven until a meat thermometer registers about 140°F internal temperature, at which point it will be cooked to medium doneness. It is important not to eat bear rare since trichinosis is a very real danger. Freezing the meat also mitigates this danger. It is important not to overcook bear meat, as it will become gamey in taste, even though, unlike most meats, the ample fat will prevent the meat from drying out.

4. Let the meat rest about 20 minutes before carving.

If you like, you can also line your roasting pan with chopped carrots, onions, celery, and a sprig of thyme, and when the bear is cooked, remove it to rest on a platter, pour off the grease, and deglaze the vegetables with some red wine. Pour this through a fine sieve and serve as a sauce for your bear.

Further Reading

Morgan, Chris. *Bears of the Last Frontier*. New York: Stewart Tabori and Chang, 2011.

Peacock, Doug, and Andrea Peacock. *In the Presence of Grizzlies*. Guilford, CT: Lyons Press, 2009.

Storer, Tracy I., and Llyod P. Tevis. *California Grizzly*. Berkeley: University of California Press, 1996.

Wood, Daniel. *Bears*. Toronto, ON: Whitecap Books, 2010.

Ken Albala

Bird's Nest Soup

Bird's Nest Soup is a rare and coveted Chinese delicacy, the recipe for which incorporates a nest made of a male swiftlet's saliva. Swiftlets are the birds of the four genera *Aerodramus*, *Hydrochus*, *Schoutedenapus*, and *Collocalia*, making up the Collocaliini tribe within the Apodidae family. This group contains approximately 30 species, which are found mostly in the tropical and subtropical regions of south Asia, the South Pacific islands, and northeastern Australia. These birds roost and breed in caves, and have the rare ability to navigate in complete darkness using echolocation.

Swiftlets naturally construct their nests in nooks and crevices high above a cave floor. Over a period of 35 days, the male swiftlet weaves a shallow, cup-shaped structure about the size of a human ear out of a thick, rope-like saliva that hardens when exposed to air. The final product typically holds two eggs.

Natural swiftlet nests are harvested primarily when the season peaks during the months between February and May from coastal limestone caves in Borneo. Gatherers use scaffolding made of bamboo as they ascend to the top of the cave, sometimes as a high as 300 feet from the floor. They hold a light between their teeth, and use a three-pronged tool called a *rada,* which they believe to be blessed by the cave spirits. One of the common taboos held by nest gatherers is that one must not make any sound while harvesting. If the gatherer should disturb the cave spirits, he would be punished. Each gatherer might procure 50 to 60 nests a day. Nest harvesting is dangerous and requires extensive training and skill. Death and injury are not uncommon. However, this danger does not seem to deter harvesters from their commitment to the trade.

Nests are harvested three times a year, and birds are typically given time to raise their young in the nest before it is removed. The first nest harvested each season is the cleanest, most pure, and therefore most highly prized. Later nests have raised young and require more cleaning.

Nests harvested for consumption are acquired mainly from the White-nest Swiftlet and the Black-nest Swiftlet. White nests are thought to be the most pure because they contain only saliva. Yellow, red, and black nests acquire their color from

A sweet Bird's Nest Soup. (© Kuan Chong Ng | Dreamstime.com)

Nest Quality and Imitators

Nests on the market represent varied quality and authenticity. Due to the high cost of birds' nests, many counterfeit or adulterated nests are on the market. Imitation nests can be constructed using rubber, resin, unbleached laver, animal skin, seaweed, and sometimes include scraps of real birds' nests. Unscrupulous nest producers might then apply cleansing chemicals or enhancing dyes and coatings of egg white or jelly. Treated nests can be potentially harmful if consumed, particularly for children, pregnant women, and the elderly. Consumer awareness is encouraged and there are some clues to look for to ensure informed purchase and consumption of pure birds' nests. A true nest is transparent, breaks into small dust-like pieces, and contains occasional feathers in the fibers. An imitation nest is often uniform in shape, reflective and opaque, breaks into chunks, and has a slight chemical or medicinal odor. Also, if the nest is authentic, its size will double when soaked in water, and the water will remain clear while foam appears on the surface of the bath when stirred. Fake nests cause the water bath to turn cloudy and produce no foam.

elements in the bird's diet or other environmental contaminants. White nests and red blood nests have a reputation for the variety of health benefits they offer. Consuming these birds' nests is said to enhance skin complexion, digestion, libido, respiration, vocal ability, and general immune system function. Furthermore, nests have significant calcium, iron, potassium, and magnesium content.

The typical Bird's Nest Soup recipe can be either savory or sweet. The savory version uses ingredients such as chicken broth, mushrooms, and ham, whereas the sweet version is much less complex—nest in a simple syrup. The nest adds a gelatinous and rubbery consistency to the broth.

With the growth of the industry, and demand that exceeds supply, swiftlet farms have been used to accommodate the market since the 1990s. Farms are made of wooden or reinforced concrete structures, and are placed in urban areas along the coast. The nest farming business is a significant component of the economy of the Indonesian province of North Sumatra, from which nests are exported mainly to Hong Kong. Products of the manmade caves have the same properties and health benefits as the naturally produced nests.

Hong Kong is the center of the swiftlet nest trade, with approximately 70 percent of nests imported from Indonesia and the remainder coming mostly from Thailand and Malaysia. Malaysian nests are known to be the finest on the market. Second to Hong Kong, the United States is the largest importer of swiftlet nests, where the soup is marketed in the various Chinatowns located in urban areas in the country. A serving of Bird's Nest Soup in Hong Kong can cost up to $100, while a pound of the ingredient itself can be a four-figure investment. There is no sign of a threat to the market in spite of the current global economic crisis.

Although sources estimate the popular consumption of Bird's Nest Soup to have begun about 400 years ago, Yun-Cheung Kong, professor of biochemistry in the Chinese University in Hong Kong indicates swiftlet nest trade might date back to the T'ang dynasty (618–907 CE). Chinese supply of nests began to diminish, and foreign nests were brought to the Imperial court of China during the Ming dynasty. During the Cultural Revolution against the bourgeois mentality, the Communist Party outlawed the buying and selling of Bird's Nest Soup as it did not conform to the ideological roots sought by the regime. The market is thriving currently, however, there is growing controversy regarding the ethics of the trade. Discourse focuses on overexploitation, corruption, and violence in the market. Main concerns include the dangerous working conditions that characterize nest harvesting, protection of the swiftlets and their nests, and legal issues regarding farming permits, particularly in Malaysia. Other common concerns include the prevalence of nest consumption related food allergies suffered by East Asian children, tainting of commercial nests with karaya gum, red seaweed, or a variety of fungus, and absorption of toxic metals from the cave walls.

Simple Bird's Nest Soup

Ingredients

1 tsp vegetable oil
1 tbsp fresh ginger root, chopped

2 quarts rich chicken stock

½ lb. birds' nests, rehydrated, then
drained

1. Heat the oil in a medium saucepan.
2. Sauté ginger until aromatic.
3. Add chicken stock, and bring to a boil.
4. Reduce heat, and add the birds' nests.
5. Simmer 5 minutes, stirring gently.

Variations: sautéed fresh or dried mushrooms, Chinese ham, or chicken breast
meat may be added.

Further Reading

Bird Nest Farm. "Quality and Authentic Bird
Nest from Indonesia, Malaysia, and South
East Asia." http://birdnestfarm.wordpress.
com/.

Cost, B. "Dried and True." *Gourmet* 65, no.1
(2005). http://www.gourmet.com/magazine/

DeGroot, R. A. "On the Trail of Bird's Nest
Soup: Caves, Climbs, and High Stakes."
Smithsonian 14 (1983): 65–75.

Gausset, Q. "Chronicle of a Foreseeable Tragedy: Birds' Nests Management in the Niah
Caves (Sarawak)." *Human Ecology* 32
(2004): 487–506.

Hobbs, J.J. "Problems in the Harvest of Edible
Birds' Nests in Sarawak and Sabah, Malaysian Borneo." *Biodiversity and Conservation*
13 (2004): 2209–2226.

Longchuen Bird's Nest Trading. "Frequently
Asked Questions." http://www.longchuen-
birdsnest.com/faq.htm.

Valli, E. "Nest Gatherers of Tiger Cave." *National Geographic* 177 (1990): 106–133.

Christen Sturkie

Bitter Melon

The bitter melon or bitter gourd is a green
fruit that resembles a wrinkly cucumber. It
is actually the fruit of a vine that thrives in
tropical and subtropical climes, although
its exact origins are unknown. The scientific name is *Momordica charantia*, and it
is known in East Asian (mostly southern
China and southern Japan), South Asian,
Southeast Asian, African, and Caribbean
cuisines. As it is so widely known, bitter
melon goes by many other names as well.
In English, it may also be called the Bal-
sam pear or bitter cucumber. Other names
include *fu gwa/ku gwa* (Cantonese/Man-
darin), *goya* (Japanese), *mara* (Thai),
peria (Indonesian), *cerasse* (Jamaican),
balsamina (Spanish), *margose/assorossie*
(French), and *kerala* (Indian).

All parts of the plant—fruit, leaves, and
seeds—are bitter. When sliced open, the
interior pith is white in the young fruit. As
it ripens, the fruit yellows and eventually
becomes a vibrant orange and softens. Bitter melon is usually eaten young, when the
green flesh has a clean, bright, bitter taste,
and retains its bell pepper–like crunch. The
bitterness intensifies with ripeness until
the fully ripe fruit is no longer eaten for
its flesh, but for its pith, which becomes
sweet and orange-colored at this stage. In
the Philippines, the leaves are eaten as a
vegetable as well.

Different varieties are cultivated in different countries; for example, the Chinese
variety is relatively smooth, with the undu-
lating ridges appearing closer to the body of
the fruit and rounded ends. The Indian variety is distinctly knobby, with jagged points
interspersed along the body and pointy
ends. Miniature and white varieties also
exist, with the former often eaten in South
and Southeast Asia stuffed with mixtures
of meat or fish and then fried or steamed.

Bitter melon. (© Jianghongyan | Dreamstime.com)

In the United States, bitter melon may be purchased in the vegetable sections of most Asian grocery stores. Indian or Pakistani groceries will tend to stock South Asian varieties, while Korean or Chinese groceries, for example, will usually have the Chinese variety. Selection of the fruit depends on the intended method of preparation. As noted before, the ripe fruit is eaten for its sweet pith, an ingredient that is popular in Southeast Asian salads. The unripe fruit is usually sliced open and the pith and seeds scraped out. The flesh is then sliced or diced and blanched in hot and/or salted water to remove some of the bitterness. The bitter melon may then be eaten raw, in soups, stir-fried, steamed, stuffed, cooked in a curry, deep-fried, or pickled.

Both traditional and modern medicine have associated bitter melon with positive health effects. The leaves may be used as a tea to expel gas, promote menstruation, and as an antiviral tonic. Its antibacterial properties makes it useful as a topical treatment for sores, wounds, and infections, and it is used both internally and externally to remove worms and parasites. Additionally, bitter melon is said to reduce blood pressure, blood sugar, cholesterol, and inflammation.

In recent years, bitter melon extracts and supplements have begun to appear in health food stores. Studies have shown that bitter melon improves the body's ability to absorb glucose from the blood, thus making it a candidate for the treatment and control of Type 2 diabetes. Bitter melon has been shown to have positive effects on certain types of cancer, and there are indications that it might improve immune cell function in cancer patients. Its antiviral properties have also led to studies on its effectiveness in treating herpes and HIV, with promising results.

Interestingly, the fruit is not widely consumed in Japan—most of the climate is too cool for its cultivation—except on the warm southern island of Okinawa, whose occupants average an even longer life expectancy than that of the rest of Japan, which is already ranked among the longest in the world. There has been speculation that this is due to the popularity of bitter melon and other yellow-green vegetables in the Okinawan diet.

Okinawan-Style Goya

In Japan, bitter melon is known as goya. In general, when selecting a young bitter melon of any variety, the exterior should be firm and smooth, and there should be no bruises. Once purchased, store refrigerated for three to five days at most.

Ingredients

1 tsp vegetable oil
2 bitter melons, seeds removed, sliced, soaked in salted water, and drained
3 tbsp soy sauce
1 tbsp mirin (sweet rice wine)
1 brick medium tofu, cut into large dice
2 eggs, beaten
1 scallion, thinly sliced

1. Heat the oil in a wok.
2. Stir-fry bitter melon until softened.
3. Add soy sauce and mirin, and stir to incorporate.
4. Add tofu, and continue stir-frying until tofu is thoroughly warmed.
5. Pour eggs on top, and continue cooking until eggs have set. Garnish with chopped scallions.

Further Reading

Jiratchariyakul, W., C. Wiwat, M. Vongsakul, A. Somanabandhu, W. Leelamanit, I. Fujii, N. Suwannaroj, and Y. Ebizuka. "HIV Inhibitor from Thai Bitter Gourd." *Planta Med* 67, no. 4 (June 2001): 350–353.

Kim, J. H., E. M. Ju, D. K. Lee, and H. J. Hwang. "Induction of Apoptosis by Momordin I in Promyelocytic Leukemia (HL-60) Cells." *Anticancer Res* 22, no. 3 (May–June 2002): 1885–1889.

Lee-Huang, S., P. L. Huang, H. C. Chen, P. L. Huang, A. Bourinbaiar, H. I. Huang, and H. F. Kung. "Anti-HIV and Anti-Tumor Activities of Recombinant MAP30 from Bitter Melon." *Gene* 161, no. 2 (1995): 151–156.

McGee, H. *On Food and Cooking: The Science and Lore of the Kitchen.* Rev. ed. New York: Scribner, 2004.

National Library of Medicine. *PubMed Central.* Bethesda, MD: NCBI, U.S. National Library of Medicine, NIH, Dept. of Health and Human Services, 2000.

Schneider, Elizabeth. *Vegetables from Amaranth to Zucchini: The Essential Reference; 500 Recipes and 275 Photographs.* New York: Morrow, 2001.

Zheng, Y. T., K. L. Ben, and S. W. Jin. "Alpha-Momorcharin Inhibits HIV-1 Replication in Acutely but Not Chronically Infected T-lymphocytes." *Zhongguo Yao Li Xue Bao* 20, no. 3 (1999): 239–243.

Karen Taylor

Black Chicken

The silky bantam chicken, *Gallus domesticus*, also known as silky or black chicken, black-boned chicken, *taihe*, *zook see gai*, or *wu gu ji* in Chinese, and *poulet soyeuse* in French, has also been dubbed the flower garden of the poultry world, due to its wispy-like feather coat that can be found in several colors including black, white, blue, and buff, making them popular as an ornamental bird. Most notable about the silky bantam are its black skin, feet, and bones, whereas other breeds of chicken may typically have white skin and yellow feet. Silky bantams are a small breed of chicken that as an adult weigh not more than 3 pounds, with the average weight being 1½ to 2 pounds.

Silky bantams likely trace their roots to Asia, where they are thought to have been brought back from Europe in the 13th century. Now found in the United States and other countries where there are Chinese populations, black chicken is used primarily by the Chinese, but is also used in Cambodian, Japanese, and Korean cooking. Typically, they are purchased live and butchered and cleaned at poultry markets in Chinatown neighborhoods such as in San Francisco and in New York. Generally, Americans raise silky bantams for pets and for show due to their friendly and gentle temperament, and for their adaptability to human handling, but their use in cooking has not yet caught on in most of the United States.

In Appalachian folklore, the blood of a black chicken is used to cure the skin disease milaria ("wildfire"). It is also used

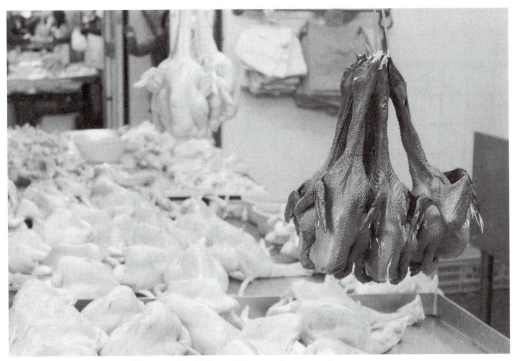

Black chicken (hanging). (© Angelika Krikava | Dreamstime.com)

as a cure for snakebite. In this instance, a poultice made of its intestines is thought to draw out venom from the bite.

The Chinese consider black chicken to be a curative, magical, restorative, supplementing, and highly nutritious food due to the black skin and bones. Black chicken provides high quality protein with lean meat, low in fat content. It contains about 1 gram less fat (per 100 grams edible meat) than standard broiler chickens. Curiously, black chicken contains nearly six times more phosphorous and nearly 10 percent more niacin than standard broilers. As black chickens have a higher water content than standard broilers, they provide less overall energy (calories) than a standard broiler chicken. Chinese women may eat black chicken and drink the broth after giving birth in order to restore their depleted energy. The broth is like chicken soup and is used for colds, headaches, to minimize stress, to promote balance between yin and yang, and also by some undergoing cancer treatment.

The small amount of dark meat is considered fine, tender, and also highly flavorful. Considered to possess a gamy flavor, black chicken is used primarily in variations of chicken soups, as well as a base for Mongolian hot pot and in curries, but is seldom roasted.

Various ingredients are used when cooking black chicken and may include Chinese yam, dried wolfberries, dried red dates, garlic, ginger, ginseng, lime, orange peel, onion and scallions, olive or canola oil, and rice or white wine. Seasonings used to cook black chicken include bay, thyme, and rosemary (made into a bouquet garni), cardamom, chilies, cinnamon, clove, coconut milk, curry paste, galangal, lemon grass, soy sauce, star anise, and salt and pepper. In making a soup, trimmed pork loin may also be used.

Black Chicken Soup

Ingredients used in this recipe may vary.

Ingredients

2 small cleaned, well-trimmed, and washed black chickens
3 to 4 cups cold water
½ cup white or rice wine
¼ cup olive or canola oil (per preference)
3 to 5 garlic cloves, smashed
1 small onion, diced
2 tbsp wolfberries
2 to 3 tsp fresh ginger, grated
2 to 3 small hot chilies (more or less per preference)
Kosher salt, to taste
Crushed black pepper, to taste

1. On the stovetop, pour oil into a Dutch oven or soup pot and let heat over a medium-to-high flame until hot.
2. Add chilies, garlic, and onion, and sauté until tender.
3. Add chicken, water, wine, wolfberries, ginger, salt, and pepper, and cover the pot.
4. Bring soup to a boil, then stir, and reduce flame to low.
5. Then let the soup simmer for 45 minutes. More or less time, will vary, until the black chicken is tender.
6. Remove chickens from the soup, and cut or pull apart into serving pieces. Serve in soup bowls with broth ladled over chicken. Steamed rice may be served on the side or in the soup.

Further Reading

American Silkie Bantam Club. http://www.americansilkiebantamclub.com/.

Brand, Eric. *Thieme Almanac: Acupuncture and Chinese Medicine—a Yearbook.* New York: Thieme, 2008.

Burum, Linda. "Black Bird." *Los Angeles Magazine,* April 2002, 96.

Louie, Elaine. "Now, a Chicken in Black." *New York Times,* January 17, 2007, F1.

Milnes, Gerald C. *Signs, Cures, and Witchery: German Appalachian Folklore.* Knoxville: University of Tennessee Press, 2007.

Mounts, Samia. "Black Chicken with Red Ginseng: A Holiday Gift for Him or Her?" *Korea Herald,* December 9, 2006.

2010 Hatching Season. Iowa: Murray McMurray Hatchery, 2010.

Young, Grace. *The Wisdom of the Chinese Kitchen: Classic Family Recipes for Celebration and Healing.* New York: Simon & Schuster, 1999.

Jenny Frémont

Blood

For as long as humankind has slaughtered animals for their meat, we have also consumed their blood. Pig, cow, horse, dog, rabbit, and even goose blood form a prominent part of food history the world over from Mexico to France to Thailand.

Recorded consumption of blood dates back to ancient times of Greece and Sparta and projects forward into our modern diet. During the Mongol conquest of Asia and Eastern Europe in the 13th and 14th centuries, the story goes that soldiers would live off the blood of their horses during long journeys. Some scholars suggest that soldiers could consume enough to nourish them for 10 days without having to eat solid food nor light a fire, an incredible advantage in battle.

However, eating blood often comes with a stigma. Considered the life force, consuming blood is explicitly banned in Christian religious texts as well as the Qur'an. Before the Islamic bans, Arab travelers combined camel hair and blood in patty form to sustain them across the desert. Still today, the milk and blood from herds of cattle are used for the same purpose by the Masai population of Africa.

Blood is also thought to have medicinal properties. As legend explains, Elisabeth de Bathory, an upper-crust Hungarian noble from the early 1600s, punished her servant with a backhanded slap that caused the servant to bleed onto Bathory's arm. Later, Bathory claimed that the blood-spattered section of skin was whiter and younger that the rest. She subsequently ordered the slaughter of hundreds of women, just so she could luxuriate in an age-defying bath. It is thought that nearly 650 virgins met their demise before Bathory was arrested. Some scholars have even deemed Bathory the first real-life vampire.

In addition to its anti-aging properties, blood is a nutritional powerhouse, attributed with many curative properties. In 100 grams, cow or pig blood has roughly 78 calories, 19 grams of protein, and very little fat. Gram for gram, it packs more protein than meat. Historically blood was also thought to bring sexual vitality, restore physical prowess, and cure everyday ills, no doubt due to its properties as a life force. During the Victorian era in England, drinking a glass of blood was a common preventative trick for tuberculosis. Today, blood is used in its very elemental form to prevent the physical and mental effects of serious malnutrition like bulging stomachs and bloated limbs. In Brazil, groundbreaking research has mixed prothemol, the primary ingredient in cow's blood with egg white protein to create a powder that helps build strength between human muscles. This powder can be baked into or sprinkled over any food or mixed into a drink.

There are many ways that blood can be eaten. A few common forms include sausages, pancakes, soups, and sauces. Most blood sausages, also called blood puddings, follow a typical pattern: blood is cooked over the stove and then a thickener is added. This can be anything from barley to rice to dried fruits, depending on the country. Then spices are added, and the mixture is poured into the sausage casing and cooked, usually by poaching. For the best flavor and minimal metallic taste, only fresh blood should be used. Traditionally, blood sausage was a made during a slaughter, as a part of a nose-to-tail approach to eating that didn't let anything edible go to waste. Typically, a 1,000-pound steer will yield up to 40 pounds of blood, and a 200-pound hog about 10 pounds of blood—and slightly more than that weight in blood sausage once thickener is added.

In Europe, every country has a different way of preparing blood. One of the most widely known blood sausages is English Black Pudding, a sausage of pig's blood, pork fat, and oatmeal. It makes up a key component in a Full English Breakfast. In Spain, morcilla is a thick pig's blood sausage seasoned with paprika. *Morcilla de burgos* is enhanced with onions and rice and is popular both for its flavor and its economy.

The French have *boudin noir*, similar to the English variety but mixed with cream for a lighter texture. Rabbit blood is also used in many traditional French casseroles and soups for its rich flavor and as a thickening agent. In Ireland, a blood cake is made by alternating layers of coagulated blood with salt and then slicing it into squares. In northern European countries like Finland, where blood sausage is called *mustamakkara* and Estonia, where it goes by the name *verivost,* the delicacies are Christmas traditions and eaten with lingonberry jam, butter, and sour cream. Other names for blood sausage include the German *blutworst* with oatmeal, the Norwegian *blodpolse* with raisins and apple, and the polish *kaszanka* with buckwheat. In Mexico the sausage is called *moronga* and contains chili peppers, fresh mint, and onions and is served with chili rojo and chili verde.

In Europe, blood is used in soups like *swartsoppa* from Scandinavia. South America, especially Argentina, takes the Spanish *morcilla* both in name and recipe. In France, rare roast duck is pressed in a specialized piece of dining room equipment called a duck press, and a sauce made from the blood and juices that are released.

The use of blood as nourishment does not stop in Europe. In the Isaan region of Thailand, fresh cow's blood is mixed with beef and noodles or added to curries for a hearty meal. The Mahouts, or elephant trainers, of the region drink the wild boar blood for breakfast before going to work. Nearby in Vietnamese markets, different varieties of blood including cow, pig, sheep, and dog are mixed in a large pot until they coagulate. Cubes of the blood mixture are then cut and placed in soup or fried until crunchy

Black Pudding with apple slice, potato pancake, and sauerkraut in Germany. (© Birgit Reitzhofmann | Dreamstime.com)

½ tsp pepper
2 cups fresh pork blood
1 cup diced leaf lard
Hog casings, rinsed

1. Sauté onion in vegetable oil until translucent.
2. Chill and add remaining ingredients.
3. Using a sausage stuffer, loosely stuff hog casings.
4. Poach in 180°F water until firm, about 25 minutes.
5. Chill.

Further Reading

David, Elizabeth. *French Provincial Cooking*. New York: Penguin, 1999.

Marianski, Stanley, and Adam Marianski. *Home Production of Quality Meats and Sausages*. Seminole, FL: Bookmagic, 2010.

Eleanor Barczak

as perfect treat at outdoor markets. Around the world, the tradition of consuming blood was born out of necessity but still persists today in deeply cultural foods.

Black Pudding

Ingredients

1 cup onion, chopped
1 tbsp vegetable oil
½ cup cream
½ cup bread crumbs
2 eggs
2 sprigs fresh thyme leaves
1 tsp salt

Bone Marrow

Bone marrow is the soft fatty tissue found in the center of animal leg bones, and in some cultures, it is considered a delicacy. Bones used for marrow are typically from the straight portions of leg bones, with some suggestion that the best source is from the femur in particular. Fresh marrow is often described as having a consistency similar to that of butter, whitish in color with streaks of red. Bone marrow is sourced from a number of different animals, which is also influenced by cultural variation, but is commonly sourced from cow (beef or veal), lamb, and even caribou or moose (particularly among Alaskan natives).

While it was once common to eat bone marrow in the United States, it has faded from popularity in recent years. However, it is still commonly eaten throughout parts of Europe and Asia. It is also suggested that there is a long history of consuming bone marrow, with some evidence found of early hominids collecting bones for their marrow, and traditional people such as Native American hunters and indigenous populations in northern Canada consuming marrow as it is believed to be highly nutritious and easily digested. Bone marrow is used in a number of preparations, from simply roasting it in the bone and spreading the softened and melting marrow on toast, to using it as a main ingredient in soups, as is done in the staple soup of Vietnam known as *pho*. It is also used as a filling for tacos and tostadas in Mexico and is an important aspect of the Italian dish *ossobuco*, which features a braised veal shank, where the marrow can be removed from the bone at the table with a table knife or a small spoon designed for that purpose.

There is little nutritional information available for bone marrow but it is commonly believed to be both nutrient dense and easy to digest. Bone marrow from cows contain approximately 120 to 150 milligrams of cholesterol per 100 grams of marrow, which is less than half of the cholesterol of egg yolks. It is also considered to be a good source of protein and high in monounsaturated fats, which are considered to be beneficial to health in moderation. Bone marrow contains other important nutrients including vitamin B complex, minerals, lecithin, and methionine. While there have been some concerns over the practice of eating bone marrow and possible links to bovine spongiform encephalopathy (BSE), more commonly known as mad cow disease, recent reports from the Centers for Disease Control (CDC) suggests that consumption of bone marrow does not pose a greater risk than any other part beef products. Thus no additional precautions for eating marrow are necessary.

A common and simple preparation of bone marrow is roasted marrow bone. The recipe is as follows:

Ingredients

12 3-inch pieces of veal marrow bone, available from a butcher
Salt and pepper to taste

1. Preheat the oven to 450°F.
2. Arrange the bones in a roasting pan. Roast for approximately 20 minutes depending on the thickness of the bones. The marrow should begin to loosen but not melt away.
3. Season with salt and pepper just before eating, and serve with toast.

Further Reading

Bittman, Mark. "A Little Bit of Work and a Lot of Satisfaction." *New York Times,* October 31, 2007.

Green, Aliza. *Field Guide to Meat: How to Identify, Select and Prepare Virtually Every Meat, Poultry and Game Cut.* Philadelphia, PA: Quirk Books, 2005.

McLagan, Jennifer. *Bones: Recipes, History and Lore.* New York: William Morrow Cookbooks, 2005.

Christine Caruso

Brains

Animal brains have long been consumed by cultures around the world. Part of the central nervous system, the brain is considered part of the food category offal reserved for entrails, internal organs, and the other edible parts of animals, as opposed to muscle flesh like steaks, roasts, and chops. However, the brains of lamb, sheep, cows, monkeys, and even gorillas are enjoyed in various preparations that cater to the taste of every culinary tradition.

Called *sesos* in Spanish, *cervelles* in French, and *nàosui* in Chinese, eating animal brains is common. The Dogtown Tavern in Evansville, Indiana, is famous for their deep-fried cow brain sandwich with the brains accompanied by mustard and pickled onions. This traditional preparation came from Germany and Holland near the end of the 19th century. Also in the United States, *Woman's Day Encyclopedia of Cooking* recommends brains with scrambled eggs, a common pairing since the two have similar textures when cooked. In France, brains have very strong roots. They can be prepared *an buerre noir* (in black butter), *en croutes* (baked in pastry shells or day old bread), or with glazed onions, mushrooms, and red wine. Nearby, in Italy, *capuzzella*, a baked sheep's head, was considered a common comfort food in the 1900s. The heads were soaked in saltwater to remove the excess cartilage, skin, and blood, then stuffed with rosemary, oregano, and tomato sauce, then baked. Further to the east, lamb or goat brain curry in India and Indonesian cow brains cooked with coconut cream continue to feed the populations. The Americas are not left out of this tradition. Throughout Mexico and Central America, visitors might smell cow heads barbecuing overnight to make *barbacoa*

de cabeza, especially delicious in the form of brain or head meat tacos for breakfast served with cilantro and onions.

In Africa, the brain of a gorilla is a highly prized commodity. The Anyang people of Cameroon revere the gorilla and only hunt it when a new chief takes over the tribal leadership. He is given the gorilla brain to eat, and another high-level official consumes the heart. Another African culture, the Fang people in the Congo, use brains as two kinds of charms for men, one for strength during the hunt, and one for luck with women.

The myth and mystery that surrounds eating brain is prominent in China where the adventuresome eater may run across the controversial monkey brain on a menu. The legend goes that a small monkey is strapped alive to the middle of a large table to immobilize it while the chef or host of the party saws off the top of its head. The diners then enjoy warm cerebrum for dinner. Allegedly, this service costs about $300 for a small monkey. Eating monkey brains has been well documented, if falsely, in documentaries, ghost stories, and the Hollywood smash hit *Indiana Jones and the Temple of Doom* when Indy dines on the chilled tissue as a dessert somewhere in India. For sanitary preparation however, there are certain steps that must be followed to ensure that the meat is clean and healthy to eat. The brain, whether of a large or small animal, should be plump and whitish pink on the day of usage. First, the meat is washed in cold water with a small amount of vinegar; next, the outer membranes and blood vessels must be removed, followed by a cold-water soak and one more washing, sometimes with saltwater.

Barbacoa/Barbacoa de Cabeza

Classic *barbacoa* is done pit-style and is perhaps best known for its barbecued cow head, *barbacoa de cabeza,* though it is also done with a whole sheep, goat, or pig. It is popular in ranching regions of Mexico, especially northern Mexico and the southwestern United States where there are large Mexican immigrant populations, but a type of barbacoa can be found throughout Mexico and Central America. To generalize, in the North, beef head (*cabeza*) or goat (*cabrito*) are common, with lamb popular in central Mexico and pork (*cochinita pibil*) in the Yucatan peninsula. At home, it is often cooked by men beginning on Saturday night in a back yard, slow roasting overnight, and eaten on Sunday as tacos with corn tortillas, salsa, and toppings like chili, lime, cilantro, and sliced onion.

To cook *barbacoa*, dig a hole in the ground and light a wood fire. Mesquite is often used in desert regions, though the flavor is strong so it is often blended with other hardwood. When the fire is mostly coals, the meat or head is seasoned with salt, pepper, and sometimes chili, wrapped in burlap, or with banana or agave leaves, depending on the region, often along with onions, garlic, lime halves, or other flavoring ingredients and buried in the pit on top of the coals. It then cooks overnight. While not necessary for a successful outcome, some cooks include a pot of water (sometimes flavored with onion, garlic, and chili) in the pit to steam the meat and catch the juices. This liquid can then be eaten as a soup or used to cook beans with a profound flavor.

Barbacoa is sold in restaurants or served for festive occasions but is also popular among backyard barbecuers.

Nutritionally, animal brain is like sweetbreads or liver; it provides close to 11 grams of protein per 100 grams of tissue and is a good source of potassium and phosphorus. However, it is very high in saturated fat and cholesterol. The health issue that has brain tissue on in the spotlight is the transmission of mad cow disease (MCD). Humans cannot contract MCD but are instead inflicted with a fatal version technically called Creutzfeld-Jakob disease. Contrary to popular thought, the disease cannot be transmitted through the meat or milk products of contaminated cows; the mutated proteins called prions that are responsible for the disease are transmitted only through nervous tissue, namely the brain and spinal cord.

Scrambled Eggs and Brains

Ingredients

3 tbsp butter
8 oz. veal brains, washed
8 eggs
Salt and pepper to taste

1. In a nonstick skillet, heat butter until frothy but not browned.
2. Add brains and cook about 2 minutes, until beginning to set.

3. Add eggs, and cook until the mixture resembles traditional scrambled eggs.
4. Season to taste with salt and pepper. Serve with toast.

Further Reading

Dolce, Joe. "A Brain Is a Terrible Thing to Waste." *Gourmet* (January 2009). http://www.gourmet.com/magazine/2000s/2009/01/growing-up-italian.

Gelfand, Jonathan L. "The Basic Guide to Mad Cow Disease." Webmd.com. http://www.webmd.com.

Graber, Karen H. "Wrap It Up: A Guide to Mexican Street Tacos—Part I." *Access Mexico Connect—Current Issue—the Electronic Magazine All about Mexico.* http://www.mexconnect.com/.

Hefling, Kimberly. "Craving Brain Food, Mad Cow or No, Indiana Diners Chow Down on a Disappearing Delicacy." MSNBC Business. http://www.msnbc.msn.com/.

Hopkins, Jerry, and Anthony Bourdain. *Extreme Cuisine: The Weird and Wonderful Foods That People Eat.* Minneapolis: Periplus Editions, 2004.

Meder, Angela. "Gorillas in African Culture and Medicine." *Gorilla Journal.* Berggorilla & Regenwald Direkthilfe. http://berggorilla.de/english/frame.html.

USDA. "Animal Brain Nutrition Information." http://www.nal.usda.gov/fnic/foodcomp/search/index.html.

Eleanor Barczak

Brunswick Stew

Brunswick Stew is a stew traditionally made from squirrel, though in many restaurants and food products today chicken is used. It has been commonly consumed in the American South, however, as people migrated north and west, so has Brunswick Stew.

Squirrels have been hunted for food on the North American continent for thousands of years, providing a key protein source for Native Americans long before Europeans settled the continent. Native to the eastern and midwestern United States, both the Eastern Gray Squirrel and the Fox Squirrel now populate a variety of environments, from densely populated urban areas to the most remote forests of the American South.

The origins of Brunswick Stew can be traced back to Brunswick County, Virginia. It was an African American chef named "Uncle" Jimmy Matthews who, in 1828, first created what was to become known as Brunswick Stew. According to Brunswick County historians, Dr. Creed Haskins, a member of the Virginia state legislature, took several friends out on a hunting trip. While the group was out hunting, Haskins's chef, Matthews, went about hunting squirrel for their supper. "Matthews slowly stewed the squirrels with butter, onions, stale bread, and seasoning in a large iron pot. When the hunting party returned they were reluctant to try the new, thick concoction but, one taste convinced them to ask for more." Today, most Brunswick Stew recipes replace squirrel with chicken and add vegetables such as lima beans, corn kernels, and potatoes to the mix as well. However, even today, many squirrel hunting enthusiasts with a connection to this stew or the American South, stay true to the origins of the dish and include squirrel meat instead of or in addition to chicken.

As its name suggests, Brunswick Stew is cooked slowly and demands attention and care throughout the cooking process. Most recipes for Brunswick Stew require anywhere from four to six hours of cooking time. First, the proteins are simmered, chicken, squirrel, or both. Next, the vegetables and seasonings are added to the pot, which simmers for up to six hours. While the vegetable and seasoning vary slightly among different recipes, one instruction remains the same, constant stirring throughout the entire cooking process. Due to the long cooking time and attention that is required, Brunswick Stew is most often prepared for "church functions, local fund raisers, family reunions, and political rallies." In 1988, Virginia's General Assembly passed a resolution "proclaiming Brunswick County, Virginia, as The Original Home of Brunswick Stew." To celebrate the resolution, the first annual Brunswick Stew-Fest was held in the Virginia state capital of Richmond and continues to be held annually to celebrate the unique heritage of Brunswick Stew.

While no adverse health effects are attributed to the consumption of squirrel meat, the consumption of squirrel brains has become a cause for concern. In 1997, doctors in Kentucky issued a warning that humans who consumed squirrel brains were in danger of contracting a variation of mad cow disease, officially called Creutzfeldt-Jakob disease.

Brunswick Stew aka Squirrel Muddle

By Grandma Hazel Newsome

Ingredients

6 squirrels
1 to 2 whole chickens
½ lb. bacon
2 to 3 lb. onions, diced
5 lb. potatoes, peeled and sliced thinly
2 quarts canned tomatoes
1 to 2 pkgs. fresh or frozen lima beans
1 to 2 pkgs. frozen corn kernels
1 to 2 10-oz. cans condensed tomato soup
3 to 4 chicken bullion cubes
Salt and pepper
Water

1. Boil squirrel and chicken in separate pots, with enough water to cover the meat. Save chicken broth for liquid additions.
2. De-bone meats and return them to the squirrel broth, along with sliced potatoes and diced onions.
3. Fry bacon (save grease) and crumble into small pieces; add to squirrel broth along with 1 tbsp of reserved bacon grease.
4. Bring to a boil, add chicken broth as needed.
5. Simmer at medium-low heat for 30 to 45 minutes.
6. Add lima beans, corn, and tomatoes. Return to a simmer; stir frequently.
7. Add salt and pepper to taste.
8. Add 1 teaspoon of sugar to cut any bitterness from the vegetables. Simmer in a covered pot for 2 to 3 hours, stirring occasionally.
9. Add chicken broth, bacon grease, and sugar as needed. Simmer until the center of the stew is thick enough to eat with a fork.
10. Stir in tomato soup, and stir frequently during the last few minutes of cooking.

Further Reading

Brunswick, County, VA. "Brunswick Stew: A Tradition with Taste." http://www.brunswickco.com/html/history_of_brunswick_stew.html.

Kelly Newsome

C

Cactus

There are more than 2,000 species of cactus, but the prickly pear cactus is the only one that is edible. The prickly pear is a staple of Mexican cuisine, but is also native to South America. There is evidence of indigenous populations cooking with the plant prior to Spanish colonization. Spaniards brought the plant to Europe with them, and today it is grown around the world from North Africa to Australia, Italy, and Madagascar.

Both the leaf pads, or paddles, of the plant and the fruit are edible. The leaf pads are sold under the name *nopales*. When choosing a paddle, firm and brightly colored ones should be sought to ensure finding the ones with the best taste and crispness. They can be boiled, grilled, or fried until tender.

Like other forms of cacti, prickly pears have spikes. These can be removed by scraping the leaves of the plant with a knife. Nopales can be used similarly to other vegetables in salads, with eggs, and in meat dishes.

Prickly pear cactus fruit is also known as *tunas* in the Spanish speaking world, and *sabras* in Israel. Regardless of whether you buy a purple or green fruit, they are best if they are an even color on the outside, and have a little give when pressed. The skin of the fruit is covered in glochids, tiny, nearly invisible spikes. To remove them, it is best to rinse the fruit in cold water, then peel with gloves before eating.

The fruit of the cactus can be eaten immediately after being peeled, pickled, candied, or as the base for a jam. The fermented fruit of the prickly pear cactus is also used to make *colonche*, an alcoholic drink. Because the fruit is a red-purple color, it has also been marketed as a cocktail mixer.

Both the paddles and fruit of the prickly pear are high in fiber and vitamin C, low in calories, and have no saturated fat or cholesterol. The plant is believed to lower cholesterol and blood glucose levels for diabetics. It has also been found to contain flavonoids, antioxidants that can help fight the effects of free radicals.

Cactus Tacos

Ingredients

2 cactus paddles, peeled
6 corn or flour tortillas
½ cup of cilantro, finely chopped
1 large tomato, diced
½ medium white onion, finely chopped
2 jalapenos, minced
⅓ cup queso fresco, crumbled
Olive oil
Dash of salt, to taste
2 radishes, sliced (optional)
Salsa verde (optional)

1. Rinse peeled cactus in water, then dry on paper towel.
2. Season with a dash of salt. These steps should help remove some of the slime that comes on fresh cactus.
3. Slice cactus into ¼ inch strips. Place in a large frying pan with a little olive oil, and cook on medium heat.
4. Turn during cooking, and cook until cactus starts to brown and begins to become tender.
5. Set aside on a paper towel to absorb the juices from cooking.
6. Reserving the juices from the cactus, heat the onion and jalapeno until they begin to brown. Set aside.
7. Before assembling, heat the tortillas.
8. Place equal parts of cactus, and onion and jalapeno mixture in each tortilla.
9. Top with tomato and cilantro, then the queso fresco. The tacos can also be topped with salsa verde and radishes.

Further Reading

Midey, Connie. "A Magical Plant." *Arizona Republic*, May 31, 2005. http://www.azcentral.com/health/diet/articles/0531prickly0531.html.

Niethammer, Carolyn J. *The Prickly Pear Cookbook*. Tucson, AZ: Rio Nuevo Publishers, 2004.

Caroline Erb Medina

Camel

Camel are herbivores, or plant-eating mammals, used for transport, meat, and milk around the world. They have a long neck and legs, a hump or humps in the center of the back, and are covered all over in coarse hair. They can reach up to 11 feet tall and weigh as much as 1,500 pounds.

There are two main species of camels, dromedaries (Arabians) and bactrians. Dromedaries have one hump and are native to the Middle East and northern Africa, while bactrians have two humps and are native to the central and western parts of Asia. The hump is made up of fat and body tissue, not bone, and is considered a delicacy in many Middle Eastern countries.

A camel's natural habitat is the desert, as it can go for many days without food or water in the heat, and still maintain and produce quality milk. However, the ancestors of camels originated in the prairies of North America, and it is suspected many moved to Africa and Asia during the Ice Age, where they were later domesticated. Today, camel meat and milk are consumed in the Middle East, northern Africa, central and western Asia, and parts of the Australian Outback.

Camels produce a red meat that tastes similar to beef, but with a slightly sweeter taste. Approximately 50 percent of the camel's body weight is meat, and much of the meat is tough, which is why it is often ground up into sausages, burgers, or kebabs. Camel meat is rich in minerals and has a lower fat content than beef, which helps reduce the risk of developing heart disease. Research even shows that camel meat contains antioxidants that help fight cancer.

Camel milk is a light, white color and tastes slightly salty due the animal's varied diet. The milk can be drunk fresh, fermented into yogurt, sour cream, or cheese, or turned into butter. Cultured camel milk products have lower lactose levels and are more digestible for those who are lactose-intolerant. Camel milk is nutritional because it has low saturated, easily digestible fats and high amounts of amino acids, proteins, and minerals.

Camel eating is traditional in Muslim areas of the Middle and Near East and northern Africa. Tradition says that the prophet Muhammad declared people who did not eat camel meat to be un-Muslim, so Muslims in these areas try to eat camel meat at least once a year. One ancient camel recipe is like a precursor to the popular American dish, the turkducken; it involves a baby camel stuffed with a lamb stuffed with a chicken, and the cavities are filled with rice, spices, raisins, and nuts. For special occasions, often a whole baby camel is purchased, cut up, and roasted for a special meal, especially the stomach, hocks, and hump. Another special occasion meal is *lubia bishmi*, which is a stew of camel, green beans, and tomatoes served with rice pilaf and yogurt.

There are also more modern and easier ways to consume camel in these areas. Camel meat is not available in grocery stores or restaurants, but rather at specialty butchers, who will sometimes signify they sell camel meat by hanging a small sign with a camel on it or a real severed camel head outside their shops. If asked, the specialty camel butchers will take a piece of fresh camel meat, mince it, grill it, and serve it as a kebab or kefta right in the shop.

Even though camel is rarely served at restaurants, a restaurant in Dubai called The Local House has started offering camel hamburgers as a healthy alternative to the traditional cow-based burger. The camel burgers are fat and cholesterol-free, require a special process to tenderize the meat, and are covered in cheese and burger sauce.

Approximately 150 years ago, English settlers brought dromedary camels to Australia to help travel, haul, and explore, and a few got loose. Today, the largest pack of wild dromedaries lives in the Australian Outback, which is a giant desert. Estimates suggest there are anywhere from 200,000 to 1 million of these wild camels, and they are considered a nuisance to native species and plants, so Australia is encouraging its people to eat more camel meat. Traditionally, camel meat was only consumed by Aboriginal Australians in the Outback, but it is starting to become trendier. Occasionally, camel meat pies (which mimic the famous English/Australian meat pies) can be found at popular snack shops around the Outback, and a few companies are trying to sell gourmet camel steaks and sausages around the country. Much of the camel meat produced in Australia, however, is exported to other countries.

Camel Kefta Burgers

Inspired by a recipe found at Anissa Helou's Blog, http://www.anissas.com/blog1/?p=76

Ingredients

1 medium yellow onion, chopped
1 large clove of garlic, minced
½ cup flat leaf parsley, finely chopped
1 lb. ground camel meat
½ tsp Chinese five spice powder
¼ tsp ground cinnamon
Salt and pepper to taste

1. Mix all of the ingredients together in a bowl until thoroughly blended; then make a small patty and fry it to taste.
2. Divide the meat into 10 equal portions, then roll into balls and slightly flatten.
3. Heat up a pan or charcoal grill, then cook the meat 2 to 3 minutes on each side, or until it is done to your desired temperature. Serve hot with pita bread and yogurt.

Further Reading

Bulliet, Richard W. *The Camel and The Wheel.* New York: Columbia University Press, 1990.

Heine, Peter. *Food Culture in the Near East, Middle East and North Africa.* Westport, CT: Greenwood Press, 2004.

Helou, Anissa. "Camel Hump, Finally." *Anissa Helou's Blog.* http://www.anissas.com/blog1/?p=1301.

Katz, Solomn H. *Encyclopedia of Food and Culture.* New York: Charles Scribner's Sons, 2002.

Leena Trivedi-Grenier

Cannabis Soda

The brand savvy Soda Pot is available in five bright flavors, each a spin on another popular soft drink. However, unlike Coca Cola, Canna Cola boasts 37 to 65 milligrams of THC. Pop the top and cheer to laced carbonation.

Canna Cola "soda pot" is the newest edition to the edible (or drinkable) medical marijuana segment. A product founded by Clay Butler, a commercial scientist in Soquel, California, Canna Cola flavors include Orange Kush, Grape Ape, Canna Cola (Coca Cola), Dog Weed (Dr. Pepper/cherry soda), and Sour Diesel (Sprite/ the lemon-lime variety).

Canna Cola isn't the first carbonated marijuana-laced beverage, but it is the first to focus so heavily on the packaging and flavor. Butler, who has never indulged in cannabis himself, says that besides the average ingredients found in any soda pop: sugar, water, carbonation, and coloring, Canna cola contains only 2.5 grams, about one-third of the THC included in some spiked sodas. "It's got a mild marijuana taste. But the taste factor is really negligible compared to some competitors with three times the THC. When you get to that level, you really have a heavy aftertaste," Butler comments.

Perhaps it is fitting; Butler hails from Soquel. After all, in 1996 California was the first American state to legalize medical marijuana. Since then Alaska, Arizona, California, Colorado, Hawaii, Maine, Maryland, Michigan, Montana, Nevada, New Jersey, New Mexico, Oregon, Rhode Island, Vermont, and Washington have followed suit. Of these, Colorado will be the first to host Canna Cola, which will only be available at medical marijuana dispensaries.

Patients are often approved to use medical marijuana to battle some of the most painful diseases like HIV/AIDS, Cancer, Crohn's disease, glaucoma, and muscle spasms (among others). "The evidence is overwhelming that marijuana can relieve certain types of pain, nausea, vomiting, and other symptoms caused by such illnesses as multiple sclerosis, cancer, and AIDS—or by the harsh drugs sometimes

Clay Butler, cofounder of Canna Cola, poses on the beach with his product in Santa Cruz, California. (AP Photo/Marcio Jose Sanchez)

used to treat them. And it can do so with remarkable safety. Indeed, marijuana is less toxic than many of the drugs that physicians prescribe every day," says Joycelyn Elders, MD, a former U.S. surgeon general.

While the most popular form of ingesting THC has been through smoking, there are actually three ways to indulge: smoking, eating, and vaporization. Vaporization is ingestion through the use of heated air and produces no cough. While there is nothing in cannabis that will harm the lungs, ingesting marijuana while smoking can do harm. On the same coin, smoking can be inconvenient and time consuming. Patients in a rising number of cases are

beginning to prefer the use of edibles for convenience sake.

Smoking versus eating marijuana results in two very different types of high. When consuming marijuana, the drug travels through the intestines to the liver, where it is converted into 11-hydroxy-THC before traveling to the brain. This chemical stays in the body for a much longer time at a lower intensity. For patients battling pain, this is the ideal type of painkiller, one that is long-lasting, with manageable side effects. Generally, smoking imparts a more intense and short-lived high.

In addition to contributing to a more controlled experience, patients appreciate edibles, such as soda pop, which can be taken anywhere. In the category of edibles, Gonga spiked lemonade is the most popular so far, but Butler is convinced that his 12-ounce drinks, selling for $10 to $15, each will soon challenge this statistic. If the Canna Cola label is nothing else, it is convincing.

Further Reading

Baine, Wallace. "Pot Meets Pop: Local Entrepreneur Plans to Market Line of Smartly Branded Medical-marijuana Soft Drinks." *Santa Cruz Sentinel*, January 24, 2011. http://www.santacruzsentinel.com.

"Canna Cola, Doc Weed: Pot Meets Pop." *Associated Press*, January 24, 2011. http://www.msnbc.msn.com/id/41232607/ns/business-consumer_news/.

Gierach, Ryan. "Medical Marijuana For Dummies: Soda Pot." *WeHo News*, July 6, 2006. http://wehonews.com.

Justin, S. "States That Allow Medical Marijuana in 2011." Canna Central, January 10, 2011. http://cannacentral.com/news/states-that-allow-medical-marijuana-in-2011/.

Parloff, Roger. "How Marijuana Became Legal." CNN, September 18, 2009. http://money.cnn.com.

"Top 10 Pros and Cons." ProCon.org, May 6, 2009. http://medicalmarijuana.procon.org/view.resource.php?resourceID=000141.

Erica Hope

Carob Syrup and Caramels

Carob syrup is a mildly sweet liquid that looks like dark honey or treacle and is extracted from carob pods. Carob pods are the fruit of the carob tree (*Ceratonia siliqua*)—a sturdy evergreen tree indigenous to the Mediterranean region and some parts of the Middle East and southwestern Asia. Nowadays, this tree is also found in other countries where it was transported primarily by maritime nations. These include Mexico, South America, South Africa, India, and Australia. Carob trees are also mainly found in California, Arizona, and Florida in the United States.

The name carob is derived from the Arab word *kharoub,* which means pod. This pod (technically a legume) is flat, dark reddish-brown and leathery, and contains from 5 to 15 seeds. The seeds are similar to large melon seeds and are surrounded by a saccharine pulp. Both carob syrup and the

Carob pods. (Photo by Suzanne Piscopo)

caramels (similar to boiled sweets) made from the syrup rely on this pulp for their sweetness.

Interestingly, carob seeds are quite uniform in weight and are thought to have been the original gauge for the carat used by jewelers.

In many countries around the Mediterranean basin, the carob pod has been used to produce carob syrup. On the islands of Malta and Sicily, and possibly other countries in the region, a type of caramel is also made from the syrup.

Carob syrup is typically made by soaking roasted carob pods in water, then boiling the mixture to extract the syrup. Next, the mixture is strained, sugar is added and the liquid is simmered for a while and eventually re-boiled until it becomes syrupy. During the boiling stage, one can add some natural flavorings, such as spices and fruit zest. (See full recipe below.) In the Near East, syrup is extracted from carob pods by pressing them through mangles when they are very ripe. Carob syrup is not to be mistaken for carob honey, which is made from the nectar of carob tree flowers.

Carob caramels are made by reducing carob syrup over high heat until it reaches the hard-crack stage. The syrup has to be boiled to the correct temperature (716°F/380°C) as boiling at a lower temperature will result in a white syrup that does not harden, while boiling at a higher temperature will result in a black syrup that hardens but has a bitter taste. The mixture is then poured onto a cool surface, such as a marble slab, and while still supple, it is marked out in squares. This is done by crisscrossing the caramel using a rolling pin that has circular blades from right to left. Once hardened, a knife is used to lift the caramel and the squares are broken off gently.

For centuries, carob pods have been used as a source of food for humans and animals in countries bordering the Mediterranean. Evidence of this dates back to ancient Greece and Egypt. There are also numerous references to the carob pod in the Christian Bible. Both the prodigal son and St. John the Baptist are believed to have subsisted on carob pods. In fact, the carob is also known as St. John's bread, or locust beans, as it was once thought that the pods were the locusts eaten by John while living in the desert. The Jewish Talmud also references carob. A legend similar to that of John the Baptist exists for Rabbi Shimon bar Yochai and his son.

Nowadays, the carob is mainly processed to produce carob bean gum or carob powder. The gum is used as a stabilizer, emulsifier, and thickener or to prevent crystallization in many foodstuffs, especially confectionery. The powder is derived from the milled dry roasted pods and is used as a substitute for cocoa powder in confectionery products and drinks, as well as a general sweetener.

Carob syrup is sometimes used as an alternative sweetener instead of honey. But it is mainly still used as a cough remedy, mixed with hot water to produce a drink for soothing sore throats and easing bouts of coughing. One can also make a refreshing healthy drink by blending together carob syrup, ice cubes, and water and serving with a slice of lemon. In a number of Mediterranean countries the production of carob syrup is seeing a revival due to the increasing promotion of local, traditional foodstuffs and culinary crafts and as part of agro-tourism initiatives.

On the Mediterranean island of Malta, carob sweets are traditionally available during the Christian period of Lent and on Good Friday. For centuries, they have been the only type of sweet allowed during this period of fasting, some say due to their alleged medicinal properties. In the past, during Good Friday sacred processions, it was very common to see street hawkers carrying cane baskets selling little bags of square-shaped carob caramels. Each caramel used to be wrapped individually in grease-proof paper, and then packed in handfuls in a paper bag. Unfortunately, carob caramels are scarcely available any more, with only a few artisanal producers making them. However, some enterprising local companies are now producing them in a more up-market concoction to sell to tourists and as specialty food gifts.

Based on an analysis of carob flour, carob is highly nutritious. It is a good source of various vitamins (e.g., vitamins A, B_1, B_2, and B_3), minerals (e.g., calcium, phosphorus, potassium, and manganese), and fiber. It is low in fat and is free of the addictive caffeine and theobromine present in cocoa. Hence, it is often considered a healthy substitute for cocoa. Carob syrup and caramels are by nature a concentrated source of carbohydrates in the form of sugar.

Carob Syrup

Ingredients

2¼ lb. carob pods
2¼ lb. sugar
2 quarts or 2 liters of water
Cloves
Cinnamon sticks
Lemon zest

1. Wash the carob pods well and pat dry.
2. Place the pods in a single layer on baking trays and roast them at 375°F/190°C/gas mark 5 for 10 minutes. Leave to cool.
3. Chop the pods into 1-inch/2 1.2-cm pieces and soak overnight in the water.
4. Next morning, transfer the pods and soaking liquid to a large pot. Add the cloves, cinnamon sticks, and pieces of lemon zest and bring to a rolling boil. Boil rapidly for a further 5 minutes.
5. Turn down the heat and leave the pot to simmer for 30 minutes.
6. Strain the water into a clean saucepan, pressing down on the pod pieces to extract all the syrup.
7. Add the sugar to the pot and stir the mixture over a low heat until the sugar is completely dissolved.
8. Turn up the heat again and boil for at least 30 minutes, or until the mixture thickens to a syrupy texture.
9. Allow the syrup to cool and then pour it into sterilized jars or bottles.

Further Reading

Cremona, M. "Cooking with Carobs." *Taste*, 2008. http://taste.com.mt/2008/08/features/cooking-with-carobs.

Hamilton, T. *Carob Cookbook*. Santa Fe, NM: Sunstone Press, 1990.

Suzanne Piscopo

Casu Marzu

Casu marzu, also known as *casu modde*, *casu cundhidu*, or *formaggio marcio*, a

Sardinian delicacy, is an unpasteurized sheep's milk Pecorino cheese, which is intentionally infested with maggots.

The cheese begins as Pecorino Sardo, a white, sheep's milk cheese that is typically left to ripen in cool, dark cellars. In order to produce the prized casu marzu (Sardinian for rotten cheese), it is instead left to ferment uncovered outdoors in the Sardinian sun, where it attracts the *Piophila casei* cheese fly. To attract the fly, some producers drill holes and deposit oil into the center of the cheese. As it ferments, each fly lays hundreds of eggs inside the cheese. The newly hatched larvae then digest the aging pecorino, their enzymes breaking down the cheese's fats. This results in soft, oozing, almost liquid goo, now ready for consumption.

The pungent cheese must be eaten while the maggots are still alive and is considered toxic once the maggots have died. Some remove the larvae before consuming by placing slices of the cheese into brown paper bags and suffocating the larvae. Others prefer to eat the cheese, maggots and all. Aficionados prize the unique taste and texture of the resulting product, which has been described as possessing similar flavor and bite as Gorgonzola cheese.

Locals believe casu marzu is an aphrodisiac that can produce hallucinogenic effects. The Sardinian government has banned the product for health reasons, including allergic reactions, burning of the esophagus and stomach, and enteric myaisis, an intestinal larval infection. It is said that the maggots, which are resistant to human stomach acid, may be able to pass into the stomach, creating lesions and other ailments.

Casu marzu is available on the black market, where it sells for two to three times the price of regular Pecorino. It is often served at homes of friends and relatives during celebrations such as weddings and birthdays. A goat's milk version of the cheese is also produced in northern Italy's Piedmont and Lombardy regions.

Cazu marzu is usually served at the end of the meal, spread on pane carasau, a water-moistened Sardinian flatbread. The sandwich is folded in half and served with a strong red wine such as Cannonau. It is important to protect one's eyes while eating the sandwich, as the larvae are able to launch themselves up to six inches into the air.

Further Reading

Clark, David. "Casu Marzu: The Maggot Cheese of the Mediterranean." *Mental Floss* (blog). http://www.mentalfloss.com/blogs/archives/21465.

Loomis, Susan Herrmann. "Sardinia, Italy." *Bon Appétit*. http://web.archive.org/web/20060409031053/http://www.epicurious.com/bonappetit/features/travel/sardinia.

Overstreet, Robin M. "Presidential Address: Flavor Buds and Other Delights." *Journal of Parasitology* (Halifax, Nova Scotia, Canada: American Society of Parasitologists) 89, no. 6 (December 2003): 1093–1107. http://www.bioone.org/perlserv/?request=get-document&doi=10.1645%2FGE-236&ct=1.

Natalya Murakhver

Caterpillars

At the end of every May, after the first rains of the season, the Shea trees (scientific name *Butrospermum parkii*, *Vittelaria paradoxa*, or *Butrospermum paradoxum*) of the Southwest region of the West African state of Burkina Faso are invaded by caterpillars (scientific name *Cyri-butyrospermi vuillet*) who feast on the leaves of this fruit-bearing tree, before closing into a cocoon and coming out as a beautiful butterfly. The caterpillars are about four centimeters long and one centimeter wide and are quite meaty. According to the Bobo informants, if the caterpillars are left on the trees they quickly eat all the leaves and the tree will die off, no longer producing the Shea fruit, which is used for making Shea butter, used both in local cuisine and for the production of beauty products, both locally and internationally. However, since the Shea tree is grown and the fruits used for Shea butter production also in areas where the population does not consume caterpillars, the danger of the caterpillar for the tree is not a proven fact.

In the Bobo area, few of the caterpillars survive the transformation into the butterfly, because their meat its much appreciated by the local population, and soon after they appear on the trees, the local women gather them, by shaking the trees, picking them off the ground, and filling their buckets and straw baskets with these small creatures. Once the caterpillars have been gathered, they are killed and dehydrated by boiling in water and rinsing with water mixed with potash. They are then left to dry in the sun, which gives them a black coloring and a taste, according to various informants, of a fried egg or fish. Thus preserved, the caterpillars can be stored for a long period of time without spoiling.

Known in the local language Dioula (Jula) as *situmu* (pronounced either as see-too-moo or she-too-moo) and in Bobo language as *kpwiye*, these caterpillars are the main source of protein in the period form May to August for the populations living in the Southwest of the country, particularly for the Bobo ethnic group, which is autochthonous in this part of the country. Many other ethnic groups, especially the Mossi (Moose), Peul (Fulani or Fulbe) of Burkina Faso view this Bobo eating habit with some disgust. However, while originally only consumed by the Bobo, caterpillars are now appreciated by Burkinabé of various ethnic origins, some of whom live on the other side of the country and will make an effort to travel to the region to buy the delicacy. Selling caterpillars is an important source of income for local women in the period from May to August or September.

The caterpillars are a very important source of protein and are also rich in other important elements. They contain up to 63 percent protein, 15 percent fats, 0.16 percent calcium, and 2.25 percent potassium, which is more than the level of protein of some of the other main foods consumed in Burkina Faso, such as dried and smoked fish. The protein aspect of this food is visible also in the great decline of the sales of other meats in the period of caterpillars.

The aficionados of the Shea tree caterpillars claim that the caterpillars also have medicinal value, such as curing constipation and blood tension among humans and rabies in the dogs, however, so far no studies have been made to prove these claims.

The preparation of the caterpillars is simple. The insects are already dead upon purchase and they simply need to be rinsed before one sautés or fries them in oil and with finely chopped onions. When cooking, the smell is similar to that of fried or sautéed liver or kidney. Prepared in this way, the caterpillars can be eaten as a side dish to a vegetable or starchy staple or as an ingredient in a sandwich, lightly seasoned with a Maggi stock cube, another West African favorite. The caterpillars can also be used in the local sauces, in the same way as one would use pieces of dried fish. In the period of great abundance of caterpillars, the Bobo prepare caterpillars with rice in a manner similar to a pilaf or a seafood risotto.

Further Reading

Agence, Syfia. *L'Afrique, côté cuisines. Regards africains sur l'alimentation.* Paris: Syros, 1994.

Akpossan, Raphaël Amon, Edmond Ahipo Dué, Jean Parfait, E. N. Kouadio, and Lucien Patrice Kouame. "Valeur nutritionnelle et caractérisation physicochimique de la matière grasse de la chenille (Imbrasia oyemensis) séchée et vendue au marché d'Adjamé (Abidjan, Côte d'Ivoire)." *Journal of Animal & Plant Sciences* 3, no. 3 (2009): 243–250.

Fadel, Par. "La chenille ou l'agrobusiness." *L'opinion,* no. 330 (January 28–February 3, 2004). http://www.zedcom.bf/actualite/op330/Nation_nutritionf330.htm.

Şaul, Mahir, Jean-Marie Ouadba, and Ouétian Bongnounou. "The Wild Vegetation Cover of Western Burkina Faso: Colonial Policy and Post-Colonial Development." In *African Savannas: Global Narratives and Local Knowledge of Environmental Change*, edited by Thomas Bassett and Donald Crummey, 121–160. Oxford and Portsmouth, NH: James Currey and Heinemann, 2003.

Liza Debevec

Cavy

Cavy or Cavey are a family of rodents native to South America. They include small and large animals. The most familiar rodent of the Cavy family is the domestic guinea pig. The scientific name for the guinea pig is *Cavia porcellus.* The guinea pig, a traditional part of the Andean diet, is known as a *cuy* in Spanish. The name comes from the squeaking sound the guinea pigs make.

Guinea pigs are used for food most commonly in Peru, Bolivia, Ecuador, and Columbia. They may have been domesticated as early as 5000 BCE and have been a significant source of protein in South America for millennia. More recently, cuy are being raised and eaten in the United States and Europe as an exotic delicacy. However, the taboo against eating rodents still exists in much of the Western world, where guinea pigs are commonly kept as pets.

As an animal high in protein and low in fat and cholesterol, guinea pigs are a healthy choice among other animal proteins. Because they are small and easy to care for, guinea pigs can be raised in urban spaces as well as in rural areas. Guinea pigs eat lawn clippings and vegetable scraps so they are inexpensive to feed, a sustainable meat. They also have short gestation periods and mature quickly so they are inexpensive to breed for food.

Guinea pigs are served in a variety of preparations. They are small animals, but a single mature one is appropriate for a single serving. Traditionally, they are plucked, not skinned. Before being fried or grilled, the guinea pigs are eviscerated, washed, and quartered. After cooking, the meat is served with chilies, peanuts, and potatoes. In restaurants, guinea pigs are often served formally as part of a complicated dish like a casserole. Traditionally in Ecuador, they are served in a soup or simply grilled.

For alternative preparations, substitute guinea pig meat in recipes that call for chicken or rabbit, as the taste and texture of the meat is comparable.

Further Reading

Morales, Edmundo. *The Guinea Pig: Healing, Food, and Ritual in the Andes*. Tucson: University of Arizona Press, 1995.

Schwabe, Calvin W. *Unmentionable Cusine*. Charlottesville: University of Virginia Press, 1979.

Ansley Watson

Cephalopods

Cephalopods are the group of sea faring animals that includes octopus, squid, and cuttlefish. Cephalopods are boneless cartilaginous creatures that can rapidly change in shape, from as big as several basketballs to the size of a tennis ball in seconds to squeeze thorough narrow passageways. They are jet powered and with the help of three different hearts, different species have adapted to survive in climates from warm tropical oceans to the freezing waters surrounding the North and South Poles. When cephalopods first appeared in the late Cambrian period nearly 3 million years prior to the earliest bony fish, they were the dominate life form in the oceans. Currently however, there are less than 800 species surviving. Humankind likes to eat at least three of those, octopus, squid, and cuttlefish.

Cephalopods are sought after for their flesh and their ink alike. When selecting an animal for grilling, frying, or harvesting the ink, it is important to find the freshest available for optimal flavor. Most grocers receive squid, octopus, and cuttlefish pre-frozen, in which case the buyer should make sure not to purchase the thawed version. However, if you are lucky enough to find their fresh counterparts, look at the eyes, which should be bright and clear. A grey color doesn't mean that the fish is dangerous to eat, but it will be past its peak.

Most people think of squid as deep-fried calamari; and while this is excellent, there are numerous other ways to enjoy this oceanic creature, including its ink. Squid ink is a dark and viscous liquid evolutionarily designed to give the cephalopod a quick getaway. When a squid, octopus, or cuttlefish is faced with a predator, it releases a dark cloud allowing it ample time to escape. Other than a spirited defense mechanism, ink is also used in pastas, breads, soups, and even ice creams all over the world. Contrary to common thought, although it may say squid ink, dishes commonly use ink from the cuttlefish sometimes known as sepia. A cuttlefish is slightly larger than a common squid and covered in light-reflecting cells, which help it blend into the ocean floor. Sepia ink is considered far more appealing to the palate than squid ink. The latter is harsh and pungent. The Italians consider squid ink the least desirable portion of the marine animal they so love in their cooking. Cuttlefish ink on the other hand has as soft warm mouth feel and a mellower aroma. Its color too, is gentle. Sepia ink has been used in paintings and dyes since the early Roman times of Pliny the Elder. The ink yields a warm brown color with red undertones. It is still in use today and sepia has become the generic name the color.

Fervent fans of squid ink dishes will defend it enthusiastically, though many without

Dried fish and squid are featured at this market near Seoul Tower in the Republic of South Korea. (Department of Defense)

knowing why. The exact chemical make up of ink was largely unknown until recently; melanin gives it its deep, opaque color, and it is chock full of amino acids, but this hardly solves the mystery of its addictive deliciousness. Scientific analysis of the ink might have yielded the answer. Cephalopod ink has a very high concentration of glutamic acid, known colloquially, though incorrectly as glutamate, the chief component of umami. Umami is the fifth taste, accompanying sweet, sour, bitter, and salty. It is found in foods from all over the world including soy products, Parmigiano Reggiano, and fish sauce. Umami's main role is to

incite deliciousness, melding and intensifying flavors, and ultimately imparting richness to every dish.

Squid ink features prominently in many regional cuisines, but the rice and pasta dishes of Spain and Italy are among the most widely recognized and visually impressive uses of the black liquid. *Chipirones en su tinta* is a Spanish dish in which baby squids, called *chipirones*, are served in a black sauce made from their own ink. The sauce is a rich combination of ink, leeks, and onions that can also be used for *arroz negro* (black rice) or as a sauce for grilled fish. The dish is emblematic of Basque cooking, where the squids are stuffed with their own tentacles. This is essentially the aquatic version of head to tail eating. In Italy *spaghetti al nero di seppia* is a popular dish in which squid ink, tomato sauce, and tons of parsley unite in a combination that has the population completely hooked. The Italians enjoy a rich *risotto al nero di seppia* commonly made with Arborio rice, but regional grains like *farro* also make their appearance lending a crunchy texture next to the soft seppia.

The Japanese also feature squid in their cuisine, though they admit some Italian influence. In Japan, many squid ink dishes are a part of traditional Shinji cuisine eaten for medicinal purposes. *Ika Sumi* is a pork and bitter vegetable soup seasoned with dashi in an ink broth that is said to help fight fever, combat exhaustion, and alleviate anemic symptoms. While the exact roots of this soup are unknown, many believe Christian missionaries brought a version of this recipe with them from Italy. The Japanese have also tried incorporating ink into breads, curries, soba noodles, and even ice cream.

For a home cook, harvesting the ink is no easy matter. While one hand holds the body of the squid, the other grasps the head and gently pulls it way. The entrails, including stomach, intestines, and ink sack should follow the head. The ink sack is very thin, silvery, and easy to puncture. There is an easier way, however. Squid ink is available at quality fishmongers and sold in jars at specialty grocery stores.

Grilled Octopus

Ingredients

1 lb. baby octopus, cleaned
1 lemon, halved
1 clove garlic, crushed

Live Baby Octopus (Sannakji)

Sannakji, or live baby octopi, are considered a delicacy in South Korea. Preparing sannakji is simple. Octopi are pulled from water and immediately cut up into small pieces. Then they are seasoned, tossed in sesame oil, and served immediately with chili or other sauces. After being cut up, the baby octopi still move around on the plate. As expected, the dish is known for being very chewy. Because the dish primarily consists of octopus, it is high in protein.

Sannakji can be found in both restaurants and bars serving a full menu. Reception usually varies between extreme love or hate because of the unique texture and presentation of the food. It has become popular among tourists in South Korea because it is considered to be so unusual.

There is a risk associated with eating sannakji. It is important to chew all pieces fully so that the suction cups on the tentacles do not remain intact. If they remain intact, they can get stuck on the roof of the person's mouth or throat, and become a choking hazard.

Caroline Erb

2 tbsp olive oil

1 dash red wine vinegar

Salt and pepper to taste

1. In a small saucepan, bring cold water to a boil.
2. Add the octopus and lemon and simmer until the octopus is tender, about 20 to 40 minutes, depending on the size. Drain.
3. In a medium bowl, toss together octopus, garlic, and olive oil. Allow to marinate at least 1 hour (best overnight).
4. Remove octopus from oil and grill on a hot grill until brown. The octopus is already cooked so there is no need to worry about doneness.
5. After removing from grill, place on a plate and top with marinade and a splash of vinegar. Season to taste, and serve hot or at room temperature.

Variation: this recipe can be made with larger octopus—just increase the simmering time.

Suggested Reading

Barrenechea, Teresa. *The Cuisines of Spain: Exploring Regional Home Cooking*. New York: Ten Speed Press, 2005.

"Cuttlefish Basics." *TONMO.com: The Octopus News Magazine Online*. http://www. tonmo.com/articles/basiccuttlefish.php.

Kelsey, Charles. "Sleuthing Squid Ink." *Gourmet* (February 11, 2009). www.gourmet. com.

Eleanor Barczak

Chicken Feet

Though to many American diners, the thought of consuming chicken feet may seem off-putting, they are in fact a part of culinary traditions throughout the world, including Asia, Africa, South America, the Caribbean, and the American South, as well as in Jewish cooking.

The preparation of chicken feet usually involves an extended cooking process because of their tough texture. In contrast to the other parts of the chicken, the feet have little edible meat, mostly skin and tendons, which makes them especially chewy unless properly cooked.

Generally, chicken feet are eaten in three ways: simmer-boiled in soups to add body, as an ingredient in stew, or as a dish in their own right, usually as an appetizer or snack. In appetizers, they are usually braised or deep-fried, and occasionally pickled.

No matter how they are prepared, cooking with chicken feet almost always begins the same way: the raw feet are scalded for 10 to 15 minutes in order to soften them, and then the claws, which are inedible (not to mention unappetizing in appearance), are broken or snipped off.

There are several reasons for using chicken feet when making a broth for soup. The primary one is the cartilage in the feet, which has gelatin-like properties that gives body to act as a thickening agent for the broth. Some chefs also claim a nutritional benefit for using the feet, saying the bones also add calcium and minerals.

Another reason is economic: in poor communities where budgets are tight, such as in rural South American countries like Ecuador, Peru, and Colombia, chickens are relatively cheap to raise, and no parts of an animal are wasted. In the past too, families in Jewish shtetls (villages) in Eastern Europe would use not only the feet (called p'tcha) but also the head, neck, gizzards, skin, and fat in various dishes.

Immigrants living in relatively wealthy societies where poultry parts other than breasts, thighs, and legs are generally considered undesirable can take a similar economic advantage of using chicken feet, which sell for as little as 50 cents per pound in places like New York's Chinatown. In one anecdote, a daughter of Jewish immigrants recounts that during the Great Depression, her mother used to collect chicken feet for free from New York butchers, who would have otherwise thrown away these parts.

The preparation of chicken feet for soup is fairly simple. After the initial step of scalding the feet and snipping off the nails, the feet are boiled with water to create a broth, along with various herbs. In Eastern Europe, these might include dill, as well as garlic, salt, and pepper, as well as any vegetables desired, such as carrots, onion, and celery. In South America, leeks, garlic, bell peppers, green beans, and cilantro might also be added, with avocado or sour cream as a garnish. In Jamaica, the feet are simmered along with such ingredients as yams, pumpkin, green bananas, potatoes, breadfruit, thyme, allspice, chili, and dumplings, often for as long as two hours. At the end of the slow cooking process, scallions or *cho cho* are added for additional flavor.

Some people remove the feet at the end of the cooking process. People from various cultures (Czech, Jewish, Ecuadorian) report that older members of their family would remove the outside skin and then snack on the feet to the delight and/or horror of their grandchildren.

Chicken foot stew, or souse, is a preparation unique to the Caribbean island of Trinidad (the stew can also be made with pigs' feet.) It is a dish sold by street vendors at large celebrations or soccer games. One Trinidadian describes seeing vendors stirring the souse with a big spoon in a large pigtail bucket in order to scoop up any feet from the bottom of the bucket.

In chicken foot souse, the de-clawed feet are boiled in seasoned water and then removed. Next, they are soaked along with cucumbers, onions, peppers, and green seasoning and allowed to cool. The souse is served at room temperature.

The main areas in which chicken feet are eaten as a snack or as a small plate are Nigeria, South Africa, the Philippines, and the American South. They are also a part of the dim sum meal, popular in Cantonese cuisine.

In most of these areas, chicken feet are eaten between meals as snacks. For example, in Nigeria, the feet are simply deep fried and served to children. In the Philippines they are a popular street food, and are popularly referred to as adidas, because of the German athletic shoe. In the Durban and Soweto districts of South Africa, the feet are called walkie talkies (because feet are served along with chicken heads) or chicken dust (because the chickens scratch up dust with their feet when alive). After the feet are boiled and the skin and claws are removed, they are seasoned and then grilled. In Hong Kong, vendors sell a similar version during intermissions at the movies.

Many Americans might be surprised to know that chicken feet are also a popular snack in their own country, though primarily in the South. The feet are deep-fried and served like chicken wings in a spicy sauce that may include oyster sauce, soy sauce, ginger, chili and crushed pepper, or brown sugar.

Perhaps the most well-known and certainly one of the most varied uses of chicken feet occurs in Cantonese-style dim sum dining, which originated in the area in and around Hong Kong. Generally, the feet are eaten in the middle of the meal, after lighter, steamed dishes, but before dessert.

The simplest way to serve the feet is pickled. The feet are served cold, and the scaly skin is gnawed from the bone.

The most traditional way to make the feet is to fry them first, to puff them up. Next the feet are marinated in a spicy sauce, and then finally are steamed and served with a black bean sauce. Another option is to braise them, often with ginger, mushrooms, and garlic. Some cooks add sugar to the mix, claiming that it softens the feet.

Further Reading

"Braised Chicken Feet with Mushrooms and Ginger." *Taste of Home* (blog), May 8, 2009. http://www.smokywok.com/2009/05/braised-chicken-feet-with-mushrooms-and.html.

Parker, Sidney. "Chicken Feet: Five Ways to Serve This Exotic Food." Associated Content. http://www.associatedcontent.com/article/2492629/chicken_feet_five_ways_to_serve_this.html.

Wang, Chichi. "The Nasty Bits: No Mean Feet." Serious Eats, August 4, 2009. http://www.seriouseats.com/recipes/2009/08/cantonese-chicken-feet-jalapenos-black-bean-sauce-dim-sum-recipe.html.

Watanabe, June. "Chicken Foot Fetish." *Honolulu Star-Bulletin*, June 3, 1996. http://archives.starbulletin.com/96/07/03/features/index.html.

Aaron Hamburger

Chuños

Chuños are potatoes that have been frozen repeatedly overnight for a series of days, and dehydrated by the sun in the interim days. The food can be found in many areas of South America including Peru, Bolivia, Chile, and Argentina but is a traditional food of the Quechua and Aymara people. More than 2,000 years ago, chuño products may have been developed accidentally in the foothills of the Andes. In the autumn, small potatoes would be unearthed and washed, then laid out on straw to be exposed to frost in the below zero temperatures of the night. People would walk on the potatoes as they thawed during the day, leaving the skins intact, but rupturing the cells and releasing moisture. Thirty percent of the fluid would be lost in the first pressing cycle, and the night-freezing and day-trampling/drying cycle would be repeated for about three to five days. After the fifth day, the potatoes were covered with enough straw to prevent freezing and impact. At this point, the rock-hard potatoes could be stored for long periods of time without being spoiled by minor exposure to moisture. This is the final stage of the chuño.

Because chuños are dried, they can be stored for months or even years with little loss of quality, as long as they are kept dry and free from bugs. Chuños are used in recipes by adding water and heating. Chuño products are used in a variety of dishes from stews to desserts. Critics state that the chuño is used as a starchy filler because it has no particular flavor of its own. Two dishes native to La Paz that incorporate the chuño are chairo, a Bolivian vegetable and meat stew, and *picana de navidad*, a dish of lamb, beef, and chicken with root vegetables and seasonings. A related potato product is tunta. The process is similar, with an additional soaking stage. The potatoes are submerged in a pond for two months, followed by a period of sun drying. Tunta is also known as white chuño. Tunta is pure white in color and easily decomposes into fine white flour. It is also frost-proof and can be stored indefinitely.

Chuños are high in carbohydrates, low in protein vitamins, and minerals. The chuño is also low in the toxic glycoalkaloid compounds, which cause bitterness in potatoes and protect the plant from predators. If ingested, glycoalkaloids can cause headaches, cramps, and even coma and death—although occurrence of death from potato poisoning is rare. The highest concentrations are found just beneath the skin.

Although the chuño has been around for thousands of years, it is currently most significant as a component of Novoandina cuisine. Bernardo Roca Rey founded Novoandina cuisine in 1986 with his signature dish: *la gran olla Huacachina*. The recipe was born after his participation as a judge at a food festival organized by the Gastronomic Association of Peru (Agape). In response to a challenge from the other chefs whom he judged in the festival, he set out to acquire fresh ingredients for a new dish. He ventured to a market the city of Ica, capitol of the Ica region in the south of Peru, know as the land of the sun due to its consistent summerlike climate. Thus begins the history of Novoandina cuisine, which applies modern techniques to traditional Andean and Peruvian raw materials. The emerging cuisine is characterized by light, fat-free brews and includes ingredients such as quinoa, passion fruit, and various flavoring herbs.

Further Reading

Carberry, S. "Alpaca: It's Not Just for Sweaters Anymore." *International Reporting Project* (blog). http://www.international reportingproject.org/fellows-editors/blog_detail/1400/.

Gootenberg, P. "Carneros y Chuño: Price Levels in Nineteenth-Century Peru." *Hispanic American Historical Review* 70, no. 1 (1990): 1–56.

Robertiello, J. "Peruvian Delights in the U.S. Northwest." *Americas* 58, no. 3 (2006): 50–51.

Christen Sturkie

Civet Coffee (Kopi Luwak)

Civet coffee, the world's most expensive and exotic coffee, is brewed from coffee berries, called cherries, that have passed through the digestive tract of the civet, a nocturnal tree-dwelling mammal found in Southeast Asia, southern China, southern India, the Philippines, and Sri Lanka. In Sumatra, Java, Bali, and other parts of Indonesia, where much of this coffee originates, the drink is known as *kopi luwak*, kopi meaning coffee and luwak referring to the Asian palm civet, or common palm civet, found throughout the region. In Vietnam the drink is known as *caphe cut chon,* translated as fox dung coffee or sometimes weasel coffee, and in the Philippines it is called *kape alamid*. The coffee's fame and fascination derive from the fact that the beans are harvested from the animal's feces. Aficionados say this unusual natural processing results in a uniquely smooth, flavorful, and aromatic brew.

The civet, a member of the Viverridae family often likened to a cat or weasel though more similar to the mongoose

Filipino farmer Eleuterio Balidio displays Civet cat droppings of mostly coffee beans, which he retrieved from a coffee farm in Indang, Cavite Province, south of Manila. (AP Photo/Bullit Marquez)

or raccoon, feeds on pulpy fruits, rodents, and insects, with a particular predilection for ripe, red coffee cherries. In the wild, civets presumably seek out the sweetest, choicest berries, a selection process some say accounts for the superior quality of civet coffee. As the berries pass through the animal's digestive tract, most of the pulpy flesh of the fruit is digested but the inner seeds (the coffee beans) remain intact, covered still by a papery skin and small outer layer of sticky mucilage and fruit pulp. The undigested beans are excreted in elongated clumps resembling nut brittle. These droppings, or scat, are collected, washed, and sun dried, and the parchment is removed by mortar and pestle or machine. The beans are then roasted, a light or medium roast generally being recommended as a darker roast might interfere with the coffee's delicate yet complex flavor notes.

In his seminal article on kopi luwak in the early 1990s, food writer Chris Rubin describes the coffee as "incredibly full bodied, almost syrupy, thick, with a hint of chocolate" and extols its "long, clean aftertaste." Connoisseurs note an earthy, musty, almost gamy quality and a marked lack of bitterness. The coffee's aroma has been described as sweet and nutty with a hint of honey and sometimes, perhaps owing to suggestion, a whiff of zoo or barnyard.

Originally, all civet coffee was collected in forests, jungles, and coffee plantations where civets, originally considered pests, feasted in the wild. Once this delicacy was discovered, producers began farming civets to expand production. Farmed civets, particularly those that are caged rather than free roaming, are often fed berries of varying ripeness and quality, eliminating the natural selection process said to account, in part, for the coffee's special qualities.

The unique flavor and aroma of civet coffee may come not only from the pre-selection of the beans by the picky civet, but also from changes induced by digestive enzymes and stomach acids as the coffee cherries pass through the civet's gastrointestinal tract. Food scientist Dr. Massimo Marcone, of the University of Guelph in Canada, has demonstrated that proteolytic enzymes penetrate the coffee beans as they make their way through the civet's digestive system, breaking down storage proteins that can give coffee a bitter taste. (A Vietnamese coffee producer, Trung Nguyen, aided by German scientists, has developed a special enzyme treatment mimicking this natural effect. They use this patented process to create a simulated civet coffee marketed as Legendee that is available at coffeehouses throughout Vietnam.) In addition, the coffee undergoes natural fermentation by lactic acid bacteria in the civet's gut, akin but possibly superior to water fermentation in the wet method of coffee processing.

The Asian palm civet's scientific name, *Paradoxurus hermaphroditus*, may hold another clue to the allure of civet coffee. Taxonomists in the late 1700s chose the species name because both males and females possess beneath their tails small glands resembling testicles. The odiferous secretion of these perianal scent glands has been variously cited as a territory marker or defense mechanism, but given its musk-like properties and proximity to the genital area, one might assume it has a role in sexual attraction—perhaps accounting for what some connoisseurs tout as the aphrodisiac allure of civet coffee. Lending credence to this hypothesis is the fact that this civet musk has long been used in perfumery.

Contrary to expectation, civet coffee may come from any variety of coffee bean, depending on what types the civet has at its disposal, the final product being influenced by such factors as altitude, soil, and shade, as with any coffee. In Sumatra, the largest producer of both farmed and wild kopi luwak, most of the civet coffee is Arabica. Robusta, less favored, is also typical in civet coffee-producing regions, sometimes blended with Arabica, either before or after processing through the civet. In the Batangas and Kalingas regions of the Philippines, civets are often fed a combination of Arabica, Excelsa, and the rare Liberica.

While the Asian palm civet, sometimes called a toddy cat for its penchant for fermented palm flower sap known as toddy, is the species most commonly associated with "poop" coffee, other animals, including bats, monkeys, barking deer (producing coffee known in Indonesia as *kopi muntjak*), and birds (especially the Jacu bird of Brazil) ingest and excrete, or sometimes spit, coffee beans that are then collected and cleaned for human use.

Because of the careful cleaning process and the fact that the civet is not a known host for *E. coli* bacteria, most experts agree that civet coffee does not pose a health risk for humans. Indeed, when Marcone was asked to test a batch of kopi luwak, the civet beans were found to contain fewer bacteria than the control samples. Viral contamination has been another hypothetical concern. In 2004, the Chinese government ordered the killing of thousands of civets, eaten as meat in China, in an effort to control an outbreak of SARS, Severe Acute Respiratory Syndrome. However, subsequent research suggested that the civets were not the source of the virus, which seemingly jumped from bats to humans and then to civets. Furthermore, the civets in question were the Himalayan, or masked palm civet, *Paguma larvata*, a different genus and species from the *Paradoxurus hermaphroditus* of kopi luwak fame.

Civet coffee sparks fascination as much for its rarity and price as for its esoteric mode of production. Some sources state that only 500 to 1,000 pounds of civet beans are harvested each year, though other estimates are much higher. The lower figures may represent the output of wild, vs. farmed, civets, though this distinction is rarely cited. Compounding the confusion, and skepticism, over the quantity and even very existence of kopi luwak, is the practice by some unscrupulous purveyors of blending in or substituting altogether ordinary beans for the civet beans, perhaps throwing in a piece of civet turd for good measure. While no formal process has been adopted to document the provenance of what is sold as civet coffee, more reputable dealers source their supply from single plantations or collectors they personally inspect, and some have even

sent their beans to Marcone in Ontario for authentication—his lab has analytic techniques, including an electronic nose, that can detect the characteristic changes induced by transit through the civet's innards. Marcone estimates that as much as half of what is passed off as civet coffee is fake. The intrepid consumer can purchase raw, unprocessed kopi luwak from select online outlets for the ultimate guarantee of authenticity: just clean and roast the beans at home.

With its short supply and storied origin, civet coffee commands lofty prices, selling for $100 to $500 and more per pound in Japan, the United States, and Canada through specialty coffee retailers. Mark Mountanos is credited as the first to import kopi luwak in the United States; and J. Martinez & Company in Atlanta, Porto Rico Importing Company in New York City, and Raven's Brew in Ketchikan, Alaska, have all had a hand in educating and supplying the rare beans to retail customers in this country. Occasionally, a daring café owner in North America, Australia, or Europe will offer a special cupping where the brew can be sampled for $10 to $50 per cup, and coffeehouses throughout Southeast Asia routinely sell civet coffee, typically local production, by the cup for tourists and locals alike.

Not surprisingly, civet coffee occasions a fair bit of fun-poking and punnery. Journalists can't resist such headlines as "Poo Brew," "Doo Process," "Crappuccino," and "Good to the Last Dropping," one writer noting, fairly enough, that "the end justifies the beans." But perhaps the truth is in the cup of the beholder. One reverent convert exclaims, "This is the kind of coffee you renounce your religion and sell your child for."

Further Reading

Marcone, Massimo. "Composition and Properties of Indonesian Palm Civet Coffee (Kopi Luwak) and Ethiopian Civet Coffee." *Food Research International* 37, no. 9 (2004): 901–912.

Pendergrast, Mark. *Uncommon Grounds: The History of Coffee and How It Transformed Our World*. New York: Basic Books, 1999.

Rubin, Chris. "Kopi Luwak: An Indonesian Island Treasure." Excerpted from *Café Ole Magazine*, found at *Sally's Place*. http://www.sallybernstein.com/beverages/coffee/kopi_luwak.htm.

Schoenhalt, Donald. "Kopi Luak: the Stercoraceous Coffee of Indonesia." *Tea & Coffee Trade Journal* (September 1, 1999): 142–146.

Meryl Rosofsky

Crawfish

The crawfish is a decapod crustacean similar, anatomically speaking, to the lobster, which accounts for the resemblance. This tiny treasure goes by many names. If you're in the northern United States, you should order a plate of crayfish; in Texas you'd better make it an order of mudbugs; in Australia, you'd be asking for some yabbies; but if you want to be sure that you're getting the right thing when you sit down in a Cajun restaurant, you'd best say crawfish.

Taking roughly 4 years to reach maturity, they have a lifespan of 20 to 30 years and average 4 to 6 inches in length, although some varieties can top out at 10 inches. The largest crawfish can be found in Tasmania and have been reported to have weighed as much as 11 pounds! The bodies of these freshwater crustaceans are comprised of 20 individual segments, most of which are too tiny to be of any culinary significance. Like their larger crustacean cousin, the lobster, it's the tail meat that is of most interest to diners. The abdomen of the crawfish holds a tiny, delicious morsel of sweet, salty goodness.

Sometimes kept as pets in home aquariums, these animals are typically used either for food or as bait, but they serve yet another purpose. Similar to canaries in a coal mine, crawfish serve as an indicator species as they are intolerant of polluted water. Environmentalists use the crawfish population of various waterways as a means of monitoring water quality.

Like some other crustaceans, crawfish molt, which means they shed their exoskeleton (shell) and grow a new one. Expert recyclers, they eat their discarded shells, which are made primarily of calcium. The nutrients afforded them by the discarded shells helps them to grow a new, slightly larger shell. Molting crawfish are extremely vulnerable to predators in their soft bodies while they grow their new shells, and since they are cannibalistic, molting crawfish have to beware not only of predators, but of their less-than-sympathetic brothers who will eat anything they can get their claws on. Crawfish are not discriminating eaters. They eat vegetation, small aquatic animals, and the carcasses of dead animals.

There are hundreds species of crawfish that can be found the world over in bodies of freshwater that run year round without freezing to the bottom. In the 1960s, technological advances and market demands aided the development of crawfish farming which is the leading form of shellfish aquaculture in the United States, and Louisiana alone produces nearly all of the domestic supply. While more than 330 varieties exist within the United States, only two species are commercially available, the red swamp (*Procambarus clarkii*), and the white river (*Procambarus zonangulus*). The meat of the red swamp and white river crawfish is very similar, but between these two varieties, the red swamp variety is widely preferred for culinary use based solely on its red appearance.

These creatures have been part of the U.S. culinary landscape since long before the arrival of the early European settlers. Crawfish are central to the creation myths of the Creek and Yuchi Indians. They're said to have burrowed underwater to retrieve the mud that would serve as the foundation of the earth. Crawfish were part of the natural diets of these tribes and were often dried and stored for use when food was expected to be scarce. Naturally low in fat, the tail meat is an excellent source of protein and a nutritious food source in lean times

Among Houma Indians, who take their name from them, crawfish are considered sacred, and according to their creation myth, it is from the crawfish that the tribe descended. For modern Houmas, who are largely Catholic, crawfish are an important part of their Lenten diet, so much so that eating them becomes almost a religious experience similar to the Christian act of taking communion. Their traditional Good Friday crawfish boil, where the crawfish are boiled alive, is said to symbolize the crucifixion of Jesus. Crawfish are also an important part of the Lenten diet of the larger Catholic population in Louisiana. Incidentally, Vatican II, a revision of Roman Catholic doctrine within which changes were made around the fasting and abstention from animal products during Lent to allow seafood, coincided with the advent of the crawfish farming industry contributing to its rapid development and long-term success.

Crawfish are synonymous with Louisiana. They are such an integral part of the landscape that in 1983, the crawfish was named the state crustacean. The animal figures prominently in the history and culture of Louisiana's Cajun community, in particular. Breaux Bridge, a Cajun enclave, is known as the Crawfish Capital of the World. Legend has it that after the Acadians (ancestors of today's Cajuns) were driven out of Nova Scotia in the 1700s, the lobsters, which were part of Acadian culture, missed the Acadians so much that they set off on a quest to find them. The journey was an arduous one and by the time they found their beloved Acadians in the bayous and swamps of southern Louisiana, the lobsters had shrunk in size to what we now know as crawfish. Their arrival was celebrated with a festival and is commemorated annually to this day, and these tiny crustaceans are featured in the many harvest festivals and social gatherings popular among Cajuns. From late February to mid-May, crawfish season in Louisiana, you're likely to find that there is no shortage of crawfish boils.

Crawfish can be prepared as any other shellfish, though most Louisianans would say that the best way is the boil. A boil consists of potatoes, corn on the cob, seasonings, and of course, crawfish. The ingredients are boiled together and then drained and the contents of the pot poured over newspaper-covered tables. The usual accompaniment is beer. How does one eat a crawfish? To begin with, the head is separated from the body. The shell is peeled back from the start of the tail and the end of the tail is pinched, which releases the meat from its confines. Hardcore crawfish aficionados then suck the seasoning-infused fat from the head, hence the saying, "Suck the head, pinch the tail."

Crawfish can easily replace lobster, shrimp, and crab in most recipes. Generally, only the tail meat is used; however, the claws of larger specimens may yield enough meat to be worth the effort required to extract it. The heads and shells are also great for making soup or stock. The recipe below is simple and straightforward.

Crawfish Cakes

Ingredients

3 eggs, beaten
2 lb. crawfish tail meat, chopped
2 cups long grain rice, cooked
2 slices bacon, cooked and crumbled
1 cup bread crumbs
1 bell pepper, finely minced
½ onion, finely minced
½ tsp Old Bay seasoning
½ tsp thyme
½ tsp kosher salt
¼ to ½ tsp hot sauce (optional)
Extra virgin olive oil

1. In a mixing bowl combine crawfish, rice, bacon, bell pepper, onion, Old Bay, and thyme.
2. Add eggs and mix well. Refrigerate for 20 to 30 minutes.
3. Combine salt and breadcrumbs in a dish for dredging.
4. Add olive oil to a heated skillet.
5. Using hands, form small patties from the crawfish mix, dredge in breadcrumbs and place in hot skillet.
6. Cook 5 to 7 minutes per side. Serve on a bed of lettuce chiffonade with lemon wedges and a remoulade or cocktail sauce.

Further Reading

Ladewig, Kathleen, and Senae Schaer. *Crawfish: A Healthy Choice*. Stoneville, MS: Southern Regional Aquaculture Center, 1993.

Pitre, Glen. *The Crawfish Book: The Story of Man and Mudbugs Starting in 25,000 B.C. and Ending with the Batch just Put on to Boil*. Jackson: University Press of Mississippi, 1993.

Hayley Figueroa

D

Dog Meat

Like it or not, man's best friend is more than just a pet in some parts of the world—he's dinner. While its moral appropriateness—and even its legality—is debatable, there's little hope that the consumption of dog will be disappearing anytime soon.

While eating dog meat is legally outlawed in most countries, its ingestion—legal and illegal—has not disappeared. Dog meat is seen as comparable to chicken or pork in Vietnam and a delicacy in parts of Ghana. It is also knowingly consumed in southern and far northeastern China and in parts of Korea, Polynesia, Nigeria, the Philippines, and Switzerland. Keep in mind, though, that the percentage of these populations that consume dog meat is small, and even those that do so claim only to indulge rarely. Still, it's estimated that 13 to 16 million dogs are killed and eaten in Asia each year.

The meat is typically obtained from breeding farms where specific breeds are raised—in Korea, for example, the *nure-ongi* breed—or obtained from routine raids of rural regions known to have large populations of stray dogs. It can be argued that seizing these stays dogs is helping these communities, not only financially, as the farms receive a small amount of money per raid, but for health, sanitation, and safety reasons.

While there are records of dog meat consumption dating back to 500 BCE in China and Korea, its place in history during times of famine is widespread. It was a vital part of sustenance during each German crisis, deemed blockade mutton. In cold climates such as Alaska and northern Canada, sled dogs were occasionally used as a source of food in emergencies.

Just as varied as feelings on the issue of consuming dog meat are the ways in which it can be cooked: cooked over open charcoal flames, then eaten off of the bone as at any other barbeque; stewed, boiled and covered in sauce; prepared in soup; or grilled, sliced, and wrapped inside leafy greens with a sauce for dipping. The meat has also been turned into sausage or jerky in Switzerland. While commonly eaten during the summer months in Korea and claimed to balance one's gi, or energy, dog meat has been praised for its warming qualities, ideal for the cold winters.

And it's not just about taste. In both Vietnamese and parts of Chinese culture, eating dog meat is associated with a raised libido in men. In Vietnam, it is ritualistically consumed during the last half of the lunar month for good luck. Taiwanese culture praises it for its help with circulation and a raised body temperature. The philosopher Mencius was even a fan due to dog meat's pharmaceutical properties, and finally, rural areas of Poland are known for rendering dog fat into lard for its medicinal properties.

While the majority of the world's population condemns the act (morally and legally), it also has religious banishment: under Muslim and Jewish dietary law, the consumption of dog meat is forbidden.

While providing protein, dog meat is notoriously high in fat. Due to the animal's typical lack of vaccinations, the chance of spreading rabies or even cholera has been an ongoing issue.

In the end, people are for it, and people are against it. Be it cruel, inhumane, delicious, or downright gross, eating dog meat isn't going anywhere.

Korean Dog Meat Stew

Ingredients

2 lb. dog meat

6 cups chopped greens, such as perilla leaf, spinach, or collard greens

4 tbsp red pepper

Eating Dog in Burkina Faso

Among the Bwaba of Boni, a village situated in southwest Burkina Faso, dog-related sacrifice and consumption of dog meat is particularly important. While this meat is not consumed on an everyday basis, it is prepared on various special occasions. Thus dog meat is consumed by a group of male friends, often members of the same clan, to strengthen the bonds that tie them together. The men eat food in the privacy of a house, away from the eyes of other villagers. It is mostly men who prepare dog meat among the Bwaba, boiling it in water seasoned with salt, pepper, and soumbala (a local condiment, known also as traditional stock cube, made of the seeds of the *parkia biglobosa* tree [Debevec 2005]). Bwaba also eat dog food in case of a dream indicating death in family. If an elderly woman dreams of death in family, the morning after the dream, the family carries out a ritual, sacrificing a family dog, and asking ancestral spirits to take this offering in place of a family member. The dog is killed at the village altar, and a small piece of meat must be eaten by every person in the family.

Further Reading

Agence, Syfia. *L'Afrique, côté cuisines. Regards africains sur l'alimentation.* Paris: Syros, 1994.

Debevec, Liza. *Through the Food Lens: The Politics of Everyday Life in Urban Burkina Faso.* PhD diss., St Andrews, University of St Andrews, 2005.

Şaul, Mahir. "Islam et appropriation mimétique comme ressource historique de la religion bobo." *Journal des Africanistes* 67, no. 2 (1997): 7–24.

Liza Debevec

8 cloves chopped garlic
1 cup green onion, chopped
Salt and pepper

1. Boil dog meat, cut into sections, until cooked through.
2. Cut into bite-sized pieces. Salt and pepper to taste.
3. Transfer to large saucepan, adding chopped greens, red pepper, garlic, and enough stock just to cover the ingredients. Simmer for 20 to 30 minutes. Bring saucepan to table and serve hot, topping with green onions.

Emily Callaghan

Duck Tongue

Yes, duck tongues are edible. In fact, they are considered a delicacy in Chinese cuisine. Although duck tongue has a strong ducky odor when being cooked, the tongue, unlike beef or pig tongue, does not taste like duck meat. Additionally, duck tongues contain a long, thin, gently curved bone than ends with a small length of clear cartilage at the tip. The bony core is covered by skin and fat with a tiny sliver of meat in the middle, tucked close to the bone. All parts of the duck tongue are edible except for the bone. The meat on the tongue is succulent and could be compared to eating the skin around braised pigs' feet, while the bit of cartilage at the tip offers a satisfying, contrasting crunch. As they make only very small tidbits, eating duck tongue is more about textural enjoyment than anything else.

Common ways of preparing duck tongue include stir-frying, braising, saltwater pickling, and deep-frying. The high ratio of skin to meat means that duck tongues are relatively high in fat (and cholesterol). When deep-fried, the skin becomes satisfyingly crisp, rather like pork cracklins or fried chicken skin. At the famous roast duck specialty restaurants in Beijing, all parts of the duck are eaten during a multi-course banquet, including the tongue. In recent years, it has become fashionable to include a course of duck tongue in aspic (clear jelly) that has been fancifully dubbed crystal duck tongue. In all cases, before cooking in its seasonings, the tongues should always be placed in cold water and brought to a simmer to remove some of the strong duck smell and any scum, which floats to the top. Duck tongues pair well with strong flavors, the classic preparation being with Chinese loh sui sauce (see recipe below), but are also good cooked with aromatic vegetables and herbs such as onion or basil.

Duck Tongue in Loh Sui Sauce

Duck tongue is usually sold in one-pound packages in the poultry section of Asian grocery sections. Select a package with pink, plump-looking tongues. A brownish or grey cast is not desirable. Loh sui sauce may be found in the sauce section of Asian grocery stores, near the oyster sauces and soy sauces, and is sometimes called "Chinese Marinade." The characters 滷水 should be on the label. The recipe usually consists of dark and light soy sauces combined with warm spices (star anise, dried tangerine peel, Chinese cinnamon, ginger, white pepper, and others), Shaoxing wine, and sugar, which creates a sweet and savory braising liquid or sauce that is used for everything from chicken wings to duck tongue. Each family or restaurant will have its own preferred blend of spices, and the sauce only gets richer and more delicious the more often it is used and replenished. Some restaurants in Hong Kong and China are renowned for their decades-old loh sui sauces, which are used every day to flavor a variety of meats and are replenished at night with additional soy sauce and secret spices. These old sauces are prized much as an old sourdough might be.

The recipe below suggests several spices that may be added if a headier sauce is desired, rather like doctoring up store-bought pasta sauce with additional ingredients. The loh sui sauce may be saved for future use; just strain, cool, skim off fat, and refrigerate in a covered container. The sauce should be used at least once a week if being stored in the refrigerator. Otherwise, the sauce should be frozen.

Ingredients

1 lb. duck tongue
1-inch knob of ginger
1 tbsp vegetable oil, preferably peanut or canola
1 cup bottled Chinese loh sui sauce
1 cup water

Optional Seasonings

3 small pieces of *chan pei* (dried mandarin orange peel)
1 stick of cinnamon
3 to 4 star anises
1 tbsp additional grated ginger
1 tsp Sichuan peppercorns
¼ cup additional dark soy (darkens and sweetens the sauce without too much salt)
1 sprig parsley, for garnish

1. Set a small pot of water to boil.
2. Meanwhile, place the tongues in a bowl and rinse. When the water is boiling, slip the duck tongues into the water and blanch 5 minutes to remove any scum. Drain and rinse with cold water, then place on paper towels to drain further.
3. Using the edge of a spoon, scrape off the peel on the knob of ginger. Smash the ginger with the blunt side of a knife and set aside.
4. Heat oil in a wok or frying pan until hot but not smoking. (Check temperature by dipping end of dry wooden chopstick into oil; small bubbles will gather around chopstick when oil is hot enough.) Fry ginger until fragrant and just turning brown.
5. Place duck tongue in wok and toss with oil and ginger. Cook for ~7 minutes, until tongues are dry and take on the ginger fragrance. Add the optional seasonings at this point, if using.
6. Pour loh sui marinade into the wok. Bring to a boil, then reduce heat and simmer for 15 minutes. Taste and adjust for salt or sugar at this point. The sauce should be slightly sweet.
7. If additional spices are used, remove the *chan pei*, cinnamon stick, and star anises before serving. Duck tongues may be served immediately, or prepared a day ahead, cooled, and

refrigerated. Duck tongues will taste even better the next day, and the sauce is delicious spooned over rice. Bring sauce back to a simmer and cook for at least 10 minutes before serving.

Further Reading

Boshoff, Yan-kit. *Classic Chinese Cooking.* New York: Penguin, 2006.

Ouei, Mimie. *The Art of Chinese Cooking.* New York: Random House, 1960.

Karen Taylor

Durian

Durian is an exotic fruit native to Indonesia. While the fruit is highly prized for its flesh, few can get past its stench. Also heralded as the king of fruits and the caviar of fruits; is durian really as odorous as the deceased?

Perfuming the air with the scent of onions, garlic, wet feet, and sweaty socks, the stench is derived from a sulfur compound and it is truly potent. Many countries in Southeast Asia prohibit taking the fruit into hotel rooms or onto public transportation. Despite laws, ferries in peak Durian season chug daily from Bangkok to Nonthaburi in central Thailand, bringing boatloads of people eager to for an unforgettable meal in the durian groves.

Durian also uses its musky aroma to attract animals. During the mast fruiting period in West Sumatra's Tapan Valley, villagers report an influx of tigers entering the forest, leaving behind clawed trees and newly opened ripe durian fruit in their stead.

With a heritage seemingly of blue roots, durian is a relative of both the cocoa plant and the cola nut. Covered in a spiked husk, the root of its name *duri* fittingly means spine. As the fruit reaches full maturity, it plummets to earth. Forming on tall trees resembling elms, the drop is long and potentially harmful to whomever may be standing beneath.

Unlike its offensive aroma, the fruit's flavor is unique and extremely complex. It is most comparable to almonds and vanilla with nuances of cream cheese, onions, or even a hint of roasted garlic. The texture of the flesh is creamy, like custard, which when coupled with a funky aroma, creates an eating experience comparable to eating a pungent runny cheese.

Besides its incredible flavor, durian is nutritious, packed with high amounts of protein, a substantial fat content, carbohydrates, and vitamins A and C.

Possibly the first to take extensive record of durian was the British naturalist Alfred Russell Wallace. Encountering the caviar of fruit in Borneo, he wrote, "Durian . . . is a fruit of a perfectly unique character; we have nothing with which it can be compared, and it is therefore the more difficult to judge whether it is or is not superior to all other fruits."

When not dropping from the trees from April to July, durian is transformed into a variety of products used year-round. Freeze-dried in chunks or dehydrated into chips, durian is the key ingredient in *lempuk*, a product used in cooking. Durian flavored *dodul* candy has found great popularity in Thailand, while durian moon cakes, cookies, and tarts are made across the world.

If one in America desires a taste of raw durian, a venture into Chinatown or an Asian market should yield results. But what should one look for? Durian is green and covered in telltale spikes. It can grow up to a foot long, weight from three to five pounds, and can cost up to $10 each.

When durian is ripe, it cracks along internal fault lines, which can be noticed when examined carefully. While it may be eaten at this point, some chose to wait several days after these cracks appear allowing the flavors to deepen in complexity. One of the best indicators of freshness is the stalk. If still attached, the stalk must be solid and not at all dried out.

Just like a pineapple, one must get beyond durian's spiny hull to delve inside. Wearing heavy-bottomed rubber shoes, one can step on the durian, allowing it to crack further along those lines before prying it apart with fingers.

If a more controlled approach is preferred, place the fruit stem down and, using a cleaver or sturdy chef's knife, make a vertical cut, top to bottom. Insert fingers into the cut and pull both sides of the hull away from each other. Much like a large pomegranate, the fruit will snap open, revealing the cream-colored pods beneath.

If one has ventured this far in the battle, the spines, and stench, chances are the effort will be well rewarded. In the words of Wallace, "If I had to fix on two only as representing the perfection of the two classes, I should certainly choose the Durian and the Orange as the king and queen of fruits."

Durian Cookies

Recipe Adapted from Periplus Mini Cookbooks: Indonesian Cakes & Desserts *and provided by Pei-Lin's Dodol Mochi blog, http://dodol-mochi. blogspot.com/2010/01/unwritten-dilemma-durian-tarts.html*

For Filling

1 cup durian flesh, pitted
¼ cup palm sugar, finely chopped
2 tbsp caster sugar (Adjust the quantity of caster sugar according to the sweetness of the durian pulp and your preference.)

1. Place ingredients together in a small heavy-bottomed saucepan. Cook over low heat stirring constantly to prevent burning at the base. Cook until mixture becomes thick and sticky, about 15 minutes.
2. Transfer filling to a shallow plate and set aside to cool completely. Once it stops steaming, move to the fridge, chilling until it firms up completely. This helps a lot with handling this gooey filling later on.

For Pastry

½ cup butter, softened
3 tbsp powdered sugar
¼ tsp salt
2 egg yolks, at room temperature
1 cup all-purpose flour, sifted once
1 tbsp water, or adjust the quantity as necessary
1 egg yolk, slightly beaten for glazing

1. Cream butter, sugar, and salt together until pale and creamy. Gradually mix in the egg yolks, beating well after each addition, then beating entire mixture until light and fluffy.

2. Using a spoon or plastic spatula, fold sifted flour into the creamed mixture until just incorporated. Do not over-work the dough! Add a few drops of water if the dough is somewhat thick to work with; however, the dough should be just right to work with without having to flour your hands too much.

Tip: Whenever you're not working with the dough, keep the dough covered with plastic wrap to prevent it from drying out. This is a crucial step to affecting the texture of the cookies later on.

To Assemble

1. Flour your hands extremely well. Divide the chilled filling into 1 tsp balls and place on a well-floured surface. Set aside.
2. Lightly flour your hands and divide the dough into 1 tbsp balls. Form a well in the center of each and place one portion of the filling inside. Carefully pinch the pastry dough shut, enclosing the filling. Shape the filled pastry into an oval and repeat procedure to rest of cookies.
3. Place filled cookies 1 inch apart on lined baking trays.
4. Glaze the surface of the cookies with slightly beaten egg yolk.
5. Bake at 350°F for 15 to 17 minutes or until the cookies look crisp and golden brown.
6. Remove the cookies from the oven. Let them cool on the trays for 1 to 2 minutes to set their underside and transfer onto the cooling racks to let cool thoroughly before storing in an airtight container.

Further Reading

Bourdain, Anthony. "No Reservations—Indonesia 3." YouTube video, 8:40, September 4, 2007. http://www.youtube.com/watch?v=1PNmuExjlEM.

"Durian—the King of Fruits Durian Fruit Information and Facts." Tropical Fruits. http://tropical-fruits.biz/.

Holden, Jeremy, and Matthew Linkie. "The Enigma Surrounding Tigers in Tapan Valley, West Sumatra." Chat 11. http://www.chat11.com/Tigers_Eating_Durian_Fruit.

Pei-Lin "An Unwritten Dilemma & Durian Tarts." *Dodol Mochi* (blog). http://dodol-mochi.blogspot.com/2010/01/unwritten-dilemma-durian-tarts.html.

Polprasid, Piroj. "History of Durian Cultivation in Thailand." DIT. http://www.dit.go.th/agriculture/durian/history.htm.

Wallace, Alfred Russel. "On the Bamboo and Durian of Borneo." *Hooker's Journal of Botany* 8 (1856). http://people.wku.edu/charles.smith/wallace/S027.htm.

Yeap, Kiat Soon. *How to Choose a Durian*. Yeap Orchard Ltd., 1998–1999.

Erica Hope

E

Earth

In Burkina Faso and other regions, we find that the practice of eating clay and soil, scientifically known as geophagy, is commonly known. The practice is not linked to a particular ethnic group. This is a practice that is most common among children and pregnant women, but we find it also among other adult women and men. Many people recall that as children they consumed earth, both simple soil and clay and earth from termite mounds, but they also say that this is a practice they have outgrown in adult age.

In Jula, the local language in the Southwest of Burkina Faso, people refer to this type of clay as *aloko*, and in French they call it *caolin*. Kaolin is a special clay that contains a silicate with aluminum. It is the main component of the clay used to make porcelain. The medicinal and food use of kaolin is not limited to Burkina Faso or even Africa. In the United States, the anti-diarrhea medicine Kaopectate is made with it (as the name suggests). It is/was consumed by African American women from the southern United States.

Apart from kaolin, people in Burkina Faso also speak about eating clay (*l'argile* in French). Furthermore, many people have spoken about eating plain soil, especially after the rain, when the rain drops on the hot soil make for a special smell that apparently gives people a craving for this soil.

Kaolin (aloko) is particularly favored by pregnant women who eat it to subdue the feeling of nausea, or as in the case of the Ghanaian woman, to subdue the feelings of hunger, without getting morning sickness. Some young women eat it as well, even when not pregnant. It has been said to be addictive, and people have compared it to cigarettes. One young man even has claimed his sister-in-law when pregnant would wake him up at night to go and search for aloko. Another woman spoke about her brother, who if he would not get his regular dose of aloko would search for termite mounds around the village and eat those.

One of the interesting issues related to geophagy in Burkina Faso is the diverging opinions about the harmful and beneficial effects of this practice on people's health. Some people believe that it may make you sick, either with stomachaches or other diseases, although there are no documented cases of people becoming sick or unwell from it. Others say that eating clay is recommended for pregnant women and is a part of doctors advice, which further research has shown to be a false belief.

It should be noted that even among scientists there is no consensus on whether this practice has beneficial effects. Osseo Asare writes that "researchers claim that there may be good reasons to eat clay that include meeting nutrient deficiencies such as iron-deficiency anemia and calcium deficiency" (2005: 45). Trevor Stokes, on the other hand, writes that some researchers claim that the nutritional benefits of clay are lost due to the stomach's acidity (2006: 543).

The price of edible clay in the market is very low, between 2 and 5 cents, and thus available to people of all social classes. Various qualities of the clay are available in the local markets, with those from Ghana and Burkina achieving higher market value than those from Mali. The clay is typically harvested and stored by the consumer or sold and stored in patties or cakes, often mixed with oil, salt, and/or sugar. Pieces are broken off and eaten as is or hydrated in warm water.

Further Reading

Hunter, J. M. "Geophagy in Africa and in the United States: A Culture-Nutrition Hypothesis." *Geographical Review* 63 (1973): 170–195.

MacClancy, Jeremy, Jeya Henry, and Helen Macbeth. *Consuming the Inedible: Neglected Dimensions of Food Choice*. New York: Berghahn Books, 2007.

Osseo-Assare, Fran. *Food Culture in Sub-Saharan Africa*. Westport, CT: Greenwood Press, 2005.

Stokes, Trevor. "The Earth-Eaters." *Nature* 30, no. 444 (2006): 543–544.

Wiley, Andrea S., and Solomon H. Katz. "Geophagy in Pregnancy: A Test of a Hypothesis." *Current Anthropology* 39, no. 4 (1998): 532–545.

Liza Debevec

Eels

For many, the thought of eating eels conjures up gruesome images of slimy, snakelike creatures teeming in shallow waters. Movie and television cameos have not helped their reputation as a tasty treat. From *Fear Factor* to the classic scene in *The Tin Drum*, the West doesn't look upon eels fondly. However, from a culinary perspective, eel meat can be luscious and can fetch a high price at market. There are hundreds of types of eels (Anguilliformes order), many of which are edible.

The common eel is a tremendous traveler. Female eels spend the first seven years of their lives maturing in freshwater in Asia, Europe, and North America, then join with their male counterparts at river deltas where they mate. Then the journey begins. European and American eels gather in the warm waters of the Sargasso Sea off the island of Bermuda in early spring, deposit their eggs and die. Asian eels have a similar meeting point. The eel larva then floats for nearly three years to reach European shores, by which time they have become elvers, the thin, three-inch, glass-like eels which are highly prized in many cultures. Finally, when the elvers have gained strength, they fight their way inland, mature into full grown eels, and the process begins again.

All this swimming makes for some very tasty and nutritious eel meat, at least the Japanese think so. Japan is the top consumer of eel, or *unagi* in Japanese, in the world. Much of the dining happens in the middle of summer on a holiday called *doyou no ushi no hi,* which roughly translates to day of the ox at the height of summer. This holiday falls in mid-July, when temperatures climb to the upper 90s and the air is thick with moisture. In the week proceeding this day, more than 2 million eels are imported from Taiwan, China, and Europe. One legend explaining this eel eating frenzy says that an eel restaurant owner noticed his business was flagging so to boost sales, he concocted a tall tale. On this day, ushi no hi, he said, people should eat foods that start with the letter *U*. Naturally, unagi was first on the list. However, there is a more practical, albeit historical, reason behind the feasting. Eel meat is extremely high in vitamins B and A and rich in omega-3 fatty acids, the same compound found in salmon, almonds, and olives. The Japanese believe that these nutrients will fight lethargy and prevent illness in the hot, humid environment. Some also believe that eating eel increases fertility, an added bonus to the fish's succulent meat.

Most westerners know unagi as a type of sushi, but in Japan, there are many different preparations. In Tokyo and the surrounding plains, the *sei-biraki* or back splitting method is used to fillet the eel, leaving the meat attached to the belly. The eel is steamed then grilled with mirin and soy. This preparation produces a soft and tender texture. The *hara-biraki* or belly splitting method on the other hand leaves the meat on the backbone and yields a deeper grilled flavor and crisp texture. The Japanese also eat eel bones deep-fried and sprinkled with salt. Elvers, known as glass eels, also feature prominently on high-end menus. During the economic boom of the 1990s they were priced at more than $300 a pound. No culture, however, is better known for eating buckets of elvers than the Basque people of northern Spain.

Basque cuisine has featured elvers deep-fried and sautéed for centuries, however, the Spanish word *angula* only entered into Castillian within the last 100 years. The Basque word for eel, *txitxardin*, had trouble catching on. From October through February, anguleros (elver fisherman) wade into the cold waters off the northern coastline with large rectangular baskets to capture the glass eels. At this stage in their lives, the eels can breathe both in an out of water so they are killed in buckets of deoxygenated water steeped with tobacco. The most traditional way to prepare the angulas is *a la Bilbiana*, meaning in the Bilbao style, the Basque country's capital. First, olive oil is heated in a ceramic casserole dish until very hot; then dried chilies and garlic are sautéed to flavor the oil. The elvers are added at the very end and cooked for just a few seconds. This dish, because of its harvest time, is a common holiday treat throughout the country.

In neighboring Italy, eating eels also means it must be Christmas season. For Italians all over the world, the Feast of Seven Fishes happens on December 24, *La Vigilia* (Christmas Eve) when Christians avoid eating meat. There are several different explanations of what the seven fish courses represent; most commonly, they stand for the number of sacraments in the Christian Bible. Depending on one's outlook, they could also signify the seven deadly sins, the seven days of creation, or the seven virtues of Christian theology. Each of the seven fish courses is prepared a different way, and the menu might include linguini with clams, deep fried smelt, or stuffed calamari. Certain dishes, however, are considered essential to a traditional feast, including baked eel. *Anguilla Livernese* is the traditional preparation in which the eel is baked with tomatoes, capers, and olives, and emerges from the oven very tender and swimming in sauce.

The eel's oily and unctuous flesh makes it an ideal candidate for grilling and *Capitone alla griglia/arrosto,* served with vinegar, salt, and pepper, is a common dish on Christmas Eve.

Eel with Olives, Chilies, and Capers (Anguilla Livernese)

Ingredients

¼ cup olive oil

1 pinch hot red pepper flakes

2 large eels, gutted and cut into 3-inch sections

2 cups tomato sauce

1 cup dry red wine

2 tbsp capers

¼ cup olives, pitted

Salt and pepper to taste

1. Preheat oven to 375°F
2. In a Dutch oven, toast red pepper flakes in olive oil. Add eel and remaining ingredients and bring to a boil.
3. Bake in oven until tender, about 25 minutes.

Season to taste.

Further Reading

Schweid, Richard. *Consider the Eel: A Natural and Gastronomic History.* Cambridge, MA: Da Capo Press, 2004.

Tesch, Friedrich-Wilhelm. *The Eel.* New York: John Wiley and Sons, 2003.

Eleanor Barczak

F

Fish Bladder

Fish bladder, also known as the gas bladder, air bladder, or swim bladder is the buoyancy organ that helps boney fish maintain a buoyant state in the water without sinking or rising. The boney fish category includes all fish except cartilaginous fish like sharks and stingrays. The organ, which is an extension of the digestive tract, must remain at a constant volume for the fish to float comfortably. As the fish dives deeper and the pressure in the water increases, oxygen and nitrogen gases are secreted into the bladder to allow the fish to continue swimming downward. This process is reversed as the swimmer nears the surface.

In addition to its biological function, fish swim bladder is considered a delicacy on menus in China. Sometimes referred to as *maw,* meaning stomach, throat, or jaw, swim bladder is considered a luxury in restaurants, yet is attainable in its dried form for home cupboards. While the swim bladder itself has very little flavor, it draws in and enhances the tastes of many time-honored dishes. Maw is sold in dried tubular shapes that are slightly yellow in color. It must be soaked for at least four hours, or preferably overnight before cooking. As it bathes, the maw expands up to three times in size and is then ready to be used. Gristly and green after rehydration, it eventually takes on a texture similar to cooked okra. Swim bladder sometimes accompanies the rather controversial shark's fin in shark fin soup. It can be used as a lower-priced substitute if fin is unavailable or out of the home cook's price range.

Maw also appears in the Cantonese dish Double Boiled Milk, which can be served savory or sweet. In the savory, soupy version, the maw boils for two hours after its first night soaking and then goes through the process once more. The next day, it is boiled and added to the milk, yielding a slight touch of the sea to the dish despite having little flavor of its own. Fish maw can also be deep-fried into a puffy yellow balloon and eaten as a snack or used in soup.

In China, fish maw is eaten for different health reasons including fertility, blood circulation, and skin vitality. Maw is a good source of collagen, a protein commonly used in anti-aging creams to increase skin's elasticity. When boiled, this collagen yields a gelatin called isinglass, used in the fermentation of alcohol. Isinglass is added to cask-conditioned ales to clear the excess yeast from the liquid. If a pint of purified ale is held to the light and has a cloudy appearance or visible residue, it could mean that the isinglass and captured yeasts were recently stirred from the bottom of the cask.

Historically, isinglass extracted from fish maw has been used to make parchment glue. In 17th-century Russia, for example, isinglass was mixed with honey to help set the paint on Christian art. In ancient Egypt, an isinglass mixture was also used as an adhesive for wooden objects.

Further Reading

Hsiung, Deh-Ta, and Hom, Ken. *The Chinese Kitchen*. New York: Macmillan, 2002.

Inness, Sherrie. *Secret Ingredients: Race, Gender and Class at the Dinner Table*. New York: Macmillan, 2006.

Schultz, Ken. *Ken Schultz's Field Guide to Saltwater Fish*. New York: John Wiley and Sons, 2004.

Tropp, Barbara. *The Modern Art of Chinese Cooking*. New York: Morrow, 1992.

Eleanor Barczak

Fish Eyes

Have you ever been served a whole fish with the head still attached? The presentation can be stunning, but the eating, well, that's another story. Westerners tend to be a bit squeamish about eating things that still have their faces intact. Head-on shrimp, whole-roasted pig, Chinese duck, we've seen the pictures, but have you ever come face to face with your food? What would you do? Have the head removed? Eat around it, being careful to avoid the lifeless orbs and their accusing stare?

In parts of the world where fish is prepared whole, few people stop to remove the eyes, and, in fact, in some cultures fish eyes are considered a delicacy and are reserved for honored guests. Fish eyes might not actually appear on a menu, but if you are dining in the Philippines, China, Japan, the Middle East, or the Caribbean, don't be surprised if a pair of eyes shows up on your plate or in your bowl.

Eyes are symbolic in many cultures. Fish eyes, in particular, may hold religious or mystical significance. The concept of the evil eye, a look that is believed to cause injury or harm to the person at whom the look is directed, cuts across geography, religions, and cultures. To be the recipient of the evil eye is to be cursed and is therefore something to be avoided. Because fish are submerged in water, they are protected from the evil eye and are, therefore, associated with blessings in many cultures. In Jewish mysticism, or kabbalah, fish eyes are symbolic that God's providence or divine guidance is constant, as they have no lids and remain open at all times. Fish eyes are often incorporated in kabbalistic jewelry such as bracelets and pendants that are meant to confer to the wearer a measure of protection against curses or bad luck. Similarly, fish eyes may be found in *khamsa* (*hamsa*, *chamsa*), an Arabic amulet in the shape of a hand, with an eye embedded in the palm. These amulets a used to deflect the evil eye and are place in the entryways of dwellings. Fish eyes are considered both kosher and halal, meaning that there are no dietary laws prohibiting the eating thereof.

The flavor is said to be rich, salty, and fishy. Depending on the method of preparation, the texture has been described as anything from gelatinous or custard-like to crunchy. Fish eyes may be eaten raw or prepared a variety of ways. In the Middle East, they might be eaten raw, boiled, fried, or steamed (*en papillote*, baked in parchment or foil packets). Elsewhere, whole fish is grilled or roasted, the eyes might have a sweet, smoky flavor. It is common to find fish eyes floating in soup or stew and are considered a kind of surprise to the eater. The gelatinous material around eyes of smallish fish is eaten and the hard cornea discarded. In larger fish, the eye is eaten in its entirety.

Fish eyes are rich in vitamin B1, used to convert glucose into usable energy and omega-3 fatty acids, including DHA, which is associated with brain function and has anti-inflammatory properties. Fish eyes are widely regarded across the Indian subcontinent as a supplement to improve and maintain good eyesight.

Fish Head Soup

Ingredients

2 to 3 fish heads (or 1 large whole fish, head on). Use fish that have dense meat like salmon, king fish, snapper
6 cups fish stock or water
8 fresh carrots, cleaned, sliced into 1-inch pieces
4 cloves garlic, minced
1cup celery, chopped
1 small onion, minced
1 small green pepper, seeded and chopped
1 14-oz. can crushed tomatoes
2 sprigs thyme
1 bay leaf
Salt and pepper to taste

1. Wash fish heads and set aside.
2. Bring fish stock to a boil; add all of the ingredients except the fish.
3. Reduce heat and cook for 10 minutes.
4. Add fish (heads) to the pot and cook for an additional 30 to 40 minutes or until the meat has fallen off of the fish heads. Serve with crusty bread and lemon slices.

Further Reading

Bashline, Sylvia. *New Cleaning and Cooking Fish*. Minneapolis, MN: Creative Publishing International, 1999.

Cracknell, H. L., and R. J. Kaufmann. *Practical Professional Cookery*. Florence, KY: Cengage, 1999.

Hayley Figueroa

Foie Gras

Foie gras, which in French means fat liver, is the fattened liver of a goose or a duck. The liver is fattened by a process called *gavage*, or force-feeding. The average weight of foie gras is 1½ pounds. They usually come raw and vacuum-packed, and can be found in high-end grocery stores. Foie gras is a fairly expensive product. It usually retails from $8 to $11 per ounce.

Today, France is the country that produces and consumes the most foie gras. However, it is also eaten and produced in other parts the world. Besides France, the countries that eat the most foie gras are other European countries, especially Hungary and Bulgaria, the United States, China, Japan, and Canada.

It is said by many that the best foie gras in the United States comes from the Hudson Valley. This company, Hudson Valley Foie Gras, is located in Ferndale, New York. It uses Moulard duck to produce their foie gras. Moulard is a cross between the Pekin (Long Island) duck and the Muscovy duck.

To produce foie gras, typically, the bird will be force-fed by a long tube that has been stuck into its throat. It is normally fed a mixture of corn and duck fat. They are fed approximately three times every day for three to four weeks before being killed. The act of force-feeding, known as gavage, comes from the French word *gaver*, meaning to force down the throat. The birds are also kept in close quarters, more specifically in small cages, which prevents them from getting much exercise, and therefore further fattens the liver. Once the bird has been slaughtered, the liver commonly sits overnight in either milk or water before being vacuum-packed.

The method of producing foie gras that is used today has greatly changed over the centuries. Back when the process of enlarging a bird's liver was discovered, the ancient Egyptians found that this was a natural process. If the bird was slaughtered just before it migrated, its liver would have already been fattened. It would have been naturally overeating for a few weeks in preparation of its migration. It was imperative to kill the bird right before migration because as soon as the bird reached the end of its journey, the liver would have shrunk back to its normal weight and size.

Foie gras consumption has been noted as early as 2500 BCE. The ancient Egyptians not only came to enjoy the taste of the naturally fattened bird liver greatly, but they also found that they could adjust the flavors by altering the diet of the bird. They soon began to feed the birds dried figs, because they noted that they could achieve a slightly sweeter taste. Although foie gras was greatly enjoyed for generations by the food lovers of ancient civilizations, such as the Egyptians, Greeks, and Romans, it became a forgotten indulgence during medieval times. The one city that did not stop its production of foie gras during this time period was Strasbourg. This part of France is now a legendary producer of the delicacy. But foie gras was reestablished in the late 1700s. Chef Jean Joseph Close, who was working for the government of Alsace at the time, popularized what soon became one of the most common and elegant preparations of this fattened liver: Pâté de Foie Gras aux Truffes. In this method, the liver is cooked with brandy, truffles, spices, and herbs, such as thyme, tarragon, and parsley.

Foie gras is prepared and enjoyed in any number of ways. It can also be enjoyed sliced, sautéed, in sausages, as a puree, or in a terrine. Foie gras is almost always served with toast. Other typical accompaniments to foie gras are apple jelly, fig jam, whole grain mustard, and cornichons (small pickles). It can also be cooked sous-vide, which translates as under vacuum. This is a method of preparation in which the foie gras is vacuum-sealed and then poached in water at a low temperature for a long period of time.

For years, foie gras has been a topic of debate with animal rights protesters. They believe that the process of producing foie gras is very cruel and stressful to the birds. In fact, California passed a law in 2004 stating that it is forbidden to produce and sell foie gras. However, this law will not be enforced until 2012. The United Kingdom, Germany, the Czech Republic, Finland, Luxembourg, Norway, Poland, Sweden, Switzerland, Denmark, and Israel are the countries in which the production and sale of foie gras has already been banned or restricted.

If one is not deterred from eating foie gras because of animal rights, he might be when he sees the nutrition facts. This product is extremely high in fat. If consumed, it should be done in moderation. In just a two-ounce portion of foie gras, there are 250 calories and 24 grams of fat. There was also a recent study conducted by Michael Greger, director of public health and animal agriculture at the Humane Society of the United States, that may link foie gras to amyloidosis, an abnormal protein buildup. Greger found that when birds are stressed due to force-feeding, they tend to experience amyloidosis. But so far, foie gras is the only food that he knows of to have such high levels of the protein fragments. Researchers found that when fed to rats, these amyloid fibrils can enter their organs. Although Greger has yet to see any demonstration of the amyloid fibrils affecting humans, he thinks, "urgent research is now needed to ensure we are not eating food that might one day lead to amyloidosis in people"(Greger, 2009).

For those who have never made or eaten foie gras before, and don't mind spending some money on the costly ingredients, this recipe is a great starter.

Foie Gras Terrine

Ingredients

2 lb. duck foie gras
2½ tsp sea salt
½ tsp coriander
½ tsp ginger powder
¼ tsp paprika
¼ tsp cayenne pepper
1 tsp black peppercorns
1 cup dessert wine such as late-harvest
   Sauvignon Blanc
½ cup port
1 whole black truffle, fresh or preserved,
   thinly sliced

1. Clean the foie gras by removing all of the veins.
2. In a roasting pan that fits the foie gras, combine all of the ingredients except for the truffles. Place the foie gras into this marinade. Put this into the refrigerator for about 2 hours.
3. Place the pan in a 300°F oven for about 10 minutes.
4. Pour the cooking juices into a bowl and save. The foie gras should still be rare.
5. Line a terrine mold with plastic wrap, but make sure to have a few extra inches on each side in order to cover the terrine.
6. Put half of the foie gras into the bottom of the mold. Put the truffles into the mold next, mostly in the center. Put the rest of the foie gras into the mold, keeping the smooth side upright.
7. Cover the terrine with the plastic wrap. Cut a piece of cardboard into the size of the top of the terrine. Place this cardboard on top of the plastic.
8. Using beans, apply weight evenly to the top of the mold, and refrigerate for 1 hour. Place the cooking juices into a small sauce pot and bring up to a simmer.
9. Skim off any impurities, then take off heat and let it cool slightly. Take the mold out of the refrigerator and take the beans, cardboard, and plastic off.
10. Pour the liquid onto the mold. Cover again with the plastic. Refrigerate the terrine for another hour. This can be served in thin slices.

Further Reading

The Culinary Institute of America. *The Professional Chef.* 7th ed. New York: John Wiley & Sons, 2001.

Greger, Michael. "Potential Health Risks Associated with Stressed Foodstuffs such as Foie Gras." *Science News.* February 19, 2009. http://www.sciencedaily.com/releases/2009/02/090210092736.htm.

Pepin, Jacques. *Chez Jacques: Traditions and Rituals of a Cook.* New York: Stewart, Tabori, and Chang, 2007.

Rolland, Jacques L., and Carol Sherman. "Foie Gras." *The Food Encyclopedia: Over 8,000 Ingredients, Tools, Techniques, and People.* Toronto: Robert Rose Inc., 2006.

Laura Mathews

Frog

Frogs are amphibians that live in rivers, swamps, marshlands, and other damp climates, on all continents except Antarctica. Though there are more than 5,000 species, many of which are edible, but only a handful are large and meaty enough generally to be considered worth the trouble. Frog meat is typically white, tender, and slightly flaky, with a delicate taste and texture often described as similar to a cross between chicken and fish. Some of the more popular edible species include the aptly named edible frog (*Rana esculenta*), the marsh frog (*Rana ridibunda*), and the American bullfrog (*Rana catesbeiana*). Although the most common way to consume frog is to eat only the legs, some people eat them whole.

Records suggest that frogs were a common food in southern China as early as the first century CE, and that they were a delicacy among the Aztecs. In France, perhaps the country best known for its affinity for frog meat, the creature first made its way on to the plates of 13th-century monks in Lorraine by way of a loophole in Lent restrictions. Despite its meaty texture, frog was classified as a type of fish, thus people were able to better satisfy their cravings on days when meat or poultry were not allowed. Recipes for frog soups and mousselines appear in the *Le Ménagier de Paris* and were on the tables at the more fashionable restaurants in Paris by the middle of the 1600s. In modern times, the most popular preparation is to sauté them in a simple butter or cream sauce with garlic and other herbs. Each region of the country has its own take on this dish: add onions, parsley, and vinegar in Lyon; combine with chopped tomatoes, onions, pimentos, tarragon, and garlic in Nice. In Provence, they are popular served lightly floured and pan-fried in olive oil, with chopped parsley and garlic heaped on in the last minute of cooking, dressed with brown butter and lemon wedges.

Eating frog never caught on with the same gusto elsewhere in Europe, although some traditional households in northern Italy, Spain, Greece, Hungary, and Croatia consume them. They certainly weren't popular in Great Britain. When celebrated French chef Escoffier planned the menu for the Carlton Hotel in London at the turn of the 20th century, he managed to get his beloved legs on the Prince of Wales' table by re-branding them Cuisses de Nymphes Aurore (legs of the dawn nymphs). Americans were so appalled by France's appetite for the web-footed creatures that they derisively nicknamed Frenchmen frogs—perhaps forgetting that fried frogs legs are not an unusual item on dinner tables in parts of the southern and southeastern United States. In Louisiana, frog legs are sometimes a traditional component in gumbo, a stew made with andouille sausage, okra, and sassafras.

Although hunted to the point of near-extinction, the mountain chicken (*Leptodactylus fallax*), also called the giant ditch frog or crapaud, is still the national dish of Dominica, the legs seasoned with lime juice, garlic, pepper, vinegar, and thyme and then rolled in batter and deep-fried. It is also eaten on other eastern Caribbean islands like Montserrat and St. Lucia.

Sometimes listed on menus across Asia as paddy chicken, frog is often served in Vietnam in an aromatic mixture of curry and lemon grass. In the Philippines, a recipe called palaman palaka requires stuffing the eviscerated body cavity of a large frog with a mixture of finely chopped pork, crushed garlic, brown sugar, salt, pepper, and vinegar. In China, a popular Hunanese dish is a simple preparation of legs slow-cooked in their own broth with a generous helping of red chilies. One Cantonese recipe calls for chopping up one frog, stuffing it inside the mouth of another frog, and cooking the whole thing. Hasma, or the fallopian tubes of the Asiatic grass frog (*Rana chensinensis*), often pop up in sweet soups on dessert menus at high-end restaurants in China, Hong Kong, and Taiwan and are also used as an ingredient in therapeutic wines and tonics that are sold widely throughout China. Sometimes mistakenly referred to as snow frog fat, because of its whitish, gelatinous appearance, the tubes come dried and flat, and are reconstituted in sugar water until they regain their tapioca-like texture, to which jujubes, lotus seeds, or other fruits or nuts are added. Hasma is said to alleviate a number of respiratory ailments, including tuberculosis, although there is a scarcity of research to support this.

These days, most of the frogs consumed in Europe and North America are farmed in places like Central Europe, Cuba, and Indonesia and frozen for export. In France, where more than 4,000 tons of frog legs are consumed annually, the native population has dwindled over the last century as a result of the draining of swamplands and overhunting. (France outlawed commercial frog hunting in 1980.) In other parts of the world, frogs are still caught in the wild, near the rivers, wetlands, and forests. Gigging for frogs, at is called in the United States, is almost always a night-time event. Armed with a long, multi-pronged pole, called a gig, frog hunters usually take a small boat out onto a marsh and shine a flashlight into the water to find the frogs, which have reflective eyes. It is then easy to spear the frogs, temporarily stunned and blinded by the light. Throughout Asia and in Asian communities overseas, live frogs are usually available in local markets, swimming in tanks, strung up with twine, or hopping in bamboo baskets. Some conservationists have raised concerns about the impact of eating frogs on the overall population, which has been in a species-wide sharp decline for much of the last century for a multitude of reasons, including human development and a widespread epidemic of chytridiomycosis, a fungal disease that is devastating to amphibians.

The quickest method for killing a live frog involves severing the spinal cord between the head and the first neck vertebra with a knife. If purchasing butchered legs, make sure that the skin is smooth and taut and, therefore, fresh. When serving the legs only, skin the frog first by slitting the skin at the neck and pulling it back, in the same manner of removing chicken skin. Cut the backbone above where the legs meet, so they can be served in pairs. Snip off the feet, and place in a bowl of ice water to soak for up to 12 hours, changing the water a few times. The flesh should whiten and swell. Pat dry with paper towels.

Pan-Fried Frog's Legs

Ingredients

12 pairs large frog's legs (see preparation above)
2 eggs
Breadcrumbs for coating
Flat-leaf parsley
Salt and pepper to season
1 lemon

1. Season the prepared frog's legs with salt and pepper. Beat eggs in a shallow dish.
2. Dip each pair of legs in egg, and then coat with breadcrumbs.
3. In a shallow saucepan, sauté in butter on medium-high heat until legs are lightly browned, about 7 to 10 minutes.
4. Remove legs from pan, drain on paper towels. Reserve used butter.
5. Serve with chopped parsley and reserved butter. Garnish with lemon wedges.

Further Reading

Frost, Darrel R. *Amphibian Species of the World: an Online Reference.* Version 4. American Museum of Natural History. August 17, 2006. http://research.amnh.org/her petology/amphibia/index.php.

Henley, Jon. "A Short History of Frog Eating." *Guardian.* August 7, 2009. http://www. guardian.co.uk/lifeandstyle/2009/aug/07/ frogs-legs-france-asia.

Henley, Jon. "Why We Shouldn't Eat Frog's Legs." *Guardian.* August 7, 2009. http:// www.guardian.co.uk/lifeandstyle/2009/ aug/07/frogs-legs-extinction.

Hopkins, Jerry. *Strange Foods.* North Clarendon, VT: Tuttle Publishing. 1999.

Schwabe, Calvin W. *Unmentionable Cusine.* Charlottesville: University of Virginia Press, 1979.

Sidra Durst

Fugu

There is a traditional Japanese saying, "Those who eat fugu soup are stupid. But those who don't eat fugu soup are also stupid." Fugu (pronounced foo-goo) is the Japanese name for several species of edible but potentially poisonous puffer fish, also known as blowfish, from the family Tetradontidae, found mainly in the northwest Pacific Ocean. The fish puff up their bodies to ward off would-be attackers, hence their common name. Torafugu (*Fugu rubripes*), or tiger fugu, is reputed to be the most delicious—and the most poisonous—variety.

This fabled, feared, prized, and sometimes fatal delicacy is consumed primarily in Japan, where consumption tops 10,000 tons per year and diners pay as much as $450 for elaborate multicourse fugu meals prepared by specially licensed chefs. Fugu is also eaten in Korea, where it is known as *bok*, and in the Philippines, where it is called *butete*. Though previously banned in the United States, in 1989, the FDA struck an agreement with the government of Japan whereby torafugu can now be imported, under tightly regulated conditions. The torafugu must be specially processed and certified in the city of Shimonoseki—the fugu capital of the world, which handles more than 80 percent of the blowfish consumed in Japan—and imported by Wako International, the sole sanctioned supplier for the United States. The sale of fugu is banned in the European Union.

The taste and texture of this white, dense-fleshed fish are described by fans as ethereal and delicious and by others, mostly westerners, as bland and rubbery; some really do say it tastes like chicken. The carefully filleted fugu meat may be served raw as sashimi (*Fugu sashi*), the pearly translucent slices arranged in intricate patterns resembling chrysanthemum blossoms, symbolic of death in Japanese culture, or fanciful peacock tails; in soups and stews (*Fugu-chiri*) with a citrusy ponzu dipping sauce; boiled (*mizutaki*) and marinated in vinegar; or floured and deep-fried (*Fugu kara-age*). Another popular preparation is *Fugu hire-zake*, smoked or grilled fugu fins steeped in hot sake.

While blowfish aficionados tout the incomparable taste, the storied danger of the Russian roulette fish, recounted by ancient Japanese haikuists and modern gastronomic adventurers alike, may account for much of its allure. The Japanese have been eating blowfish for centuries, and many have died for the pleasure. Feudal warlord Hideyoshi, the unifier of Japan, banned fugu in the 1500s after losing too many soldiers to the delicacy. Only in the 20th century was the cause of fugu's deadliness discerned: the skin, gonads, intestines, kidney, and liver of the fugu concentrate tetrodotoxin, a deadly neurotoxin that is 1,200 times more potent than cyanide and has no known antidote. Symptoms of fugu poisoning typically begin within 20 minutes of ingestion, with unlucky diners experiencing numbness, nausea, dizziness, and headache, followed by progressive paralysis and convulsions. As many as 60 percent of victims die from respiratory failure, generally within 6 to 24 hours of eating the tainted blowfish.

Proper fugu preparation involves removing the poisonous organs—which must be disposed of in locked containers and incinerated as toxic waste—without contaminating the flesh with any of the toxin. Since 1958, when Japan began to require a license to prepare fugu, deaths from fugu poisoning have dropped from several hundred to fewer than 10 each year, most of the fatalities befalling non-professionals who prepare and eat their own catch. Misidentification and mislabeling of fugu are also issues in some markets. Licenses are awarded only after years of rigorous training to the minority who pass the grueling final exam.

Thrill-seeking connoisseurs crave the lip-and tongue-tingling sensation they say a highly skilled fugu chef can create by leaving a non-lethal trace of poison on the fish, but at least one fugu expert dismisses this as an urban myth or perhaps a placebo effect: "It is your mind playing tricks. If your lips are numb, then you are already dead."

Voodoo Fish?

One horrifying—and captivating—feature of tetrodotoxin poisoning is that, because the toxin does not cross the blood-brain barrier, as paralysis spreads throughout the body and renders the victim unable to move or speak, he or she remains mentally aware through much of the ordeal. This experience mimics that reported by voodoo zombies, leading to the controversial, but intriguing, hypothesis put forth by Harvard-trained ethnobotanist Wade Davis, that Haitian voodoo *bokors,* or sorcerers, use puffer fish in the toxic powders they inject in victims during zombification rituals, and indeed, samples of voodoo powders have been shown to contain tetrodotoxin.

The amount of poison in a puffer fish varies by species, time of year, body part, and even sex. Popular *torafugu* is the most toxic species, lending credence to the notion that people covet that which is dangerous. Puffers are less toxic in wintertime, before the spring mating season. And ovaries are more dangerous than testes, which are prized as a male virility-enhancer, though grilled blowfish testicles have landed more than one man not in the boudoir but the hospital bed. One such episode involved seven men served the dish at a restaurant in northern Japan in early 2009. Because some fugu are hermaphrodites, containing both testicles and ovaries, it is possible that the chef—who was not licensed—mistakenly served female gonads alongside the male. It should be noted that even the highly toxic ovaries can be rendered safe to eat through a special pickling process that takes three to four years.

The liver is considered the tastiest part of the blowfish, a guilt-free foie gras of the sea, but is by far the deadliest. Though its consumption is officially banned in Japan, it occasionally crops up at fugu *ryotei*, specialized fugu restaurants recognized by the inflated blowfish lanterns hanging outside. In 1975, beloved kabuki actor Mitsugoro Bando VIII went from being a living national treasure to a dead one when he insisted the chef serve him four helpings of fugu liver, a request the poor chef felt he could not refuse the great man.

In recent years, Japanese researchers have discovered how to produce toxin-free fugu by carefully controlling the puffer's diet. It appears that tetrodotoxin is not produced by pufferfish directly, but rather accumulates in the fish after a meal of small mollusks or crabs laden with tetrodotoxin-producing marine bacteria, mainly of the genus *Vibrio*. A symbiotic relationship develops whereby the bacteria gain an accommodating host and the puffer fish enjoy the defense of a lethal toxin (a mutation in the fugu's sodium channel protects the fish from being harmed by the poison themselves). Farmed fugu, fed *Vibrio*-free foods like mackerel and sardines, is not only safer but relieves the overfishing that has depleted wild fugu stocks in recent years. Nonetheless, efforts to permit the sale of fugu liver from the presumably safe cultivated fish have met with resistance, and connoisseurs continue to prefer wild fugu over farmed, despite—or perhaps because of—the greater danger and expense. Even Tamao Noguchi, the scientist who developed the poison-free farmed fugu, admits, "A fugu without its poison is like a samurai without his sword."

Is fugu so deeply desired because eating it is a death-defying act, a poetic reminder of the inherent riskiness and fragility of life? Does this pricey icon earn its status by the thrill it sets off when the tongue begins to tingle and the lips grow numb? Or is it, as the great 20th-century artist Kitaoji Rosanjin insisted, simply addictively, unnervingly delicious? "The taste of fugu is incomparable," he wrote. "If you eat it three or four times, you are enslaved. . . . Anyone who declines it for fear of death is really a pitiable person." Pity then the emperor, who is forbidden by law to even touch this most exalted, yet potentially deadly, delicacy.

Further Reading

Hiltzik, Michael. "Poisonous Fugu—Deadly Fish Still Delights Japan Diners." *Los Angeles Times*, February 8, 1988.

Light, William Haugan. "Eye of Newt, Skin of Toad, Bile of Pufferfish." *California Wild,* Summer 1998.

Newman, Cathy. "Pick Your Poison—12 Toxic Tales." *National Geographic*, May 2005.

Onishi, Norimitsu. "If the Fish Liver Can't Kill, Is It Really a Delicacy?" *New York Times*, May 4, 2008.

Meryl Rosofsky

Fungi

The world of edible fungi includes a wide range of colorful specimens with incredible diversity. In their most basic sense, fungi are eukaryotic organisms with cell walls made up of chitin, which differs from plants, animals, and bacteria that are structurally made up of cellulose. The kingdom of fungi is expansive, including microorganisms like molds and yeasts, as well as larger fruiting bodies of better-known mushrooms. More than 100,000 species of mushrooms have been identified, though not all are safely edible.

Fungi grow across the globe, from sandy deserts to arctic tundra, and can grow above ground, underground, and even under water, sea and fresh. Nevertheless, because of their small cellular structure, much fungus grows inconspicuously. Fungi are essential players in the environmental lifecycle because they decompose much organic matter, turning dead plants and animals into useable nutrients.

As food, fungi have been used for thousands of years, across almost all cultures of the globe in one form or another. Mycophagy, the act of consuming fungi is a global practice. Yeasts and molds have been used for their fermenting and growth properties since the dawn of civilization. *Saccharomyces cerevisiae*, or common bakers yeast, is used in fermentation in such applications as alcoholic beverages, bread, and other grain-based foodstuffs. Newer products marmite and vegemite are yeast-based condiments popular in the United Kingdom and Australia and are made by processing yeast with heat, salt, and other enzymes.

Certain types of molds, a species of microscopic fungi, are used to alter a variety of food products. The mold *Penicillium* aids in creating prized cheeses like Roquefort, Stilton, and Camembert. Tempeh, the Indonesian soybean cake is fermented with the help of *Rhizopus oligosporus*. And soy sauce, a thousand-year-old tradition, uses a range of *Aspergillus* molds to change soybeans into the dark, salty, umami-rich sauce, a foundation of Asian cooking.

Edible mushrooms, cultivated since Greek and Roman times, are the most familiar, if not the most widely consumed fungus. The small- to medium-sized fleshy, fruiting bodies of mushrooms play an important role in many cultures. Japanese, Chinese, and French cuisines highlight the earthy flavors and interesting textures of mushrooms, which can be cooked in a myriad of ways and encompass a spectrum of flavor. Mushrooms can be roasted, fried, sautéed, and simmered into soups and stews; notably, they are a favorite of vegetarians for their meaty texture and flavor. Many mushrooms are raised commercially, but other, more rare varieties are harvested from the wild. The white button mushroom, readily available in supermarkets across the United States, is one of the most common. Oyster, portabella, and shiitake mushrooms are some well-known types of mushrooms. Morels, porcini, chanterelles, and white and black truffles are more distinct and can carry a high price on the market.

Even to the practiced eye, wild mushrooms can be very difficult to identify for consumption. It is extremely dangerous to pick and eat wild mushrooms, unless aided by an experienced mushroom forager. Poisonous mushrooms, of which there are many, if consumed, can cause stomachaches, vomiting, or even death.

Inky cap mushrooms (*Coprinopsis atramentaria*) are a species of grayish, capped, bell-shaped mushrooms that open and curl upwards before deteriorating into dark inky goo. The shaggy ink cap (*Coprinus comatus*) has shaggy scales on its white-to-beige cap and disintegrates into black goo shortly after picking; it must be consumed quickly. The alcohol inky cap (*Coprinus atramentarius*) is a particularly interesting specimen. Similar in shape and size to other inky caps, this mushroom creates an inability to process alcohol in the body. The mushroom generates a chemical similar to disulfiram (Antabuse). When the mushroom and alcohol are consumed within 48 hours of each other, the unfortunate eater is racked with anxiety, high blood pressure, nausea, and vomiting. Because of this eccentricity, it also goes by the name tippler's bane.

The stinkhorn mushroom (*Dictyophora indusiata*) is named for its offensive rotting odor that attracts flies and other insects. Most people find stinkhorns to be too disgusting to eat though some brave cultures bear the smell. The Chinese wash off the stinky slime, which usually covers the cap, to eat in soups or dry for later eating. There are many types of stinkhorns though the ravenel's stinkhorn (*Phallus ravenelii*) and the dog's penis mushroom (*Phallus inpudicus*) look surprisingly similar to the human and dog male genitalia, respectively. *Phallus ravenelii* grows in clusters in the northeastern United States, developing from underground eggs, testical-sized balls rise up from the ground, growing further into large, capped, tan-colored phalloi. The *Phallus inpudicus* is a smaller, narrower mushroom, scarlet red in color, not dissimilar to a canine's erect penis.

False morels (*Gyromitra esculenta*) look very similar to true morels. They are potentially fatal if eaten raw but are generally acceptable to consume if par-boiled. The mimickers contain *gyromitrin*, a toxic and possible carcinogenic chemical, which can be minimized, though not completely eliminated by repeatedly boiling them in water. Some view false morels as permanently off-limits but many cultures take the risk. In some countries in Europe, the false morels are available in markets, carefully labeled and packaged as such, to avoid confusion and sickness.

Puffball mushrooms (*calvatia* and *lycoperdon* species) are smooth, white, round globes that grow up from the ground. When disturbed, puffballs sometimes explode, rocketing their spores out into the air. There are a handful of varieties that can grow from golf-ball sized to as large as a beach ball. Their firm texture and mild, nutty flavor works well with many dishes.

Chicken mushrooms (*Laetiporus sulfureus*) taste like chicken. Flat and fanning with yellowish to bright orange lobes, this mushroom can be quite large, though is best consumed while young and tender. When adapted to traditional chicken recipes, it reportedly tastes very similar to white meat chicken. This mushroom is not to be confused with hen-of-the-woods mushroom (*Grifola frondosa*) or fried-chicken mushroom (*Lyophyllum decastes*), both of which are edible but do not taste like poultry.

Caterpillar fungi are created when the fungus (*Cordyceps sinensis*) infects a moth larva, killing it, mummifying it, and growing into a caterpillar shaped-fungus. The dried fungus, a yellow caterpillar with a stem growing out of its head, looks similar to a slender, dried chili pepper and sometimes goes by the poetic name winter worm, summer grass. Several species of caterpillars from Tibet, India, China, and Nepal attract the fungus. In Tibet, the phenomenon is called *yartsa gunbu* and is an important source of income for a huge percentage of the population. Caterpillar fungi can fetch large profits on the market with some of the most pristine specimens reaching $900 an ounce. The larvae live underground on grassy plateaus, where they become infected with fungus. The fungus overtakes the body, killing it, and grows filaments throughout, which extend out through the caterpillar's forehead. In spring or early summer, the dried blackish bodies poke out of the ground and must be hand-collected. Without sharp, keen eyes, the fungus can be difficult to see which is why children make good foraging companions. The fungus is only consumed medicinally, popular in traditional Tibetan, Chinese, and folk medicine. It is believed that the fungus, because it contains both animal and plant properties, is a good balance of yin and yang, making it especially popular in traditional medicines to treat a variety of illnesses such as impotence, stress relief, liver function, even cancer. To consume, the dried fungus is ground into a powder, mixed into other tonics, or steeped in hot water or broth.

Psilocybin mushrooms are consumed for their psychoactive properties, which can include hallucinations and altered visionary and auditory states. These species of fungi have a long tradition as physical and mental healers in traditional medicine, religious divination, and spiritualism. Psilocybin mushrooms are native to South America, Mexico, and the United States. They can come in a small spectrum of colors and usually have long, slender stems, small caps, with dark gills underneath. In Mesoamerica, hallucinogenic *Psilocybe* were known to the Aztecs as *teonanácatl,* divine mushroom. Despite their mind-altering influence, psilocybin mushrooms are non-toxic and are also consumed as recreational drugs.

Mushrooms are nutritionally quite valuable. Low in calories but big on flavor, mushrooms contain lots of vitamins, minerals, zinc, iron, and dietary fiber making them a healthy addition to any diet. Medicinally, fungi play a staring role in traditional Chinese medicine. Hundreds of species of mushrooms are reportedly used to strengthen, cleanse, and detoxify the body.

Creamed Morels on Toast

Ingredients

4 cups morels, cleaned of dirt and debris
2 shallots, finely diced
2 tbsp butter
1 cup heavy cream
2 tsp fresh tarragon, chopped
Salt and pepper, to taste

1. Melt butter over medium heat in a medium saucepan.
2. Sweat shallots and cook until translucent, seasoning with salt and pepper.
3. Add morels and sauté until they begin to release their liquid.
4. Add cream and gently simmer, until cream is slightly reduced and the mixture tightens.
5. Add tarragon, salt, and pepper and serve over buttery toast.

Further Reading

Arora, David. *Mushrooms Demystified.* 2nd. ed. Berkeley, CA: Ten Speed Press, 1986.

Kuo, Michael. *100 Edible Mushrooms.* Ann Arbor: University of Michigan Press, 2007.

Scarlett Lindeman

G

Goat

Goat is a mammal in the ovine family. This is the same family as sheep. Its horns are hollow, and its hair is coarse. It is used for both its meat and its milk, and in some cases for its wool as well. Along with the sheep and the pig, the goat was one of the earliest animals to be domesticated, beginning approximately 10,000 years ago. There are two regions in which the goat was first domesticated. One is the Euphrates River valley in Turkey. The second is in the Zagros Mountains in Iran.

Kid is the name for a young goat. Kid meat has a light color, and it tends to be very lean and milder in taste than full-grown goat. The most prized goat meat is that of a kid under six months old, due to the tenderness of this meat. Older goat's meat has a darker color, is tougher, and has a much more intense, gamey flavor, similar to that of lamb. In general, the meat should have a light-pink to bright-red color and be firm to the touch. Unlike beef, goat meat does not have traces of intramuscular fat marbled throughout. Goat is generally a moderately priced meat, depending on where you buy it and the cut.

There are more than 300 breeds of goat, all of which are used for different products. However, the two main breeds that are used for their meat are Boer and Cashmere. The Cashmere is also used for its milk, but it is best known for its wool. Other goat breeds that are used for their milk include La Mancha, Nubian (from Great Britain), Oberhasli (from Switzerland), Saanen (from Switzerland), and Toggenburg (from Switzerland). A good amount of this milk is used to make cheese. Goat cheese has a very tangy flavor, and it is most commonly found as a soft, yet crumbly cheese, though firm, aged goat cheeses are available as well. Fresh goat cheese is a healthier option than cow's milk cheese, due to the lower fat content.

Unlike many other animals, goats can easily and comfortably live in the mountains and on other rough types of land. Because of this ability, goats are often found as a part of the diet of cultures that have limited land for grazing and do not have many other meats readily available. For example, goat meat is very commonly used in mountainous Jamaica. Curry goat is actually one of the national dishes of Jamaica. Goat is also frequently eaten in the Middle East, India, Africa, and parts of Europe.

Goat meat is commonly marinated first and then cooked slowly in order to tenderize the tough meat (especially in older goats).There are several flavors that work very well with the taste of goat. Some of these include bacon, cinnamon, cumin, curry, ginger, chilies, honey, jerk spice, lime, mint, and onion. Roasted kid is a very traditional method of cooking baby goat. It is still one of the preferred preparations of goat, especially in Italy. A very popular way to eat the meat in the Middle East and the eastern Mediterranean is in a dish called *Kibbeh Nayyeh*, which is raw goat (or lamb) with bulgur wheat. This dish is part of the pan-Islamic cuisine and was introduced by the Ottomans. A lot of time has been shaved off the preparation of this dish in recent years. Instead of the time-consuming task of chopping up the raw lamb, the food processor is now often used. The texture of this raw meat has a very smooth quality. When mixed with bulgur, it produces a very earthy flavor. In Nigeria, it is not uncommon to eat goat's head. The goat is cleaned and burned in order to get rid of its hair. It is then broken apart, and the parts that are to be used for cooking are set aside. Typically, the brain, ears, eyes, and tongue are cooked with a combination of onion, garlic, ginger, tomatoes, and spices. It is polite to serve the goat's eyes to the guest of honor.

Up until the last several decades, families in India, Jamaica, and the Middle East did not eat meat on a regular basis. Rice, legumes, and vegetables were the staples of their diet. However, when there was a very special occasion, a goat dish, whether a curry or a biryani, was almost always made. This is true even today when there is cause for celebration.

Since goat is very lean, it is a much healthier choice than most other meats, such as beef. Of course, much leaner goat meat can be found on a kid rather than an older goat. In a four 4-ounce portion of raw kid, there are 124 calories, 25 grams of protein, and only 2.6 grams of fat. The same portion size of one of the leanest cuts of beef—the sirloin—contains 216 calories, 23.4 grams of protein, and 12.64 grams of fat. However, goat meat does contain high levels of cholesterol. A 4-ounce portion of raw goat meat has 64 milligrams. But when eaten as a part of a balanced meal, it can be nutritious and satiating.

Goat Curry

For a flavorful recipe, this goat curry is the way to go. It serves four people.

Ingredients

2 lb. goat meat, cut into cubes
5 cloves garlic, minced
½ jalapeno pepper (without seeds), minced
1½ tbsp cumin, ground
1½ tsp coriander, ground
1½ tbsp garam masala
1½ tbsp curry powder
½ tbsp chili powder
1 small onion, julienned
1 scallion, thinly sliced
3 tbsp corn or peanut oil
1½ tsp salt
4 small potatoes, peeled and halved

1. After rinsing the goat meat in cold water, drain thoroughly.
2. Place garlic, 3 tablespoons water, and jalapeno pepper in a blender. Blend until a paste forms. Empty this into a bowl.
3. To this mix, add the ground cumin, coriander, garam masala, curry powder, chili powder, and enough water to form a thick paste.
4. In another bowl, mix the onion and the scallion.

5. Put a wide, covered pan on medium-low heat, and add the oil.

6. Put the spice paste in and cover. Occasionally, remove the lid to stir, and cook for about 3 minutes.

7. Add the meat to the pan and bring the heat up to medium. Cook the meat for about 1 minute, stirring often.

8. Add the salt to the pan and cover, cooking for about 20 minutes. Stir occasionally.

9. As soon as the juices in the pan have almost all evaporated, add 2¼ cups water and stir. Bring this to a simmer. Reduce the heat to low, and continue to cook, covered, for approximately 45 minutes.

10. Add the potatoes and cook, covered, for another 5 minutes, stirring occasionally.

11. Add 2 cups of water and bring this to a simmer. Bring the heat up to medium-low and cover, cooking for about 25 minutes.

Further Reading

"Goat Meat Nutrition." Elkusa.com. Grande Premium Meats. September 1, 2009. http://elkusa.com/Goat_meat_nutrition.html.

Green, Aliza. *Field Guide to Meat: How to Identify, Select, and Prepare Virtually Every Meat, Poultry, and Game Cut.* Philadelphia: Quirk Publications, 2005.

Hirst, K. Kris. "Goats: The History of the Domestication of Goats." About.com: Archaeology. The New York Times Company. http://archaeology.about.com/od/domestications/qt/goats.htm.

Jaffrey, Madhur. *From Curries to Kebabs: Recipes from the Indian Spice Trail.* New York: Clarkson Potter, 2003.

Sokolov, Raymond. *The Cook's Canon: 101 Classic Recipes Everyone Should Know.* New York: Harper Collins, 2003.

Laura Mathews

H

Haggis

Haggis is Scotland's national and most notorious dish. Legend states that haggis is a furry, four-legged creature that lives in the Scottish highlands. The animal is lopsided as the legs on one side of its body are shorter than the other, making it perfectly adapted to move around the tops of the Scottish hills. The haggis is known to be very shy, however, it has been noted that the best way to catch the animal—that is if one is lucky enough to spot a haggis—is to run around the hill in the opposite direction, as a haggis can only run in a clockwise path.

Although many people from outside of Scotland believe the legend, haggis is in fact not an animal. The dish is a hearty relative of the sausage family, comprised of a sheep's heart, liver, and lights (lungs). The offal meats are chopped and mixed with oatmeal and seasonings before being stuffed into the sheep's stomach and boiled for several hours. Haggis is traditionally served at the table still in its original casing. The typical accompaniment for the dish is neeps 'n' tatties, also known as capshot in Scotland—which is more commonly referred to as mashed turnips and potatoes outside of the country.

Britons have consumed dishes similar to haggis since the Mesolithic era. When prey was caught, roasting was the easiest method of cooking, since at that time the people of the area had no cooking vessels. The innards of the animal would have been eaten as well as the flesh, although the preparation was slightly different. Offal and brains were mixed with fat and stuffed into gut casings. This was then roasted in the embers of the cooking fire. These haggis-type dishes were popular in the Scottish Highlands and other rural areas well into the Middle Ages.

It is understood that the history of the haggis does not begin in Scotland, however, its exact origins are unknown. This type of cooking was also known outside of Britain. One of the more famed notations of a haggis-type dish was in Homer's *Odyssey*. Some historians believe that the dish arrived in Scotland when the Romans came to Britain, as the Romans were known to enjoy foods of the sausage family. This original dish did not contain oats or mutton; the addition of these ingredients would have taken place as the population adapted to the new surroundings.

The origin of the word haggis itself is also somewhat of a controversy. The most common belief is that the word derives from the French word *hachis*. When translated into English the word means hash, hack, or chop. However, some argue that the French term was not frequently used at the time when haggis first became common.

The second commonly believed source of the word haggis comes from the

A cooked haggis with diced turnips and mashed potatoes—the traditional "tatties and neeps" of a Burns supper. (Shutterstock)

celebration of the New Year. Some authorities suggest that the word is derived from the words *au gui l'an neuf*, which means mistletoe for the New Year. This saying was the cry of the mistletoe sellers in the Middle Ages.

It was the famous Scottish poet Robert Burns who truly made haggis the icon of Scottish culture that it is today. The story of Burns and haggis dates back to the 18th century. In 1785, Burns was a guest at a supper club. When asked to say grace, Burns rejected the traditional route and instead chose to address the haggis—which was what was for dinner that night. A year after that fateful evening, Burns completed the work. The address-cum-poem was published in the Caledonian Mercury on December 20.

On the fifth anniversary of Burns's death, nine men sat down to what became the first Burns's supper. The men recited "Address to a Haggis," and naturally one was consumed. The party met again the following year, and the tradition was born. Over the years it started to be held both on the anniversary of his birth and that of his death. This tradition dwindled down to once a year yet again, this time the anniversary of his birth.

There are many regional specialties around the world that share similarities with the famed Scottish dish. American scrapple is an example of a cousin to haggis. Scrapple is considered by many historians to be the first all-American pork food. Boiled pork offal and cooked cornmeal are combined to make the dish. This mixture is

Robert Burns's Address to a Haggis

This poem is traditionally recited over a haggis meal.

Fair fa' your honest, sonsie face,
    Great chieftain o' the puddin-race!
    Aboon them a' ye tak your place,
    Painch, tripe, or thairm:
    Weel are ye wordy o' a grace
    As lang's my arm.

The groaning trencher there ye fill,
    Your hurdies like a distant hill,
    Your pin wad help to mend a mill
    In time o' need,
    While thro' your pores the dews distil
    Like amber bead.
    His knife see rustic Labour dight,
    An' cut you up wi' ready sleight,
    Trenching your gushing entrails bright,
    Like ony ditch;
    And then, O what a glorious sight,
    Warm-reekin, rich!
    Then, horn for horn,
    they stretch an' strive:
    Deil tak the hindmost! on they drive,
    Till a' their weel-swall'd kytes belyve,
    Are bent lyke drums;
    Then auld Guidman, maist like to rive,
    "Bethankit!" 'hums.

Is there that owre his French ragout
    Or olio that wad staw a sow,
    Or fricassee wad mak her spew
    Wi' perfect sconner,
    Looks down wi' sneering, scornfu' view
    On sic a dinner?

Poor devil! see him ower his trash,
    As feckless as a wither'd rash,
    His spindle shank, a guid whip-lash,

His nieve a nit;
Thro' bloody flood or field to dash,
O how unfit!

But mark the Rustic, haggis fed,
The trembling earth resounds his tread.
Clap in his walie nieve a blade,
He'll mak it whissle;
An' legs an' arms, an' heads will sned,
Like taps o' thrissle.

Ye Pow'rs wha mak mankind your care,
And dish them out their bill o' fare,
Auld Scotland wants nae skinking ware
That jaups in luggies;
But, if ye wish her gratefu' prayer,
Gie her a haggis!

Robert Burns, "To a Haggis," *The Poems and Songs of Robert Burns* (London: Cassell and Company, LTD, 1908), 138.

then put in loaf-shaped pans to be formed before serving—similar to a meatloaf. Scrapple originated in Chester County, Pennsylvania, with the Dutch settlers.

Another cousin of haggis is kishke. This Yiddish sausage is made from beef intestine that is stuffed with matzo meal, fat, and spices. The beef used is traditionally kosher. Blood is not used, as it is forbidden by kashrut. The dish is sometimes called stuffed derma, based on the Hebrew word for gut.

Ghammeh is a dish from Lebanon that also makes use of the stomach of the sheep. The stomach is stuffed with rice, garlic, onions, pine nuts, minced lamb meat, and spices. Many other offal dishes can be found throughout the world. Greece, Italy, Germany, and France all have traditional dishes making use of organ meats.

Within Scotland, haggis has made its way into popular food culture. It is now used as a substitute for ground beef in hamburgers and lasagna. Haggis-stuffed samosas can be found in curry restaurants, pubs, and in the frozen food section of the grocery stores. Pizzas topped with haggis can be purchased in stores or from pizza chains across Scotland. Haggis can be purchased fresh from a butcher, frozen, or canned. Halal, kosher, and vegetarian versions are available within Scotland.

Further Reading

Turnbull, A. "Haggis: Great Chieftan o' the Puddin'-race, and How!" *National Post*, January 23, 2010.

Tyrrell, A., P. Hill, and D. Kirkby. "Feasting on National Identity: Whisky, Haggis and the Celebration of Scottishness in the Nineteenth Century." In *Dining on Turtles: Food Feasts and Drinking in History*, edited by D. Kirkby and T. Luckins, 46–63. New York: Palgrave MacMillan, 2007.

Wilson, A. *Food & Drink in Britain: From the Stone Age to Recent Times*. London: Constable, 1973.

Alexandra Turnbull

Hákarl

Kæstur hákarl, or *hákarl* for short, is the rotten, aged meat of the Greenland shark (*Somniosus microcephalus*), eaten in Iceland and possibly Greenland since Vikings inhabited the region. It has a high concentration of ammonia, which dominates the taste, and a secondary but no-less-noticeable fishy flavor. Some people liken the experience to eating a very ripe cheese, while others compare it to ingesting stagnant urine.

The flesh of the Greenland shark, when left untreated, is inherently inedible to humans and animals because of naturally occurring levels of trimethylamine oxide in its flesh, a toxin that when consumed breaks down into the neurotoxin trimethylamine, which causes a state akin to extreme drunkenness. How Iceland's Viking settlers discovered that the meat could be made into a snack food is a mystery. What is known is this: The process of making hákarl involves killing, eviscerating, and cleaning the shark, removing the head and cartilage, and then burying what's left in a pit dug on a gravelly beach above the tidal line, and covering it with heavy stones and sand. Under the weight of the stones, the toxic fluids drain from the carcass and a state of putrefaction sets in. It is possible that during this time people would urinate over the pit to counteract the strong smell of ammonia from the rotting meat, but this is largely hearsay. Once the meat is soft and the ammonia odor undeniable, it is dug up again after about six to seven weeks (in the summer, or about three months in the winter), and is then strung up and hung in a well-ventilated shed, where it is left to dry for several months. One modern approach to making hákarl involves forgoing a gravel pit for a large container with a drainage hole.

Ask any young Icelandic person about hákarl and you are likely to be met with an amused and slightly embarrassed response. Few people still eat the stuff; it is generally considered the domain of the elderly, who associate eating it with strength and vigor. However, it is still consumed from time to time among Icelandic people who have developed a taste for it, and by tourists and other participants in *Thorrablot*, a modern Icelandic holiday that attempts to recreate the ancient midwinter pagan feast during *Thorri*, a month on the old Icelandic calendar which begins in late January. Anthony Bourdain called it the "worst, worst, worst, worst thing" that he had ever tasted, and one traveler said of the experience, "It felt like God was pissing in my eyes and mouth." British chef Gordon Ramsay tried a bite on television, and promptly threw up into a bucket.

Hákarl has two distinct components: *glerhákarl* (glass shark), the chewy, semiopaque flesh that lays next to the skin, and the yielding, tender inner flesh, called *skyrhákarl* (skyr shark). They are equally pungent. They are traditionally served cut into small cubes, eaten with forks or toothpicks, and quickly chased down with a shot of *brennivín,* a type of Icelandic schnapps made from potato pulp and flavored with caraway seeds. *Brennivín* has earned the nickname black death (*svarti dauði*) for its distinctively somber black label and high alcohol content (37.5 percent). The liquor helps mask the taste of the shark.

Further Reading

Anthoni, U., C. Christophersen, L. Gram, N. Nielsen, and P. Nielsen. "Poisonings from Flesh of the Greenland Shark *Somniosus microcephalus* may be due to Trimethylamine." *Toxicon* 29, no. 10 (1991): 1205–1212.

"How to Prepare Rotten Shark." Jo's Icelandic Recipes. January 23, 2010. http://www.simnet.is/gullis/jo/shark.html.

Ramsay, Gordon. "The F-Word." Serious Eats. http://www.seriouseats.com/2008/01/gordon-ramsay-vs-james-may.html.

Rögnvaldardóttir, Nanna. *Icelandic Food and Cookery.* New York: Hippocrene Books, 2002.

Sietsema, Robert. "Let Us Now Praise Stinky Foods: How to Cure Icelandic Hákarl (Including Urine)." *Village Voice* (blog). http://blogs.villagevoice.com/forkintheroad/archives/2009/12/let_us_now_prai_5.php.

Sidra Durst

Head Cheese

Head cheese, known as brawn in England, is not made from milk or cheese at all. It is the meat from the head of an animal that is boiled, chopped, and pressed into a mold or form, covered with some or all of the boiling liquids and chilled. It is most commonly made with pork, but can also be made with the head of a sheep, ox, or rabbit. In medieval Britain it was made from wild boar.

The chopped meat is held together by aspic or unflavored gelatin that is a byproduct of boiling the head of the animal. The muscles of the face and head are held together by connective tissues that, when heated, slowly break down—which is why recipes call for several hours of boiling with spices and other aromatics. When the collagen in the connective tissues is heated, it hydrolyzes and becomes gelatin, present in the cooking liquid. Some or all of the liquid is added back to the chopped meat and then cooled; the meat is then

Roasted potatoes with headcheese. (© dirkr, istockphoto.com)

suspended in the gelatinized liquid. This mixture was often poured into cylindrical moulds, similar to those used for cheese, which is where the American term head cheese and French, *fromage de tête*, originate. In some regions of Pennsylvania, the dish is called souse, which is often pickled. Head cheese is not limited to Western Europe and the United States; almost every country and culture has its own version of a dish that combines chopped meats in aspic, with a wide range of names and spices.

Head cheese is usually available in some butcher shops and specialty markets in the United States, though now shaped in long rectangles and sliced, rather than rounds. The origins of head cheese are fairly simple. If one were to boil a head and chill it in the broth, something akin to head cheese would form naturally (think, for example of the gelatin that forms under a cold roast chicken). Head cheese is a refinement of this process.

Head cheese is eaten on its own, often served, like pâté, with bread or crackers, mustard, and cornichons or in a sandwich as lunchmeat.

Head Cheese

Ingredients

The Meat

1 pig's head, or
2½ lb. of pork meat and 1 to 2 pig's
   feet, or
1 calf's head

The Seasonings

4 cloves garlic
1 to 2 onions, chopped
2 celery stalks, cut in half

1 bell pepper chopped (optional)
½ cup vinegar (optional)
Cold water
Salt and pepper to taste
Optional spices: 1 tsp sage, 2 bay leaves,
   1 to 2 tsp red pepper flakes, a bunch
   of fresh parsley, 2 tsp whole allspice
   berries

1. Make sure the head is cleaned. Specifically: remove the eyes and brains, and clean the ears and teeth. (Many butchers will do some or most of this for you.)
2. Place the head and/or meat into a large stockpot and fill with water to cover the meat completely.
3. Add in the seasonings and aromatics. Only add a few pinches of salt and pepper at this time. (You will season it again later.)
4. Bring to a boil, and lower the mixture to a simmer.
5. Cook for 2 to 3 hours or until the meat falls off the bone.
6. Strain the meat, reserve the stock. (Strain out the vegetables and whole spices.)
7. Pull the meat off the head. Cut it into pieces if necessary. You are looking for pieces to be bite size or smaller.
8. Return the meat and strained stock to a pot.
9. Simmer the mixture for 30 minutes. Taste it, and add additional salt if needed.
10. Remove it from the heat. Pour the mixture into a pan or tureen lined with plastic wrap. Fold the extra plastic wrap over the edges, cover the pan, and weigh it down.

11. Chill the mixture in the fridge until it is cold and has gelled. (Overnight is best.)

12. To remove, uncover, and turn out the head cheese. If your plastic wrap worked, it should come out in one loaf. If the mixture leaked and it is sticking to the inside of the pan, just run a warm knife around the edge and pull it free. Remove the plastic wrap and cut into slices.

Serve with a vinaigrette, mustard, pickles, or condiments of your choice.

Further Reading

Ayto, John, ed. "Brawn." *An A-Z of Food and Drink*. Oxford University Press, 2002. Oxford Reference Online. http://www.oxfordreference.com/pages/Subjects_and_Titles__s9t134.

Davidson, Alan. "Brawn." *The Penguin Companion to Food*, 111. New York: Penguin, 2002.

Rombauer, Irma S., and Marion Rombauer Becker. "Head Cheese or Brawn." *Joy of Cooking*, 449. Indianapolis, IN: Bobbs-Merrill, 1964.

Kristina Nies

Hormigas Culonas (Big-Bottomed Ants)

Hormigas culonas (*Atta laevigata*) are one of the largest leaf cutter ants in the world and have been a delicacy in Colombia since pre-Colombian times. The name translates to big-bottomed ants in English. These ants, cherished for their unmistakable sour taste, get their name thanks to the disproportionate size of their bottoms in comparison to the rest of their bodies.

The first written records of the consumption of these ants dates to colonial times, 500 years ago, when the conquistadors, astonished and scared, described the important role the ants played in the diet of Indian communities who used the culonas as a good source of protein and fat. They also described their use for medicinal and ceremonial purposes, thanks to their analgesic properties and the belief among the Indians that the ants had aphrodisiac powers.

Many of the traditions involving the culonas remain the same today. These ants, only found in a very limited area in the state of Santander (northeastern Colombia), only come out of their nests during the April rains to reproduce. It is said that only after great rains followed by intense sunny mornings, will this phenomenon occur. The future queens, culonas, who are the only ones appropriate for consumption will make their first and only flight, the nuptial flight during which they are fertilized. When their bottoms are filled with eggs, they are ready for catching.

For hundreds of years, they have been hunted in the traditional manner; men have stood at the edge of the nests to get, not without an extenuating battle, a taste of these magnificent ants. The skilled hunters, protected from the ferocious pincers of the working ants by rubber boots and gloves, go out with cans, pots, and bags in search of the big queens. Once the ants are captured, following the traditions of the Guane Indians, the hunters brine them (soak in salt water) and finally toast them until dark and crunchy. This process is done in traditional clay pots, with no other fat than that which the ants release in roasting at low heat over a long period of time. Wings and legs are removed and only the

Piles of live "hormiga culonas" or big-bottomed queen ants are offered for sale by vendors on the streets of San Gil, Colombia, 145 miles northeast from Bogota. The culonas, a source of cultural pride and epicurean delight in throughout Santander Province, are now being discovered by curious gourmets in other parts of the world. (AP Photo/ William Fernando Martinez)

toasted body and the creamy butts are consumed.

Traditionally the big-bottomed ants are consumed as a snack, though a new wave of Colombian chefs is trying to incorporate them into more sophisticated recipes. Also, the demand for them in the international markets has called for more innovation, and they are now sold as a sweet snack, covered in chocolate.

Further Reading

Gutierrez, Juan Carlos. "Las hormigas culonas." *SemanaMagazine*, 2006. Semana.com. http://www.semana.com/especiales/hormigas-culonas/95477-3.aspx

Plata, Horacio Rodriguez. *Las hormigas culonas en la historia y el folklore*. Bogota, Columbia: International Monetary Fund, 1966.

Villegas, Benjamin. *El sabor de Colombia*. Bogota, Columbia: Villegas Editores, 2006.

Marcela Duarte

Horse

Inhabitants of many countries around the world have traditions of consuming horse (*Equus caballus*), both meat and milk. In Europe, horse meat is eaten with varying degrees of acceptance from country to country, and the top consumers are the French, Belgians, Swedish, and Italians. Horse meat and milk are also consumed in Central Asia, China, Japan, and South America.

At archaeological sites throughout Europe, there is evidence that prehistoric Europeans hunted horses, in some cases by deliberately stampeding them over a cliff—the first evidence of a long-standing relationship between the inhabitants of Europe and horse meat. In pre-Christian times, rituals involving the sacrifice and consumption of horse in northern Europe figured in Teutonic religious ceremonies, especially in the worship of the Norse god Odin. In an effort to spread Christianity, Pope Gregory III tried to ban the pagan practice in 732 CE. However, the Catholic Church eventually gave one notable exception to Icelanders in 999 CE, which allowed them to continue eating horse meat.

In combination with the papal ban on eating horses for food and their value in wartime activities, horse was not a substantial source of protein in the European diet until the mid-19th century when a number of campaigns popularized the eating of horse meat. The eminent French zoologist Isidore Geoffry St. Hilaire joined the cause of encouraging horseflesh eating, or hippophagy, pointing to customs from other parts of the world, the importance of horse meat among ancient Germans, the potential to increase protein for the poor and its excellent taste. Emile Decroix, the head veterinarian of the French army and later the head of a veterinary school near Paris, distributed horse meat to the poor and organized a *banquet hippophagique* in Paris in 1865. The banquet's menu featured courses like horse consommé and horse sausages, but the reception to these dishes was mixed. Nevertheless, the same year of the banquet, the first horse meat butcher shop opened in Paris.

In the 20th century, the practice of eating horse meat has typically been adopted as a wartime measure or viewed as a meat source for peasants. Even in North America, where eating horse meat is taboo, butcher shops selling horse meat opened during the 1970s when the oil shock caused a steep increase in beef prices. The M and R Packing Company of Hartford, Connecticut, tried to popularize horse steaks and horse burgers through its Chevalean brand, setting up promotional vending carts in large cities in the Northeast. At one cart in New York City, customers formed long lines to taste horse steaks, which they dubbed Belmont steaks. But eating horse meat in America proved to be short-lived after the M and R Packing Company folded under pressure from beef lobbyists and animal rights groups.

Italy is the largest consumer of horse meat in Europe with more than 48,000 metric tons eaten every year, though many Italians also associate it with wartime substitutes for unobtainable meats. The average national consumption is around 2 pounds of horse meat per person per year. Horse meat has been a delicacy in Italy since Roman times, even despite the Catholic Church's ban, and it is particularly associated with the Emilia-Romagna region around Parma. In Venice and Verona, it is featured in several dishes such as a stew called *pastissada de caval*. It is also served as a steak, *carpaccio* (thin slices of raw meat), or made into *bresaola* (thin slices of meat that have been salted and air-dried for two to three months). Horse fat is used in recipes such as *pezzetti di cavallo,* or pieces of horse meat, and slices are often served on top of an arugula salad. Horse meat sausage (*salsiccia di equino*) and cured strips (*sflacci*) of horse meat are also available.

In France, horse meat is called *viande de cheval, viande chevaline,* or colloquially, *chevaline*. Even though the French are the most famous consumers of horse, consumption has fallen over the past two decades and now represents less than 1 percent of the meat consumed in the country. Horse meat consumption is often associated with low social status and poverty, and though it was initially touted for its health benefits, it came to be considered unhealthy, especially after a salmonella scare in 1967. However, there is some specialist breeding of horses for their meat, using Ardennes and Postier Breton horses, and 95 percent of all horses in France are bred first and foremost for their meat. Traditionally, horse meat has been sold in approximately 1,000 *boucherie chevaline,* presumably so that it can't be passed as more expensive cuts of beef. French culinary tradition doesn't dictate special dishes for horse, but recipes advise that it can be substituted interchangeably in any dish calling for similar cuts of beef.

Mongolians have a long-standing relationship with horses as work animals and as a food source that continues to this day. In the 13th century, Genghis Khan's warriors conquered a swath of Eurasia from China to Hungary to create the Mongol Empire, and part of their success is credited to their speed and agility on horseback. They could travel 100 miles a day on horseback, and on forced marches, many soldiers survived by drinking their horses' blood. Each warrior traveled with a string of horses and would open a vein in a different horse at 10-day intervals, drinking some of the fresh blood and then closing the incision. Any horses that died during a march were also eaten for their meat. Today, mares are milked every couple of hours during the summer foaling season to yield about two quarts of milk. The milk is left for 24 hours to ferment while being frequently jostled to prevent spoilage and the end result is *airag*, a slightly effervescent and sour drink with an aftertaste of almonds. *Airag*, also known as *kumiss* throughout Central Asia, is slightly alcoholic, and if left to ferment for longer is turned into *arkhi*, a milk brandy with an alcohol content as high as 18 percent.

In Japan, raw horse meat is called *sakura niku*, which means cherry blossom meat. This is in reference to the intense red or pink color of horse meat when compared to beef. Sakura niku is best known as a specialty of the Kumamoto Prefecture, which was home to large horse farms as early as the 1600s. However, horse meat eating didn't gain widespread popularity until the 1960s when automobiles reduced the need for horses for transport and farming. In a preparation called *basashi,* horse meat is served raw in thin slices with condiments like soy sauce, shiso leaves, and daikon. Thinly sliced horse meat is also added to *sukiyaki*, a hot pot simmered at the table with vegetables and broth, grilled tableside in *yakiniku* or served as sushi.

Horse meat is typically sold in cuts similar to beef. It has a taste similar to beef but is leaner, has a more tender texture, and a slightly sweet aftertaste due to a high glycogen content. Pound for pound, horse meat is lower in calories than beef, with 22 percent protein compared to 14.7 percent protein in a T-bone steak, and has one-tenth the fat of beef. Horses are tender as colts, but also in old age since only horses whose muscles have recently been under strain tend to be tough. Also, horses typically do not carry diseases and parasites like tuberculosis and tapeworms, which makes their meat ideal for raw preparations like steak tartare or horse sushi.

Pastissada de Caval

This is a traditional Veronese horse meat stew, made with local Amarone wine and paprika to taste. It can be eaten alone, but is typically served with polenta and other side dishes.

Ingredients

2 lb. horse meat, cut into cubes for stewing
2 stalks celery, diced
3 carrots, diced
1 large onion, diced
4 cloves garlic
1 pinch coriander seeds
1 bay leaf
1 750-ml bottle red wine
¼ cup olive oil
Salt and pepper to taste
1 tbsp butter kneaded in 1 tbsp flour

1. In a large container, combine the meat with the diced vegetables, garlic, coriander seeds, bay leaf, garlic, and wine. Cover and marinate overnight, turning the meat occasionally.

2. Remove the meat from the marinade, reserving the marinade. Pat the meat dry and dredge in flour.
3. Heat the olive oil in a Dutch oven. Brown meat on all sides. Add the vegetables and liquid; bring to a boil and summer until tender, about 2 to 3 hours.
4. To finish, remove the meat from the sauce and, using an immersion blender, blend together the vegetables, sauce, and butter/flour mixture.

Serve with polenta or crusty bread.

Further Reading

Harris, Marvin. *Good to Eat: Riddles of Food and Culture.* New York: Simon & Schuster, 1985.

Schwabe, Calvin W. *Unmentionable Cuisine.* Charlottesville: University of Virginia Press, 1979.

Weil, Christa. *Fierce Food: The Intrepid Diner's Guide to the Unusual, Exotic, and Downright Bizarre.* New York: Penguin Group, 2006.

Leah Kim

Huitlacoche

Huitlacoche (hweet-la-KOH-chay), sometimes spelled *cuitlacoche,* is a fungus (*Ustilago maydis*) that infects corn. It has been consumed and cultivated in Mexico and Central America as a foodstuff dating back to Aztec rule. Some consider it a delicacy, while others view it as a blight that ruins crops.

The silver-gray fungus is harvested and prepared in soups, tamales, tacos, and paired with cheese in quesadillas. The term *huitlacoche* comes from two words in the ancient Azetec language Nahuatl. *Huitlatl* means "excrement," *coche* means "raven." The Latin term *Ustilago maydis* refers to the burn-like appears on the husk of the ear of corn. *Ustilago* comes from the Latin word *ustilare* ("to burn").

The fungus can be spread by insects and by wind and can infect the corn kernels and/or the corn tassels. All forms of corn, popping corn, sweet corn, and dent corn are susceptible to the fungus, which is associated with hot, dry weather, but they do require some water—usually found within the ears—to replicate. Since the spores can infect the individual kernels, traditional fungicides do not work, and the spores can withstand winter, making it more difficult to prevent or eradicate the fungus from a crop or field.

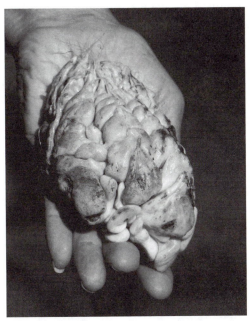

A woman holds huitlacoche in a food market in Mexico City. (AP Photo/Claudio Cruz)

Infected kernels expand up to 10 times their normal size, turning the white/yellow kernels to a silver-gray tumor filled with fungal threads and blue-black spores. These immature, slightly spongy tumors or galls can be harvested, cooked, and eaten. When cooked, the grey, stone or pebble-shaped huitlacoche becomes soft, very dark, almost charcoal in color. If it is cooked further, it will begin to leech water, like other mushrooms, turning the cooking liquid almost black. It has a woodsy, mushroom-like flavor, coming from the glucose, sotolon, and vanillin present in the fungus. Fully mature galls are dry and filled with spores that look like black dust. The slightly smoky, mushroom flavor has earned huilacoche the nicknames of Mexican truffle, Aztec caviar, maize mushroom, or *el oro negro*—black gold.

While considered a delicacy to some, others know huitlacoche as corn smut (smut meaning fungus), maize smut, or devil's corn because the fungus can ruin corn crops. Huitlacoche decreases the total corn yield and once an ear is infected, it has to be removed from the field for risk of the spores becoming airborne and infecting other plants. For this reason, many corn farmers in the United States have viewed huitlacoche as a disease rather than a delicacy.

Beginning in the 1990s, farmers in the United States began harvesting and selling huitlacoche, coinciding with the rise in popularity of Mexican food. Huitlacoche is now actively cultivated in some regions of America. Usually, it is sold fresh during corn season, but can also be found frozen or canned in specialty food stores.

A similar fungus, *Ustilago esculenta*, is an edible fungus that infects wild rice in Japan and China. The spores infect the upper stem, which swells as the fungus grows. The stems are harvested and cooked and served like a vegetable, tasting faintly of bamboo.

Further Reading

Coyle, L. Patrick. "Cuitlacoche." *The World Encyclopedia of Food*, 220. New York: Facts on File, 1982.

Davidson, Alan. "Huitlacoche." *The Penguin Companion to Food*, 467. New York: Penguin, 2002.

Herbst, Sharon Tyler. "Cuitlacoche." *The New Food Lover's Companion: Comprehensive Definitions of Nearly 6,000 Food, Drink, and Culinary Terms*. 3rd. ed. Hauppauge, NY: Barron's Education Series, 2001.

McGee, Harold. "Huitlacoche, or Corn Smut." *On Food and Cooking: The Science and Lore of the Kitchen*. New York: Scribner, 2004.

Kristina Nies

Human

It is commonly believed that cannibalism, or anthropophagy, is the ultimate taboo, that we are, by our very nature, averse to even the idea of consuming human flesh. However, throughout history, people have often eaten other people. Among the rest of us, it is often the subject of nervous jokes, rumors, and myths—in fact, cannibalism features prominently in the literature of many societies.

In survival situations, there are definite preferences as to which portions of the anatomy are eaten first. But what about the gastronomy of cannibalism? Over the years, the non-emergency eating of human flesh might have evolved into unique cuisines within the various cultures that indulge in the habit. After all, there are definite differences between the ways other meats are used by different cultures.

First, it should be understood that there has always been a distinct survival advantage in the eating of high-energy (fatty) foods. Most people prefer the fattier cuts of meat. We have since learned that it is unhealthy to eat such foods, so we have developed a conscious—perhaps even self-conscious—aversion to them.

With that in mind, we expect to see this pattern of fat seeking in the preferences of most cannibals. What are the most fat-rich portions of the anatomy? They are not the spots you might expect. Potbellies, love handles, and thunder thighs are the result of a lifestyle that has not existed in most of human history. Where would a cannibal expect to find fat on the leaner bodies he would more likely encounter?

The liver, buttocks, brains, and the marrow of the larger limb bones. The enlarged foramen magnum on many ancient skulls would seem to indicate that brains were popular among our forebears. Soft tissue, like buttocks, leave little traces—but cut marks in particular places on bones indicate removal of the desirable portions. Owen Beattie's expedition in search of the 19th-century remains of the HMS *Erebus* and the HMS *Terror* found exactly the kinds of marks one would expect to find if such soft tissue had been cut off.

When Tim White analyzed pre-Colombian bones from Mancos Canyon, he found evidence of very efficient utilization of the flesh and bones of humans. Leg

Discussions of cannibalism must always be viewed with a critical eye. Have humans been used for food in the past? Unquestionably, yes. But often accounts of cannibalism are exaggerated or totally fictitious. Accusing another culture of cannibalism has been used as a way to denigrate others, to imply that they are primitive or savage. The context of the cannibalism is important as well—religious ritual, wartime practice, sustenance food, deviant behavior, or tasty treat?

bones showed cut marks and fractures that showed how the marrow was extracted. He also found telltale pot polish, in which the broken ends of bones become smoothed by rubbing against the inside of a vigorously boiling pottery or stone container of water. Pot polish develops when the bones are boiled to extract the marrowfat, which rises to the top of the water, where it is easily collected. White also acknowledged the work of Lynn Flinn, Christy Turner, and Alan Brew, who noted that the

> bones at the top of the skull show the most evidence of burning, concluding that "Perhaps the skull itself was used as a cooking utensil, being turned upside down so that it rested in the fire pit on the frontal and parietal sections, while the brain roasted within it." (White, 1992, 171)

The archaeological evidence of cannibalism confirms these preferences. Of course, it cannot tell us if these humans were eaten as survival food.

They may have been consumed in some form of ritual or ceremonial fashion. Certainly nutritional concerns were more than incidental—the elaborate efforts to extract every bit of marrow fat form the larger

bones make it clear that this was not *only* about insulting an enemy warrior.

The Mancos Canyon site that White examined was only one of many Anasazi sites that show signs of cannibalistic activities. They all seem to date from the mid-12th century, a time in which "cannibalism was associated with violent conflict between Anasazi communities. . . . contemporary with a period of drought and the collapse of the Chaco system" (Walker, 1997, 206).

There are four basic forms of cannibalism: endocannibalism, when only people in one's own group are eaten; exocannibalism, when only people outside one's own group are eaten; survival cannibalism, when people eat others under extreme conditions in order to survive; and symbolic cannibalism, where people are not actually eaten but are consumed in other ways (e.g., the Communion rite).

The boundaries between the four basic forms of cannibalism are often blurred in practice, and it is not always possible to tell if the cannibal's motivation was primarily survival, religious ritual, military action, or gustatory pleasure.

Sophie D. Coe, in her efforts to curb the exaggeration of cannibalism reports among the Maya, gives us some insight into their preferences.

> The Maya were accused of eating human flesh, and like the Aztecs, the conquest period Maya certainly did, but again it was for ritual purposes, not as ordinary food. Reverend Father Francesco of Bologna wrote Pope Paul III in the 1530s saying that the arms and legs of sacrificial victims were given to the principal chiefs, "who ate them with joy and respect, saying they were the relics of saints" (Díaz 1838: 215). The *Littera mādata* (Anon. n.d.: 298r) is even more precise and says it was only the calves of the sacrificed captives' legs that were given to the victorious rulers to eat: hardly articles of daily diet. (Coe, 1994, 160)

Right up to the beginning of the 20th century, the Big Namba of Vanuatu ate everything except the head and entrails, but favored the buttocks especially. Nineteenth-century naturalist Carl Bock interviewed a Bahou Tring priestess in southeast Borneo about her people's preferences. She held out her hand and told him

> that the palms are considered the best eating. Then she pointed to the knee, and again to the forehead, using the Malay word *bai, bai* (good, good), each time, to indicate that the brains, and the flesh on the knees of a human being, are also considered delicacies by the members of her tribe. (Bock, 1985, 221)

A plump rump was the favorite of some Maoris, as noted by Captain Cook in the 18th century but was rejected as tasting like waste matter by some aging cannibals in the Solomon Islands. Thighs and upper arms yield a good quantity of meat, and according to the Fijians, some of the tastiest flesh. The leg was often reserved for the chief on Vanuatu.

Twentieth-century travelers learned that the head was the apple of many a headhunter's eye—in Borneo, New Guinea, and the New Hebrides. The Oba of Vanuatu preferred the breasts of young women, a dish suitable for royalty. The female breast, and the nipple, was a special favorite in the Solomon Islands, too.

Genitalia don't appear on as many *plats du jour* as other cuts—though they have been eaten by the Herero of southwestern Africa (in what is today Angola). The testicles of slain enemy warriors were fed to the newly initiated Ovaherero youth of Abyssinia.

Many anthropophagists enjoyed organ meats, not very popular among noncannibal Americans. Hearts, of course, and livers, have been eaten almost everywhere that discriminating cannibals dine—but also kidneys and the belly fat. In Vanuatu and the Solomons, the organs were simply discarded.

Dr. John Collee, writing in the Manchester *Guardian*, quoted a Papuan source, from 1939, recommending

> "the portion above the hips which tasted like opossum." The tribesmen of the Markham Valley apparently prized the feet and hands as delicacies, cooked with sago and cabbage, although I'm more inclined to believe the tour guide I once met in Fiji, who told me that the tastiest portion of a

human being was the underside of the upper arm of a young girl. (Collee, 1995, 90)

In addition to being fussy about which cuts are most desirable, many cannibals have expressed concern over the source of the meat. Women and children have had their aficionados among the Tartars, in China and in 18th-century New Zealand. In Liberia, they were thought to have a bitter taste. Eighteenth-century Maoris preferred black men to white men, as did the Chinese of the 11th century. Adult males were also the choice of the Bele of Liberia.

The eating habits of the Foré of New Guinea have been much studied, because of the incidence of kuru disease among them. Before they prepared human flesh, it had to be aged—then prepared with

> green vegetables, or small pieces of flesh might be cooked in a stew with ginger and vegetables. Even though the people of the eastern highlands eat pork and other meat in a fresh state, they appear to have preferred human meat when it was decomposed. A corpse was usually left in a shallow grave until the process was well advanced. (Farb and Armelagos, 1980, 137)

The Asmat of the swamps of New Guinea are (or were until very recently) headhunters and cannibals. Their reasons and methods came directly from myths about the dawn of their world. In the beginning, according to the story, there were two brothers, one who had physical defects and one who took care of hunting and gathering food. The first brother convinced the younger brother to kill him, and although he was dead, he explained how to cook his body (Schneebaum, 1988).

The Asmat used this ancient story to teach their young the ways of their people. That it contains a recipe is proof that food, especially properly prepared food, is one of the key elements that define a group's identity.

Jeremy MacClancy, interviewed John Peter Anahapat—a chief of the Big Nambas in Vanuatu, in 1978—about the methods used in the preparation of human flesh. Anahapat was neither shy nor uninformed about the subject.

> When man is cut, he is cut in a different way from bullock or sheep or pig or goat. Cut out the navel, then the shoulder, then cut the fingers at all the joints, then the wrists, then the elbow, then the shoulder, then all toe and foot joints, then the knee, then pull out the stomach, then cut out the neck, then cut out the legs. Then cut everything into pieces. Give the legs to the chief.
>
> . . . The body is cut up in this special way as a mark of respect. If the body is cut up like an animal, the meat is taboo. If eaten, the spirit of the dead man will spoil the village by making the people of that village go to places where people of other villages can kill them. (MacClancy, 1992, 140)

This is not so much a recipe, as instructions for the proper handling of an ingredient. Such instructions, like recipes, are means by which people attach social significance to inert matter—taking some raw material from nature and turning it into a human artifact, civilizing it, so that it can be—literally—incorporated into the community.

Freelance writer Michael Krieger, after reading an article about William Arens's book, *The Man-Eating Myth*, decided to find out for himself if there was such a thing as cannibalism. In 1987, he interviewed several former cannibals in Vanuatu and other nearby island chains. Many of his subjects were from the same Big Namba villages studied by MacClancy. Some of them told Krieger what was done with the body of a Small Namba they had killed.

> The body is split up, different parts to be cooked by three or four different families, though in all cases the method of preparation is the same. The body parts are wrapped in banana or other large leaves and are laid on top of preheated rocks in an umu, or earth oven, to steam until done, usually overnight. Then the cooked pieces are diced and mixed into laplap. Depending on the portion size, a human victim can serve, perhaps, ten warriors. Adult males are the only ones allowed to partake of human flesh. (Krieger, 1994, 73)

Apparently chief Anahapat was more concerned with proper religious behavior than Alam and the Big Nambas interviewed by Krieger. His statement of cooking methods nearly echoes their description, even if his characterization of the flesh itself does not sound like that of Seabrook.

> When you cook man, it is very yellow, very greasy and very sweet. It cannot be cooked like normal meat. It tastes better if hung for a couple of days. Put the meat in a lap-lap (grated tuber pudding wrapped in banana leaves like a long, flat packet and cooked in an earth oven). (MacClancy, 1992, 142)

The Kwakiutl Indians of the Pacific Northwest smoked human flesh (but only during specific religious/initiatory rituals)—just as they did their annual salmon catch. The Huni Kui of the upper Amazon also preferred their man smoked—but that may be because they didn't eat their victims on the spot, but rather brought the flesh back to their village after a successful war party. Keeping meat fresh in the hot moist tropics would have been impossible—and cultural preferences evolve in response to the physical restrictions of their environment.

Likewise, in the Congo,

> The popularity of smoking indicates that humans are indeed a delicacy: something to be served and savored at leisure. Hands are a special delicacy. The muscle at the base of the thumb, the thenar eminence, is highly developed in all humans . . . The fact that cannibals appreciate such delicacies proves finally, that they are far from being mad butchers. They are connoisseurs. (Sheffield, 1996)

The Aztecs seem to have eaten human flesh in a manner that we clearly recognize as Mexican food. According to early ethnographer and historian, Benardino de Sahagún, they cut it up and prepared the limbs for cooking—the favorite recipe being a stew flavored with peppers and tomatoes. . . . They put "squash blossoms" in the flesh. (Harris, 1977, 121–122)

Supposedly, some of that human flesh wound up in a dish that we would recognize as the ancestor of our chili con carne.

Sophie D. Coe believes that the cannibalism of the Aztecs was greatly exaggerated. She pointed out a recipe for human stew or *tlacatlaolli* in Sahagún that contained mostly maize and only a tiny amount of flesh. She says,

> The accounts agree that this was a communion of sorts, unity with the god being achieved by sharing the god's food and eating it. . . . The portion of flesh per person was very small indeed, about half an ounce, and some people refused it altogether. The very description of the method of cooking . . . should signal to us that this is not an ordinary meal but a religious rite. (Coe, 1994, 98)

The Asmat of New Guinea eat the thighs roasted. They are headhunters, so they have special interest in the treatment of the head. After a successful raid,

> The first night the decapitated head is roasted and put up in the eaves. In the morning, the nose skin is cut off and the jaw removed . . .
>
> With a bamboo knife, Simni cuts from the bottom of the nose, slices up over the head, and on down to the nape of the neck. He tears off the

skin and tosses aside the jawbone, which is picked up by a woman who has taken part in the ceremony. He holds the head over the fire so that the flame reaches the temple and back. He uses a stone ax to cut a hole in the side of the skull and shakes the brains and mucous into a bowl made of sago palm leaf. He mixes the brains with sago, rolls the mixture into long tubes and cooks them in the fire. When they are done, he offers them to the old men and women who eat with great pleasure, knowing this powerful food will lengthen their lives. (Schneebaum, 1988, 178)

Jack Mater, an Australian police officer in New Guinea, told explorer Jens Bjerre about the preferred methods of the highland Kukukuku tribes.

> Fresh vegetables are brought from the fields and a big hole is dug in the ground for an oven. . . . When the prisoner has been killed, his arms and legs are cut off with a bamboo knife. The meat is then cut up into small pieces, wrapped in bark, and cooked together with the vegetables, in the oven in the ground. (Bjerre, 1957, 23)

Elsewhere in New Guinea, every part would be eaten, taking care to use even the small scraps.

> the bones were pulverized and eaten with green vegetables, or small pieces of flesh might be cooked in a stew with ginger and vegetables. (Farb and Armelagos, 1980, 137)

In the South American jungles, Amahuaca women have taken the cremated bones of their dead infants stirred into a kind of banana gruel before eating them. When one Amahuaca woman was asked why she did this, she responded, "to have the dear departed closer to her." (This example is from the American Museum of Natural History.)

Understandably, various cannibal cultures have clear notions of how human flesh should be prepared. What about the cooking methods of anthropophagists who don't have the benefit of those cultural traditions?

The shipwreck survivors of the USS *Dumaru* had twice resorted to eating their shipmates in 1918. There is only one passage in the account of first assistant engineer Fritz Harmon, incidentally, that addresses the issue of the flavor of human flesh. The usable portions of his former superior, chief engineer E. Howell were

> boiled to a broth and consumed by all hands when it was served in the two enameled cups and wooden bailer. The salt in the sea water in which the flesh was boiled was absorbed by the flesh, leaving the broth free from salt and not unpleasant to taste. The flesh was like tough veal. (Thomas, 1930, 163)

The Uruguayan rugby team that was the subject of the book (and subsequent film) *Alive!* had no ritual interest in their cannibalism—but being human, they took an interest in their food, eventually air-drying it in strips on the fuselage of the plane. The Andean survivors had too little fuel to waste on cooking, so they made do with such forms of preparation. However, one time when there was not enough sun to melt snow for drinking water, they burned a few Coca Cola crates.

> The embers were still hot; it seemed sensible to try cooking a piece of meat on the hot foil. They did not leave it on for long, but the slight browning of the flesh gave it an immeasurably better flavor—softer than beef but with much the same taste.
>
> The aroma soon brought other boys around the fire, and Coche Onciarte, who had continued to feel the greatest repugnance for the raw flesh found it quite palatable when cooked. Roy Harley, Numa Turcatti, and Eduardo Strauch also found it easier to overcome their revulsion when the meat was roasted and they could eat as though it were beef. (Read, 1974, 445)

Further Reading

Allen, Gary. "What is the Flavor of Human Flesh?" http://food.oregonstate.edu/ref/culture/taboo_allen.html.

Bjerre, Jens. *The Last Cannibals.* Translated by Estrid Bannister. New York: William Morrow and Company, 1957.

Bock, Carl. *The Head-Hunters of Borneo: A Narrative of Travel up the Mahakkam and Down the Barito; also, Journeyings in Sumatra.* 1881. Singapore: Oxford University Press, 1985.

Coe, Sophie D. *America's First Cuisines.* Austin: University of Texas Press, 1994.

Collee, John. "Mind & Body and the Foe Was Soundly Eaten; Dr. John Collee Chews over the Issue of Cannibalism." *Guardian,* March 19, 1995. http://proquest.umi.com.

Farb, Peter, and George Armelagos. *Consuming Passions: The Anthropology of Eating.* Boston: Houghton Mifflin, 1980.

Harris, Marvin. *Cannibals and Kings: The Origins of Cultures*. New York: Random House, 1977.

Krieger, Michael. *Conversations with the Cannibals: The End of the Old South Pacific*. Hopewell, NJ: Ecco Press, 1994.

MacClancy, Jeremy. *Consuming Culture: Why You Eat What You Eat*. New York: Henry Holt, 1992.

Read, Piers Paul. *Alive: The Story of the Andes Survivors*. Philadelphia: J.B. Lippincott & Company, 1974.

Ripe, Cherry. *Goodbye Culinary Cringe*. St. Leonards, NSW, Australia: Allen & Unwin, 1993.

Schneebaum, Tobias. *Where the Spirits Dwell*. New York: Grove Press, 1988.

Sheffield, Emily. "Minx . . . Society Girls Leg or Breast?" *Guardian*, September 12, 1996. http://proquest.umi.com.

Thomas, Lowell. *The Wreck of the Dumaru: The Story of Cannibalism in an Open Boat*. New York: P. F. Collier and Son, 1930.

Walker, Amélie. "Anasazi Cannibalism?" *Archaeology* (September/October 1997): 26.

White, T. D. *Prehistoric Cannibalism at Mancos 5MTUMR-2346*. Princeton, NJ: Princeton University Press, 1992.

Gary Allen

I

Iguana

Iguana, known as *garrobo* in Spanish, has been a viable food source in Central and South America for thousands of years. The lizards, which are usually green to grayish, though some species can be black or speckled, are very sensitive to cold and can live only in warm weather climates, ranging from the southern United States down to the coast of Venezuela. They can range from two to four feet long, have scaly, menacing tails, and horny spines that run down their backs. In the United States, they are considered an invasive species that threatens indigenous wildlife and destroys plants. The green iguana was a popular pet in the United States during the 1980s and 1990s. Many escaped lizards bred with Latin American species. Today, Honduras, Panama, Columbia, Mexico, and El Salvador are large consumers of the lizard, which is usually caught in the wild, though there are some small iguana farms in production.

Preparing iguana for food includes gutting, skinning, cleaning, and if the lizard is female, possibly removing internal eggs. The female iguana can hold dozens of eggs internally, which are strung together with long membranous tissue; eggs can be cooked and eaten. Iguana eggs are sold hardboiled in some South American markets, along with live or prepared lizards. Like most lizard species and raw chicken, iguanas tend to carry salmonella. They must be prepared under sanitary conditions and cooked thoroughly to avoid food-borne illnesses.

Iguana can be cooked in a number of ways. Some cultures favor grilling, roasting, or frying. Simmering iguana in a broth with aromatic herbs and vegetables is quite popular. The meat is pale pink and tends to flake into large chunks like meaty fish though the flavor is more akin to chicken, giving the iguana the nickname *gallina de palo*, bamboo chicken or chicken of the tree. During Holy Week in Nicaragua, locals traditionally make an iguana stew called *Indo Viejo,* Old Indian, that includes the lizard, local vegetables, and corn meal.

Some Latin American cultures believe that eating iguana is a delicacy, not just in taste, but in the restorative qualities that consuming the meat gives. Like the fierce lizard, eating iguana meat results in strength, energy, and a burst of libido.

The legality of killing wild iguanas depends on both the country and the species. It is important to learn local laws when considering capturing iguanas for food; some species may be protected or illegal to kill during specific times of the year, resulting in harsh fines and prosecution. In the United States, iguanas are considered pests and can be freely eliminated; it is actually illegal to release a live iguana into the wild, so if you catch one, you must keep it or kill it. Fresh iguana meat is difficult to come by in the United States, though some brands of iguana soup are imported to the United States and can be found in Latin American markets.

Braised Iguana

Ingredients

1 iguana, skinned and cleaned, cut into manageable portions
1 cup vinegar
Juice of 1 lime
1 tbsp salt
2 tsp pepper
¼ cup cilantro, chopped
6 carrots, thinly sliced
2 onions, thinly sliced
1 sweet pepper, diced
½ a cabbage, thinly sliced
2 cloves of garlic, chopped
1 can diced tomatoes

1. Toss the iguana meat in the lime juice and vinegar.
2. Add salt, pepper, cilantro, and toss to coat. Let marinate for 1 hour.
3. Heat oil in a pot over medium heat.
4. Remove the meat from the marinade and add to heated oil, turning the meat so it is browned on all sides.
5. Add onions, carrots, pepper, cabbage, and garlic. Cook over medium heat until soft and lightly browned.
6. Add the tomatoes and a little water. Bring to a boil, then lower heat and simmer for 30 minutes.

Further Reading

Coles, William. "Green Iguana." U.S.V.I. Animal Fact Sheet #08. Department of Planning and Natural Resources U.S. Virgin Islands Division of Fish and Wildlife. fw.dpnr.gov.vi/education/FactSheets/PDF_Docs/08GreenIguana.pdf.

Scarlett Lindeman

Insects

Black flies, chiggers, deer flies, fleas, gnats, lice, mosquitoes, no-see-ems, ticks—their names alone start us twitching, scratching involuntarily, wondering if it's just our imagination—or is something creeping up our backs, under our shirts, just out of reach?

What can we do—we can't bite back, can we?

It turns out that we can—and we have, all around the world. We're not referring to accidental consumption of insects—the trace amounts of eggs, bug fragments, and insect filth that the FDA considers normal, "natural or unavoidable defects for human use that present no health hazard."

We're talking about the intentional ingestion of things that creep, crawl, and occasionally go bump in the night.

In the United States, insect-eating—or entomophagy—is mostly a matter of joke foods and machismo (think chocolate-covered ants, whole crickets embedded in transparent lollipops, or biting the worm at the bottom of a bottle of Mescal). Occasionally, food writers and anthropologists point out that our aversion to insects as food is irrational and culturally based, that insects can be tasty, nutritious, and a possible answer to food shortages—by providing cheap, easily-produced and eco-friendly, sustainable protein. Often these suggestions appear in the form of half-joking cookbooks, with titles like

Fried insects, street food at Central Market of Cambodia. (© Hippo Studio, istockphoto.com)

Butterflies in My Stomach or *Entertaining with Insects*. The University of Kentucky's entomology department even maintains a website devoted to the subject.

While modern Americans of European extraction may be repulsed by the notion of insectivory, their ancient ancestors were not. Aristophanes wrote about four-winged fowl (grasshoppers), and Aristotle and Athenaeus thought that large egg-filled cicadas were the best eating. Pliny noted that cicadas were still eaten in the East, but thought more highly of epicurean *Cossus* grubs (the carefully fattened larvae of *Lucanus cervus*).

In the past, Native Americans—especially in the western half of the continent—supplemented their diets with insects, sometimes in preference to foods we would consider more respectable. However, while most modern Americans remain unconvinced of their merits, insects have been consumed enthusiastically by diners in many other places—and still are in a few.

Archaeologists have shown that grasshoppers were part of the Mexican diet as early as 7,000 BCE. The earliest written account of Mexican entomophagy is that of Benardino de Sahagún, who chronicled—in 1577—Cortes's conquest of the Aztecs. The practice has not diminished in the succeeding five centuries.

In Mexico, *los gusanos*—the maguey worms found in Mescal—serve not only as an indicator of alcoholic proof (the worms decompose if the alcoholic content is too low); but as a component of worm salt.

They are fried until they are crispy, then ground together with chilies and salt. The resulting condiment has a warm, musky flavor that is reminiscent of Tequila—which makes sense, since the worms grow inside, and feed upon, the agave plants used to make mescal and tequila. Deep-fried, they are sold as a snack food, caterpillar pretzels. They are also braised or fried, and wrapped, along with a dab of guacamole, in warm tortillas like a soft taco.

Mexicans don't limit their entomophagy to larvae of the tequila giant skipper butterfly, *Aegiale hesperiaris*. They consume various stages (eggs, larvae, pupae, and adults) of more than 130 species of insects, including beetles (*Coleoptera*); flies (*Diptera*); bugs (*Hemiptera*); aphids (*Homoptera*); ants, bees, sawflies and wasps (*Hymenoptera*); butterflies, moths and skippers (*Lepidoptera*); crickets, grasshoppers, roaches (*Orthoptera*); caddisflies (*Trichoptera*); termites (*Isoptera*); and darners, dragonflies, and dobsonflies (*Megaloptera* and *Odonata*).

Escamoles, immature ants of the *Liometopum apiculatum* species, are highly favored. Fried in butter, with garlic and onions, they fill tacos in Mexico City. Various species of grasshopper are boiled with chili powder, garlic, and onion, or coated with lemon juice and salt before being toasted, or simply fried in lard. This last method could not have been made before the arrival of Cortes—lemons, pigs, and metal containers for deep-frying were not then available.

In several South American countries, insects are part of the diet. Some species are similar to those eaten in Mexico and the Caribbean, but differences from country to country merit individual attention.

For example, in Argentina, only the larvae of palm weevils (*Rhynchophorus palmarum*) are eaten, but Brazilians have also eaten beetles, flies; treehoppers, bees, wasps, and ants; termites; butterflies and moths; plus grasshoppers. The individual species are not always named because the anthropologists who reported the entomophagy were more interested in human behavior than with identification of the insects being consumed.

Larvae of beetles are highly prized, as they are large and plentiful, and are high in protein and fat—especially those that inhabit palm trees. They are roasted or eaten raw throughout the Caribbean and Central and South America—everywhere east of the Andes. Adult ants are roasted or smoked, and seasoned with salt (one account described roasted ants as tasting like crisply fried bacon). Bee pupae are eaten along with the honey in the comb, and some winged ants are fried and glazed with sweet syrup.

Colombians ate one genus of fly (*Chrysochlorina*); bees; nine wasps and ants;

"Worms" is not accurate; maguey worms are not actually worms—they are larvae, the immature stage of an insect's development.

The term is commonly misused in many other countries; almost invariably, when one finds "worms" on the menu, what is meant is "insect larvae."

termites; butterflies, skippers, and moths; dobsonflies; grasshoppers; and caddisflies.

In Bolivia, palm weevil larvae are relished (as almost everywhere else)—preferably fried. They are said to taste like fat bacon. Some fly larvae are simmered in a sauce spiked with hot chilies.

Chileans utilize a slightly wider variety of insects, including two species of beetles; mosquitoes and locusts—the last two, reportedly, made into a kind of bread.

Colombians eat more fish than insects, but insects provide more of their protein (mammals, birds, and reptiles represent a smaller part of their diet—but, gradually, insectivory is being replaced by the sort of carnivory which is more familiar to those with more traditional European tastes). As elsewhere in the region, the large grubs of palm beetles (*Rhynchophorus* spp.) are prized for their size and meatiness, as are those of the giant rhinoceros beetle (*Podischnus agenor*). Adults tend to eat the grubs roasted, though children—who generally prefer blander foods—eat them raw. Bogota cinemas sell toasted abdomens of leaf-cutter ants (*Atta* spp.) like popcorn, well-salted. They are so highly prized that a pound of the ants sold for $20 a decade ago.

Palm weevil larvae, fried in lard, are eaten in Ecuador and Guyana—as are scarab beetles (*Scarabaeidae*); the latter accompanied with small tostados that are also fried in lard. Guyanans also consume bee and wasp larvae, adult ants, termites, and roasted sphinx moth caterpillars—which have been described as "tasting precisely like soft-shelled crabs" (Verrill, 1937, 186). In the 19th century, some

Guyanans even preferred *Atta* ants over the highly esteemed palm weevils.

As late as the 1970s, the Guayaki in Paraguay received most of their nutrition from honey and beetle larvae. The Ache are Paraguayan hunter-gatherers, with honey and insects second only to game in their diets. As elsewhere, the grubs of palm weevils are much in demand (the Guayaki actually farm them, by leaving short sections of palm trunks on the ground to rot, providing ideal breeding areas for the weevils). In recent years, the Ache have been forced from much of their old forests, and the palm grubs have gone from staple food to prized delicacy. The cooked grubs were reportedly sold on the streets of Iquitos, Peru, in the 1980s. They were still a staple in Suriname in the 1950s, and among the Venezuelan Yanomama in the late 1970s. The Peruvian soup, *chupe de chiche*—made from riffle beetles (*Elmidae*)—was still popular in the 1950s. Toasted mayfly nymphs (*Ephemeroptera*) are ground together with chilies to make a sauce for fish—a nice twist since mayflies are a favorite food of trout.

In Central America and the Caribbean, insects are not consumed as frequently as in Mexico and South America—but the larvae of several species of beetles, honey bee larvae and pupae (*Apis mellifera*), caterpillars of various butterflies, and some grasshoppers appear on the menu. In Jamaica, cotton tree worms (the three-inch-long larvae of *Stenodontes damicornis*) are crusted with breadcrumbs, nutmeg, and salt, then toasted on skewers. Grougrou-worms or palm grubs were cooked in similar fashion in the 19th century, but—since they were a salable commodity—they were more often

Insects of Mexico

In Mexico, there are 57 types of edible insects that are enjoyed by local populations in tacos, sauces, soups, or as snacks. Some of the most common and popular varieties of insects are ant eggs, also know as the Mexican caviar, crickets, maguey worms, a common addition to bottles of mezcal, red ants, and crayfish. Mosquitoes, flies, dragonflies, ants, worms, butterflies, and lice are also part of the diet in many Mexican communities.

Often, Mexicans must wait for insects to be in season since sometimes only the eggs are collected while some insects are prepared full grown, and others are preferred for the honey they produce in their abdomens. For the most part, insects are only found in specific parts of the country, and many Mexicans travel to different towns just to be able to taste local delicacies.

Insects have a very high protein content and still are the main protein source in many poor Mexican communities. Insects are often inexpensive in local markets. In a country were a large percentage of the population is very poor, insects provide an inexpensive addition to the daily diet of beans, corn tortillas, and hot salsas.

During the last few years, Mexican insects have become a renowned gastronomic delicacy around the world and are now enjoyed by more affluent consumers. Upscale restaurants in Mexico City and other large cities in Mexico now serve, in season, traditional insect dishes.

Further Reading

Coe, S. *America's First Cuisines*. Austin: University of Texas Press, 1994.

Davidson, A., ed. *The Penguin Companion to Food*. London: Penguin Books, 2002.

De Foliart, G. R. "The Human Use of Insects as a Food Resource: A Bibliographic Account in Progress." Food Insects. http://www.food-insects.com/book7_31/The%20Human%20Use%20of%20Insects%20as%20a%20Food%20Resource.htm.

Ramos-Elorduy, J., and J. M. Pino. "Caloric Content of Some Edible Insects of Mexico." *Rev. Soc. Quim. Mex.* 34, no. 2 (1990): 56–68.

Velázquez Soto, I. "Flores e insectos en la dieta prehispánica y actual de México." Entomología.net. http://entomologia.net/idolina.htm.

Gabriela Villagran Backman

eaten by English gourmets than by Bajans (natives of Barbados). When toasted, they are said to taste like almonds.

In North Africa, desert locusts (*Schistocerca gregaria*) are the primary insect food, but as one travels south, the number of species consumed increases, with some 25 species being eaten between Ethiopia and Nigeria. Families of edible insects include beetles, water boatmen, bees, termites, butterflies and moths, dragon-flies, and of course a number of crickets, grasshoppers, and locusts.

One infamous species—Spanish fly (*Cantharis vesicatoria*), or blister beetle—is occasionally found in the Moroccan spice mixture called *ras al hanout*. Reputed to be an aphrodisiac, it is actually a dangerous irritant of urinary passages that has nothing to do with sexual pleasure. It is easy to remove from the mixed whole spices, since the beetle is bright metallic green.

Caterpillars of the pallid emperor moth (*Cirina forda*) are so popular that they sell for twice the price of beef in Nigerian markets. African palm weevils (*Rhynchophorus phoenicis*), closely related to the New World's palm weevil, is in nearly as much demand. They are harvested from the sub-Saharan tropics all the way to South Africa. The second most marketed family of insects in tropical Africa is termites—but some 138 species are regularly consumed in the region. Some are described as tasting like crab, lobster, or shrimp, while others are said to taste like hazelnuts.

Nearly 2,000 tons of mopane worms—caterpillars of another emperor moth (*Gonimbrasia belina*), one of many species of the giant silkworm family—are harvested commercially in South Africa each year. Botswana, Namibia, and Zimbabwe are other major producers. The larvae sell for twice the price of beef of the same weight, and are available either dried or canned in tomato sauce. Soldier termites (*Macrotermes goliath*), fried and salted, are consumed like beer-nuts in the region. Locusts, grasshoppers, and crickets are always popular, in part because of their size and vast numbers, which provide fat and protein to large numbers of people.

Southwestern Asia, from Turkey south to Saudi Arabia, is dry country—so it lacks the great diversity of insect species found in moister environments. Nonetheless, some 16 species are eaten there—including beetles, aphids, leafhoppers, wasps, and grasshoppers.

A regional exception is Israel. Insects (other than locusts) are *treyf*—profoundly unkosher, according to the laws laid down in Leviticus 11—so are unlikely to be found on Jewish tables.

The Bible tells us that John the Baptist ate locusts, but they were probably one of two species of grasshoppers still found in the area. Locusts are still popular in Iran and Saudi Arabia, where they may be seasoned with salt and spices, then consumed with dates and rice.

The manna mentioned in other biblical accounts is probably honeydew, the secretions of several different aphids (*Aphididae*), mealybugs (*Pseudococcidae*), and psyllids (*Psyllidae*). The man in manna comes from the Arabic word for aphids. The consumption of manna may sound fairly revolting—until we recall that honey could be unpleasantly, if accurately, described as bee vomit. Snout beetles, of the genus *Larinus*, use a similar sugary secretion to form their cocoons. Iranians and Iraqis boil the cocoons to make a kind of syrup used to treat colds (just as we might add honey to tea for the same purpose). Iraqi Kurds bake little cakes of manna and flour. Confections, made with manna, eggs, nuts, and sweet essences (orange blossom water or rose water) used to be sold on the streets of Baghdad as late as the 1930s.

Southern Asia (from Pakistan to Nepal, and south to Sri Lanka) has a much more varied climate than Southwest Asia (the

Middle East)—hence it supports a much greater variety of insect life. Consequently, people from the region eat more than 50 species of beetles, weevils, waterbugs, stinkbugs, cicadas, bees and wasps, ants and termites, moths, darning needles, crickets and grasshoppers, as well as caddisflies.

In India, some ants are killed before drying and being ground to a powder. The powder from the ants contains formic acid, which makes a very tart seasoning for curries. Red ants (*Oecophylla smaragdina*) are crushed with chilies, salt, and turmeric to a form a paste used as a condiment in India, Myanmar, and Thailand.

As elsewhere, the larvae of *Rhynchophorus* genus are prized for their size and fat content (Sri Lanka has two species: *R. chinensis* and *R. ferrugineus*). Likewise, larvae of giant silkworms are happily eaten. It is claimed that short-horned grasshoppers—called *Hawaii Jhinga* (or aerial crustacean) in Baluchistan—taste like crayfish.

Like observant Jews, the Jains of India are unlikely consumers of insects—but for a very different reason. Jains are so concerned about the sanctity of animate life that they sweep the path before them to avoid inadvertently stepping on an insect—and even wear gauze masks to prevent accidentally inhaling one.

Farther east—in Cambodia, Indonesia, Java, Laos, Myanmar, Thailand, and Vietnam—more than 130 species of insect are munched by humans, including ants and termites, bees and wasps, beetle larvae (such as palm weevils), cicadas, dragonflies, crickets and grasshoppers, mayflies, moths (including the ever-popular Saturnids), roaches, and water bugs. Some 15 species were found on sale in a market in northern Thailand in the 1980s. Some Thai farmers have managed to save money and feed themselves at the same time.

Thais eat more than 50 species of insects, including flying shrimp (grasshoppers), and praying mantises—which are said to taste like a mixture of mushrooms and shrimp. Many of these rural insects wind up as urban snack foods in places like Bangkok. The Thai government encourages the consumption of agricultural pests such as:

> Fried locusts or grasshoppers, known as "sky prawns," are a popular and expensive dish in urban areas as well as rural ones. Cricket and locust fritters are also one of the most common dishes sold in urban restaurants and as street foods in large markets such as the weekend market in Bangkok, the night market in the Patpong area, large markets in Chiangmai and so on. (Yhoung-aree and Puwastien, 1997, 140)

Bee pupae are eaten raw, or fried, or smoked, or served in a typical Thai curry—made with coconut milk, onion, lemongrass, chili, and citrus leaves. Tart larvae and pupae of red ants (*Oecophylla smaragdina*) are popular in Laos and Thailand—in spicy salads or in a pickle of citrus leaves, ginger, tamarind, onion, and a slightly sweetened brine. The very sour ants are often paired with the sweet rich taste of fatty pork. Thais prepare immature dragonflies with basil, fish sauce, garlic, lemongrass, and onions. Large locusts and cicadas are simply roasted or deep-fried as a crispy treat.

Continuing south and east (Australia, New Zealand, the Pacific Islands, and Papua New Guinea), we find that insectivory is alive and well—with close to 100 species on the menu. As elsewhere, palm weevil larvae are a mainstay; in New Guinea and greater Oceana, the subspecies of choice is *Rhynchophorus ferrugineus papuanus*.

The most famous insect foodstuff of aborigines in Australia are witchetty grubs, a general term for the larvae of a number of moths, but especially cossid wood moths (*Endoxyla leucomochia*). These grubs, which can be an inch and a half to two inches long, are eaten alive or barbecued—and are said to taste like a cross between shrimp and peanut butter. They are not just eaten by aborigines, either. Australian supermarkets carry canned witchetty soup. Also popular are the desserts of the insect world, stingless bees (*Trigona* spp.), and repletes of honeypot ants (*Melophorus inflatus*)—the abdomens of the latter swelling into jewel-like beads of amber-colored sweetness.

In Hawaii, a giant insect (perhaps a cricket or katydid) was driven to extinction in the late-19th century because the natives so loved them (roasted on skewers). Today all we have is the Hawaiian name for them, *'hini pa'awela*. The insect itself is long gone.

Eastern Asia includes China, Japan, Korea, Macau, Singapore, and Taiwan—where nearly 70 species of insects are regularly consumed by the inhabitants.

The Cantonese, who are well-known omnivores, sell and consume large numbers of locusts, silkworm pupae (not just domesticated *Bombyx mori*, but the wild Saturnid, *Antheraea pernyi*), and water beetles. This is not just a Chinese culinary tradition; a popular item in Korean markets is canned silkworms. Peter Menzel, a photojournalist, and his wife, Faith D'Aluisio, found urban scorpion nurseries in Kunming apartments, with cages filled with the dangerous insects, just inches from the cribs of Chinese infants.

Japanese rice farmers once gathered the grasshoppers that infest their crops, *Oxya japonica*, fried them quickly and ate them glazed with *shoyu*. Today they are an urban delicacy. Canned wasp larvae, braised in soy sauce, fetch high prices in Tokyo markets, as do caddisfly larvae cooked in sweetened soy sauce—known as *zazamushi*.

Perhaps the strangest insect food is the Chinese *Cordyceps sinensis*, which is only partly insect. During part of the life cycle of *Herialis amoricanus*, some caterpillars become infected with a fungus that ultimately kills them. Their hollow dried remains look like desiccated twigs, are sold like herbs, and are used to flavor broths made with duck and/or chicken. While *Cordyceps* does little to promote the well-being of the ghost moth larvae it infects, the Chinese believe it gives energy and longevity to those who consume soups made with the fungus.

Insects provide more high-quality protein—per pound—than do larger, more familiar farm animals. They multiply faster, and require less space and resources to produce usable food for a hungry planet. People may have begun eating insects out of necessity, but clearly insects are the food of choice in many cultures; they eat bugs because they like them.

Further Reading

"Bug Food: Edible Insects." Department of Entomology, University of Kentucky College of Agriculture. http://www.ca.uky.edu/entomology/dept/bugfood1.asp.

Chagnon, Napoleon A. *Yanomamo: The Fierce People.* 3rd. ed. New York: Holt, Rinehart & Winston, 1977.

Cutright, P. R. *The Great Naturalists Explore South America.* New York: Macmillan, 1943.

De Foliart, Gene R. Food-Insects. http://www.food-insects.com.

Holt, Vincent M. *Why Not Eat Insects?* 1885. Hampton, Middlesex: E. W. Classey, 1967.

Menzel, Peter, and Faith D'Aluisio. *Man Eating Bugs.* Berkeley, CA: Ten Speed Press, 1998.

Ramos-Elorduy, Julieta, and Peter Menzel. *Creepy Crawly Cuisine; or, The Gourmet Guide to Edible Insects.* Rochester, VT: Park St. Press, 1998.

Schwabe, Calvin W. *Unmentionable Cuisine.* Charlottesville: University Press of Virginia, 1979.

Simmonds, P. L. *The Curiosities of Food; or, The Dainties and Delicacies of Different Nations Obtained from the Animal Kingdom.* 1885. Berkeley, CA: Ten Speed Press, 2001.

Taylor, R. L. *Butterflies in My Stomach; or, Insects in Human Nutrition.* Santa Barbara, CA: Woodbridge Press, 1975.

Taylor, R. L., and Barbara J. Carter. *Entertaining with Insects; or, The Original Guide to Insect Cookery.* Yorba Linda, CA: Salutek, 1999.

Verrill, A. *Foods America Gave the World.* Boston: L. C. Page, 1937. http://www.food-insects.com/book7_31/Chapter%2008%20South%20America%20Brazil.htm.

Yhoung-aree, Jintana, and P. Puwastien, "Edible Insects in Thailand: An Unconventional Protein Source?" *Ecology of Food and Nutrition* 36 (1997): 133–149.

Gary Allen

Intestines

The small and large intestines are members of the offal category of meat, which includes the non-muscle edible bits inside an animal, like the stomach, pancreas (sweetbreads), and liver. These organs are staples in head-to-tail diets, in which every edible portion of an animal is consumed. Intestines themselves are commonly found as sausage casings, but they also appear all over the world in traditional dishes from Turkey to France, China, and the southern United States.

The most important step in preparing any intestine-based dish is to clean the organ thoroughly. The intestine, from a sheep, pig, goat, or cow, must be cut into pieces and rid of all internal material, then either turned inside out and scrubbed or well-flushed repeatedly with water. Butchers categorize intestines by the diameter, which determines the appropriate type of sausage or dish. Round is the small intestine of a cow, pig, or sheep and is used primarily for thinner sausages like hot dogs and chorizo. The middles are slightly larger, mainly cow or pig, and produce larger sausages like Spanish blood sausage called *morcilla*. Finally, bungs are the caecum of cattle or the rectum of pigs used for large sausages like mortadella. One might imagine that butchers are rarely solicited for a slice of caecum! When used for sausage casings, one small pig intestine will yield up to 102 sausages, at a rate of 2 per foot.

Nearly every culture has its own version of the pork, beef, goat, or lamb sausage, but intestines are also highlighted in many recipes on their own merits. In Turkey, around lunchtime office buildings and small shops alike empty onto the streets in search of *kokorec*, the traditional fried lamb intestine with cumin and red pepper served on toasted bread. This dish originated in the rural areas of the country where several intestines were wrapped around a large spit and roasted over a fire. More recently, however, this tradition has migrated to the cities where deli owners and street venders alike do a booming business. The lamb is thought to be better when slaughtered before the heat of summer so storeowners purchase enough meat in January and February to last through the entire year. One deli owner may store as much as 80,000 spits with five intestines each inside a large walk-in freezer, thawing a few spits at time to satisfy the daily demand. Kokorec became a symbol of national pride when the European Parliament imposed restrictions or outright bans of offal meats, including intestines. The dish has neither disappeared nor diminished in popularity.

While in other cultures, intestines don't have the status of a Turkish kokorec sandwich, they are still very visible on regional menus from France to the Philippines. *Andouillettes a la Lyonnaise* are French pig intestines prepared Lyon style, fried with buttered onions, then dressed in vinegar, and sprinkled with parsley. This dish can also be grilled, similar to the Peruvian preparation of *anticuchos*. Anticuchos are intestines that have been marinated overnight in vinegar, garlic, and hot chilies. The next day they are skewered, grilled, and coated with a mixture of the marinade, annatto paste, and lard. In China, they favor garlic and soy flavor for their intestines. *Tsu tsa so unepi kan*, a traditional intestine recipe is served over rice with fish cake

and liver. Although less common, chicken, goose, and other bird foul intestine is also used in some cultures. For example, the Filipino preparation of chicken organs in blood sauce (*dinuguan manok*) combines intestines, liver, heard, gizzard, and kidneys with the tantalizing flavors of onions, bay leaves, and hot pickled peppers.

The United States is no stranger to intestinal cuisines. Chitterlings or chitlins, sometimes called the quintessential soul food, are pig intestines marinated overnight in vinegar and chopped onion and doused with Tabasco sauce the next day. Historically an African American food, this dish dates back to the 1800s when slaves would generally only receive organ meat to eat. In the 1950s and 1960s the Chitlin Circuit, a string of clubs and bars that served chitterlings among other foods, was essential to the proliferation of black performance art because they provided venues to hundreds of young singers, actors, and story tellers whom the mainstream media refused to showcase.

Beloved for their cultural significance and meaty flavor, chitterlings can be dangerous to eat and require special care. Because of their role in the digestive tract, occasionally intestines will contain traces of fecal matter. However, the bacteria that are contained in raw intestines is the real health issue. Salmonella and yersinia are two of the most common offenders; yersinia is particularly dangerous because it can survive at cold temperatures and is therefore impervious to refrigeration. Any contact with the meat can spread these bacteria. Although most grocers and butchers sell pre-cleaned packaged intestines, they require further washing before eating.

Health departments across the South recommend boiling pieces of the intestine for 5 minutes. This does not change the flavor, but does disinfect and render them easier to clean. Even after the lengthy preparation process, intestines are not wildly healthy foods. Three ounces at about 200 calories contains 17 grams fat, over half of it saturated. It also has 80 percent of the daily recommended amount of cholesterol.

Further Reading

Coltrain, J.B. "History of Chitterlings, Chitlins, Chitlins Recipe." What's Cooking America. http://whatscookingamerica.net/History/ChitlinsHistory.htm.

Flikins, Dexter. "Istanbul Journal; Europe's on Notice: Don't Mess With Our Lunch." *New York Times*, June 24, 2003. www.nytimes.com.

Eleanor Barczak

Isaw (and Other Philippine Street Food)

In the Philippines, food vendors line the streets just about everywhere—in the markets, around the malls, on strategic corners, and wherever possible on college campuses. They know full well that Filipinos have a passion for street food and are happy to provide it, both sweet and savory.

Particularly prominent are the vendors of *isaw*. These grill masters are living proof that in the Philippines nothing goes to waste. In turn, their products illustrate—as do many aspects of life in this island nation—that wordplay is a major source of entertainment.

Consider pigs' ears, or Walkman, a great favorite, which are marinated and barbecued. Other parts of the pig are equally popular, including the skin and tail. But the pièce de résistance at the isaw booth is the intestines of both pigs and chickens. These are rinsed thoroughly, then threaded tightly up and back along a wooden skewer before grilling. While pork intestines are simply referred to as isaw, chicken guts are commonly called IUDs because of their obvious resemblance to the contraceptive device.

This is one country where no edible part of an animal goes uneaten—particularly when it comes to chickens. The egg, a favorite among both children and adults, is known as *kwek-kwek*. This is a hard-boiled egg dipped in a yellow-tinted batter and deep-fried. Beside them at the kwek-kwek stand are *tokneneg,* quail eggs that have undergone the same process.

Up one step in the chicken life cycle are day-olds. These are exactly what they sound like—day-old male chicks which are of no use to egg producers. But they are of great use to the vendors who grill and sell them as tasty two-bite snacks.

Mature chickens provide even more fodder for strolling munchers. Grilled chicken heads, known as helmets, are extremely popular as are Adidas, chicken feet which have had the nails and tips clipped off and are scrubbed in hot water to remove the skin. Every portion of the mature chicken's digestive system shows up on the grill or in the deep-fryer as well. These include the esophagus, known as *botsi,* and the proventriculus, or *proven,* a hard portion between the esophagus and gizzard, which is marinated before cooking. Gizzards themselves are popular enough to appear on the dinner table from time to time in a pot of *adobo*, but show up on the isaw grill as well. Not to be ignored is betamax, curdled chicken blood cut into cubes, strung on barbecue sticks and grilled. The name derives from the delicacy's shape, a vague resemblance to the old video player.

Many of these treats are often deep-fried, while some, like proven and gizzards, are occasionally braised. But, however they are prepared, no street food is complete without some form of *sawsawan* or dipping sauce. In the Philippines, it is up to the diner to personalize his food, and no vendor would dare to offer food without something to dip it in. Most of the street dips are extremely simple—vinegar, red chili sauce, a sweet/sour blend, or a highly popular sweet dip.

The innard category only scratches the surface of the Philippines' street food abundance. But, to a foreigner, isaw and their ilk are undoubtedly the most challenging. Who wouldn't eat a banana-cue covered with caramelized sugar hot off the grill? Or crunchy deep-fried pork skin? Or a skewer of crispy chicken wings, known popularly as PAL for Philippine Air Lines?

But it is in the passion for those things that Americans throw away, the offal, that the true Filipino character emerges: thrifty, communal, food-loving, and very, very funny.

Further Reading

Hayden, Roger. *Food Culture in the Pacific Islands*. Santa Barbara, CA: ABC-CLIO, 2009.

Rodell, Paul. *Culture and Customs of the Philippines*. Westport, CT: Greenwood, 2002.

Nancy Freeman

K

Kangaroo

Kangaroo meat has been consumed by the Arrernte tribe, which has existed for more than 20,000 years in the central part of Australia around Alice Springs in the Northern Territory. The Arrernte call kangaroo meat *kere aherre*. Historically, preparation began with spearing the kangaroo, roasting the carcass, then chopping it in such a manner conducive to shared eating by a large crowd of people: two thighs, two hips, two sides of ribs, the stomach, the head, the tail, the two feet, and then the back and the lower back. The Arrernte people also traditionally consumed the fluids drained from the kangaroo.

Conflict exists between culinary artists and environmental activists who feel that the Australian national symbol should not be featured as a part of the menu at restaurants across the country. Safe Australia is a group that works to fight potential extinction of the national animal due to hunting and consumption, although, survey data estimates an approximate 35 to 50 million kangaroos thriving in Australia today. Incidences of activism have been documented such as the display of a dead kangaroo carcass across the doorstep of Riberries, a renowned restaurant known for serving the meat, and the airing of a commercial depicting kangaroo steak infested with worms, in an effort to send the message that cattle are less likely to be infected. While many follow the ideology of Safe Australia, a more significant portion of the Australian populous considers the kangaroo to be a pest to farms and the cause of thousands of traffic accidents each year.

The kangaroo meat industry creatively answers criticisms that are directed toward it. One such example of their retort is a contest for a name for kangaroo meat that would set it apart from the animal and/or symbol. Of the 2,700 entries, *australus* was chosen, however, it has not been approved in any official capacity since the contest's conclusion in 2005. Southern Game Meat, a large kangaroo meat company, has hosted food conferences as far away as Europe, and refers to kangaroo as Australia's health meat, given its relatively low levels of fat and cholesterol. Kangaroo also has a high concentration of conjugated linoleic acid (CLA), which is attributed to anti-carcinogenic and anti-diabetic properties. Additionally, the meat is linked to a reduction in obesity and atherosclerosis. Kangaroo meat is strong in flavor, and can be minced or ground and used as a substitute in recipes that call for beef.

Hunting kangaroo is legal in Australia, but is strictly regulated. Kangaroo meat is commercially available both in Australia and for export. In 1993, the sale of the meat for consumption by non-aborigine Australians became legal in New South Wales and Victoria, and is now available across

Sydney butcher Daryl Williams holds up sealed packets of kangaroo meat in his Balmain shop in Sydney, Australia. (AP Photo/Mark Baker)

the country. Most Australians do not eat kangaroo meat on a regular basis. In fact, 70 percent of the market depends on exports, particularly to Germany and France, and until recently—Russia, which banned kangaroo imports due to contamination.

The kangaroo meat industry is fearful of ruin as Russia accounted for about 70 percent of international demand. Before the Russians imposed this restriction, Australia's kangaroo trade was $225 million annually. Currently, China and Columbia are being considered as potential alternative markets. The United States was decidedly inappropriate for marketing, according to Peter Beattie, now Queensland's U.S. trade commissioner. Exploration for marketing potential in other countries in the Americas will continue.

Kangaroo Fillets with Mustard-Cream Sauce

Adapted from http://fossilfarms.com/ recipes.htm

Ingredients

1 lb. kangaroo loin fillets
1 tbsp olive oil
Salt and pepper to taste
¼ cup shallots or green onions, minced
¼ cup dry sherry
2 tbsp whole grain mustard
½ cup heavy cream

1. Heat oil in a sauté pan. Salt and pepper kangaroo filets and sauté until brown and medium (about 140°F internal temperature). Remove kangaroo from pan and hold for service.
2. Add shallots or green onions to pan and sauté until aromatic. Add sherry and reduce until nearly dry. Add remaining ingredients and adjust seasoning.
3. Add kangaroo back to pan and warm filets in sauce.

Further Reading

"Background Information: Commercial Kangaroo and Wallaby Harvest Quotas." Australian Government: Department of the Environment and Heritage, 2007. http://www.environment.gov.au/biodiversity/wildlife-trade/publications/kangaroo/quotas-background.html

Beattie, Peter. "Qld: Colombia Could Become Kangaroo Meat Market." *AAP General News Wire*. DOI: 1880272481.

Guerrera, O. "Australus: A Palatable Name for Our Skippy." *The Age*. http://www.theage.

com.au/news/national/australus-the-dish-kangaroo/2005/12/19/1134840798480.html.

McBride, S. "Eating Right: Turning an Icon into an Entree Isn't Easy [Australia]." *Asian Wall Street Journal Weekly* 23, no. 29 (2001): 9.

Ratcliff, C. "Kanga Who?" *Special Broadcasting Service Food.* http://www.sbs.com.au/food/article/3348/Kanga-who.

"Russia Bans Australian Kangaroo Meat." *Voice of America News.* DOI: 1814671701.

Shendon, P. "Battling over a National Symbol: It's on the Menu." *New York Times*, Late Edition (East Coast), A.2.

Sinclair, A.J., K. O'Dea, G. Dunstan, P.D. Ireland, and M. Niall. "Effects on Plasma Lipids and Fatty Acid Composition of Very Low-fat Diets Enriched with Fish or Kangaroo Meat." (Truncated abstract of article only). July 22, 1987. Originally published Lipids; abstract republished by International Bibliographic Information on Dietary Supplements Database. U.S. Government: National Institutes of Health/Office of Dietary Supplements and the National Agricultural Library/Agricultural Research Service/Food and Nutrition Information Center, 523–529.

Christen Sturkie

Kokoretsi and Mayeritsa

Kokoretsi and mayeritsa (also spelled magiritsa or mageritsa) are traditional dishes served during Easter in Greece. Kokoretsi is increasingly served year round in Greece and throughout the Balkans, and among their expatriate communities within the United States. Mayeritsa, on the other hand, is only served at Easter, as it is the dish that is prepared to break the 40-day fast observed by followers of the Greek Orthodox tradition. The prepared kokoretsi is served as an appetizer at Easter, but is also eaten as a sandwich on flatbread at other times, and is more commonly served in this fashion in Turkey, accompanied by pickled peppers or cucumbers.

Mayeritsa is the first course of a large meal that breaks the Lenten fast. It is also referred to as Easter soup or Easter lamb soup by Greek-Americans and is made from lamb offal. In its traditional form, mayeritsa consists of the internal organs from the lamb before it is prepared for roasting for the Easter dinner. It is traditionally prepared in the home on the Saturday morning before Easter (Holy Saturday) and is consumed immediately after the Easter midnight mass.

Traditionally, kokoretsi was utilized so as not to waste any part of the animal and includes the internal organs of the lamb (which is the traditional main course of Easter dinner) wrapped in the intestine and roasted over hot coals on a spit along with the lamb. Kokoretsi is also sometimes prepared from goat, though lamb is more common. The nutritional profile of kokoretsi includes 178 calories per serving, with 18 grams of fat and 1 gram of protein. It also contains vitamins A and C, calcium, and iron.

The main source of flavor and body in mayeritsa is the head and neck from the lamb, and also includes vegetables and other seasonings. A common preparation follows.

Mayeritsa

Ingredients

Lamb head, neck organs, and intestine—
    thoroughly washed
1 onion

2 tbsp spring onion, chopped

2 tbsp dill, finely chopped

Salt and pepper to taste

1 tbsp rice per person

Avgolemono (egg and lemon sauce) to serve

1. Boil cleaned, whole lamb parts in water for 1 hour to make the stock.
2. Remove all with slotted spoon, and allow to cool slightly to handle.
3. Cut organ meats into bite-size pieces, and add remaining ingredients except rice, and allow to simmer.
4. Add rice and cook through. When rice is ready, remove from heat, season with salt and pepper, and add avgolemono to thicken and serve.

Kokoretsi is commonly prepared over a charcoal or gas barbeque and takes 3 to 5 hours to cook. As suggested above, the ingredients were traditionally gathered from the lamb that was to be used as the main course, but increasingly cooks purchase the individual ingredients directly from the butcher. A common recipe follows.

Kokoretsi

Ingredients

Internal organs of lamb: may include hearts, spleen, liver, lungs, testicles, and glands

Intestine, well washed, turned inside out and washed again

Oregano, salt, and pepper to taste

1. Cut organs into small pieces and feed them onto the skewer or spit.
2. Wrap cleaned intestine around the skewered organs being sure the intestine covers everything on the spit. Season with salt, pepper, and oregano, and stand the spit on end to allow some of the juices to drain.
3. Roast over a constant low heat for several hours until browned and cooked through. When done, cut in pieces, and season with additional salt and pepper to serve.

Further Reading

Bonser, K.J. "Easter in Greece." *Folklore* 75, no. 4. (1964): 269–271.

Chantiles, Vilma. *Food of Greece: Cooking, Folkways, and Travel in the Mainland and Islands of Greece.* Lady Lake, FL: Fireside Cookbook Classics, 1992.

Cowell, Alan. "The Talk of Rafina. Greek Easter: Diet of Lamb and Vice." *New York Times*, April 20, 1987.

Hoffman, Susanna. *The Olive and the Caper: Adventures in Greek Cooking.* New York: Workman, 2004.

Christine Caruso

Kombucha

Kombucha is a bracing fermented drink that originated in China during the Qin dynasty (250 BCE) where it was known as the remedy for immortality. Often incorrectly believed to derive from a mushroom, kombucha is a fungus, clinically known as a zoogleal mat, brewed using a culture (SCOBY—"Symbiotic Colony of Bacteria and Yeast") that, when fully developed, resembles a flat mushroom or pancake. While kombucha has a small following in China, the beverage emerged in the early 2000s as a celebrity-driven health food fad in the United States.

A biologically active beverage, kombucha is a celebrated folk remedy high in antioxidants, folic acid, B vitamins, amino acids, probiotics (like yogurt), and glucuronic acid (a liver detoxifier). It is said to increase energy and vitality and cure everything from indigestion to cancer, although, to date, there have been no authoritative medical studies. Kombucha is not an herb, supplement, or drug.

The tea begins with a kombucha baby, or starter culture (the mother culture creates babies every 7 to 10 days) and is traditionally obtained by passing the culture among friends. The culture can also be purchased online.

To make kombucha, the baby is added to a glass jar of room-temperature sweetened tea (caffeinated works best). The mixture is then covered with clean cheesecloth or a coffee filter, secured with a rubber band, and stored out of direct sunlight, at room temperature. After 7 to 10 days, when a creamy, gelatinous pancake has formed along the jar's rim, the drink is ready. Refrigerated kombucha lasts up to 5 days. The mother may be reserved for future batches.

Home-made kombucha is the most economical option, but making it takes time and care. Some supermarkets and health food stores carry ready-made kombucha. Popular brands in the United States include GT's Kombucha and Kombucha Wonderdrink.

Further Reading

"Kombucha Mushroom Tea Cultures Provides a Low Cost, Proactive Approach to Health & Wellness" Organic Kombucha. organic-kombucha.com.

Pryor, Betsy. "Make Your Own Kombucha Tea Safely, Easily and Economically at Home." Laurel Farms. laurelfarms.com.

"Where to Get a Kombucha Starter Culture." *Kombucha Journal*. www.kombu.de/source. htm.

Natalya Murakhver

Kumis/Airag

Mare's milk has been drunk by the people of the Central Asian steppes since before the fifth century BCE. The drink was quite popular with the Turks, Bashkirs, Kazakhs, Kyrgyz, Mongols, Yakuts, Uzbeks, and Hungarians. It is still produced and drunk today within Central Asia, more than 2,000 years later. Mare's milk is higher in lactose than cow's milk, which can frequently lead to digestive upset; it is therefore fermented before being drunk. This fermented milk beverage is known as *kumis* or *airag*.

Kumis is similar in many ways to its cousin kefir, which is produced by fermenting cow, goat, or sheep's milk. One of the key differences between the two beverages is the alcohol content. Mare's milk contains more sugars, which convert to alcohol during fermentation. Kumis therefore has a slightly higher alcohol content. Another difference between the beverages is how fermentation is provoked. Kumis uses a starter culture, where as kefir uses solid grains.

Traditionally, kumis is fermented in a horsehide bag or pouch. Mares would be milked in the spring and summer months after foaling. Approximately half of the horse's milk would be used in kumis production; the rest would be left for the foal.

The milk would be churned often during the fermentation process so that it would not spoil. An alternative to this was attaching the pouch to one's saddle, allowing the day's riding to agitate the milk.

Modern methods are quite different. Within the home, a plastic or metal container may be used in place of the horsehide. When mass-produced, the milk is fermented in a controlled environment, with the finished product containing between 0.7 percent and 2.5 percent alcohol. Occasionally kumis will be distilled to produce a beverage with a higher alcohol content called *arkhi*. Kumis is ideally drunk as fresh as possible, as it can become quite sour when it is aged. Old kumis can be up to 18 percent alcohol.

Kumis is light-bodied when compared to other dairy-based beverages. It has a sour taste, with a note of alcohol and some effervescence. It is traditionally served chilled from *piyala*—small bowl-shaped cups with no handles.

It is considered to be insulting if a guest refuses to drink kumis when offered by his host. However, a sip will suffice, the guest is not required to finish his cup.

Tradition dictates that the drags left in one's piyala of kumis should be poured back into the container in which it was originally held to ensure that there would be enough left for future guests. This practice is becoming less and less common.

Throughout history, kumis has been known as a remedy for many illnesses. By the 19th century, it became known as a cure-all, and kumis resorts become popular. Today unfermented mare's milk is known throughout central Asia to be a powerful laxative, a reputation that it has held since the first century CE. This possibly stems from that fact that it contains approximately 40 percent more lactose than cow's milk.

Gluten-Free Kumis Sourdough Bread

Ingredients

2 cups gluten-free flour blend
1 cup kumis
2 tbsp vegetable oil
¼ tsp sea salt
1 to 1½ cups warm water

1. Combine all of the ingredients in a large bowl, adding only enough warm water to create a thick dough.
2. Cover the bowl with a damp tea towel.
3. Place the bowl in a warm, moist area with no draft. An unplugged microwave with a small bowl of warm water works perfectly.
4. Allow dough to rise.
5. Transfer to a loaf pan, and allow dough to rise again for approximately 24 hours.
6. Bake at 350°F for 40 minutes.

Further Reading

Bold, Sh, and Mieegombym Ambaga. *History and Fundamentals of Mongolian Traditional Medicine*. Ulaanbaatar, Mongolia: Sodpress Kompanid Khevlv, 2002.

Ruotsala, Antti. *Europeans and Mongols in the Middle of the Thirteenth Century: Encountering the Other*. Helsinki: Finnish Academy of Science and Letters, 2001.

Alexandra Turnbull

L

Lizard

Lizards are a widespread group of reptiles with approximately 3,800 species spread all over the world. The exceptions are Antarctica and most oceanic island chains. Because they have good survival skills and a great ability to adjust to any climate, they are eaten by humans. We can find them in the forests, prairies, deserts, and rocky areas. The length of adult species ranges from a few centimeters, with the smallest being the gecko, to three meters, the Komodo Dragon. There are many suborders of lizard.

Common edible species are *Iguana*, *Gekkota*, *Autarchoglossa*, and *Amphisbaenia*. The iguana is mostly found in Africa, South Asia, Australia, and the islands of the West Pacific. *Gekkota* inhabit Australia and New Zeeland. They are both edible reptiles, while *Autarchoglossa* and *Amphisbaenia*, found in North and South America and Africa, are less known as food lizards.

In many cultures, the lizard has played a significant role in tradition and food. Lizards have symbolized something and through many centuries had a deep traditional meaning. For example, in Roman mythology, a sleeping lizard throughout the winter symbolizes death and resurrection. In Greek and Egyptian tradition, it represents divine wisdom and good fortune. In the Christian world, the lizard has a more ambivalent meaning. Like all reptiles, they are recognized as a powerful symbol represented by the snake. Moreover, it is a symbol of dreaming and conservation.

Lizard as a serving dish in a diverse form has been found in Asia as well as South and Central America. In China and Taiwan, the gecko is known as Ge Jie and is found in traditional medicine. One of the most popular uses for gecko is for the treatment of asthma and deficiency of the kidneys. It is also believed to be a good cure for impotence and to enhance sexual function in men. In alcohol, wine or vodka, it is used like an aphrodisiac to increase endurance. When served as a meal, it is roasted, fried, or made into a soup with native species. In some Arabic countries like Qatar or Saudi Arabia, it is mostly fried or roasted and served with rice or in a soup.

Mexican and Panamanian kitchens marinate lizard in sour orange juice, or in sweet orange juice acidulated with lemon juice, whole peppers, a dash of nutmeg, and seasoned with salt. It is then dipped in beaten egg, bread crumbs, and deep fried in hot fat. In Nicaragua, lizard is served up with eggs.

The lizard's smell, taste, and the way it is skinned, for some, is similar to fish; for others it's comparable to a chicken. This rich-in-protein reptile is cut like a chicken.

First, the legs are removed, then the belly is slit to open and the organs are removed. The skin is removed with a knife or peeled off after blanching in water.

Lizard Soup

*This lizard soup recipe is easy to make
and open for any invention. Cooking
iguana is like cooking a chicken stew.
It can be cooked in hot water for 30
minutes until the meat is tender with
some spices and vegetables according
to any recipe. Chinese tradition recommends cooking it with some herbs,
about a tablespoon of each:*

Jujube
Ginseng
Medlar
Tragacanth
Yam

*It also may be cooked with ingredients such
as ginger, citrus skin, jujube, chicken, or
pigeon. As it is hard to find a live lizard
at the market, one can buy a dried one in
Chinese areas of major cities.*

1. Soak lizard in water for 1 hour to
   soften a little.
2. When it is ready, cut the head off.
3. In a pot on a high flame, boil slices
   of ginger, a few pieces of jujube, and
   salt.
4. Turn down the flame and cook for another 3 hours.

After that, the lizard soup is ready to eat.

Further Reading

"Gecko (Ge Jie)." *Nutritional Wellness.* www.
nutritionalwellness.com/nutrition/herbs/g/
gecko.php.

Malgorzata (Maggie) Zurowska

Locusts and Grasshoppers

Locusts are a phase in the life cycle of one
species of grasshopper. At one time, huge
flocks of locusts and grasshoppers, thick
enough to block out the sun, regularly
swarmed in areas of the world from the
Middle East to the American West. They
stripped all vegetation in their paths of its
greenery, leaving people with no food—
except locusts. *The Guinness Book of World
Records* describes the desert locust as "the
most destructive insect in the world." But
people, who live in areas where locusts
swarm, enjoy their taste and look forward
to the swarms for a change in diet.

In the Bible, locusts were among the
plagues God sent to the Egyptians to co-
erce the pharaoh to release the Israelites
from slavery. The description, probably
dating from circa 1440 to 1290 BCE, dra-
matizes the enormity of the locusts' effect:
"They covered the face of the whole land,
so that the land was darkened, and they ate
all the plants in the land and all the fruit of
the trees . . .; not a green thing remained,
neither tree nor plant of the field through
all the land of Egypt."

Some scholars suggest that the manna
the Israelites ate during their flight from
Egypt was locusts, but other scholars and
some characteristics of manna do not agree
with this theory. Leviticus 11:22 specifies
that locusts are clean animals, permissible
to eat. The New Testament says that John
the Baptist ate locusts and wild honey.

Fortunately, modern pest control methods have almost completely eradicated locust swarms, although as recently as 2004,
swarms arose in Africa and the Middle
East, causing enormous destruction of
crops.

People have eaten locusts in the Middle East, Africa, Asia, North America,
and Australia. Many animals in these regions also eat locusts, including most

domesticated animals. In the frenzy of their swarms locusts also eat other locusts, especially injured ones.

In the American West, Native Americans ate locusts. Some early settlers of European ancestry ate them during times of famine; others starved because they could not bring themselves to eat insects.

Locusts are easy to catch. One collects them from the ground or vegetation, especially at night when cooler temperatures make them sluggish. In some areas, people cooperate to drive them into a trench or pit. Then they light a fire in the pit, which kills and cooks the locusts.

Some people eat locusts raw, removing the wings and legs (which may stick between the teeth) and the head. Ways to cook them include boiling, roasting, smoking, frying, or salting. Nowadays, people generally eat locusts as a snack. However, some cultures cook them in soups and stews, or powder dried locusts and use the flour to make bread (for people or animals) or to thicken soups and stews. In Asia, street vendors sell deep-fried locusts (good with a little vinegar) or dried locusts cooked in soy sauce and sugar. In Thailand, people make grasshopper paste, a nut butter containing two parts of locusts to one part of nuts. In the Middle East, people eat locusts with rice or couscous. Locust eggs make a good soup.

Various people have described locusts as tasting like hard-boiled egg yolks, peanut butter, fish, shrimp, or, creatively, "whitebait that, somehow, have been stuffed with buttered toast." (Leipoldt, quoted in Davidson, 1999, 459). Most sources describing locusts as food call them fattening. They are good sources of nutrition, "between 40 and 50 percent [protein], low in fat, rich in minerals (calcium, phosphorus, and iron) and vitamins (B2 and Niacin)" (Hopkins, 2004, 192).

Some ethnic grocery stores sell locusts; pet stores sell them as feed. They are also available online. Before eating locusts or grasshoppers, be sure they have not been exposed to pesticides.

Further Reading

Davidson, Alan. *The Oxford Companion to Food.* Oxford: Oxford University Press, 1999.

Hopkins, Jerry. *Extreme Cuisine: The Weird & Wonderful Foods That People Eat.* Singapore: Periplus, 2004.

Holt, Vincent M. *Why Not Eat Insects?* 1885. Reprint, Faringdon, England: E. W. Classey, 1978.

Leipoldt, Christian Louis. *Leipoldt's Cape Cookery.* Cape Town: W. J. Flesch, 1976.

Schwabe, Calvin W. *Unmentionable Cuisine.* Charlottesville: University Press of Virginia, 1979.

Simmonds, Peter Lund. *The Curiosities of Food; or, The Dainties and Delicacies of Different Nations Obtained from the Animal Kingdom.* Facsimile of the 1859 edition with an introduction by Alan Davidson. Berkeley, CA: Ten Speed Press, 2001.

Taylor, Ronald L. *Butterflies in My Stomach; or, Insects in Human Nutrition.* Santa Barbara, CA: Woodbridge Press, 1975.

Christine Crawford-Oppenheimer

Loofah (*Luffa mill.*)

What is a bath sponge doing in a food encyclopedia? Well, unlike most sponges, which are harvested from the sea, loofah is a vegetable (a gourd to be exact), and it is edible. Its relatives include cucumbers, zucchini, and watermelon. Like its more familiar cousins, loofah grows on vines on land that produce beautiful flowers, which are also edible.

There are many varieties of loofah or luffa (either spelling is correct). It is also known as sponge gourd, dishcloth gourd, vegetable sponge, and Chinese okra.

Smooth loofah (*L. aegyptiaca*) and ridged/ribbed loofah (*L. acutangula*) are typically found throughout Asia and South America. Another variety, *L. operculata*, found in Asia and Africa, looks distinctly different from the other varieties in that it has a thorny skin. All varieties are edible and they all make for great sponges. Incidentally, though most of us would look for a loofah in the shower, hanging from a piece of looped cording, in other parts of the world, the sponges are also used in the kitchen to scrub pots.

Loofah sponges are made from the mature fruit of the plant, which though edible, most people find too fibrous for culinary use. It is the immature (unripe) fruit of the loofah that is used in cooking. When used for food, the fruit of the loofah plant is harvested young, about 90 days after planting, when the fruit is just three to six inches in length. The mild, squash-like fruit can be used whole, cut into pieces, or even shredded and used like zucchini. A common ingredient in various kinds of Asian cuisine, from Indian to Vietnamese, loofah can be found in soups, stews, stir-fries, and curries. The brightly colored flowers that grow on loofah vines can be fried or served raw in salads. In some countries, even the young shoots, leaves, and flower buds of the plant are eaten.

Loofah is also believed to have healing properties, and both the smooth and ridged varieties are used for medicinal purposes.

Across Asia and South America, it is used to treat a variety of illnesses, including, but not limited to, fevers, anemia, prevention, insulin irregularities, and skin irritation. The fruit can be taken in the form of juice, tea (tisane), or soup. It can also be used as a paste or poultice, applied topically to the affected area.

Loofah grows very quickly and with one plant yielding more than 20 fruits within a single growing season, it is a sustainable and eco-friendly food source. Seeds from the fruit can be saved for planting in subsequent growing seasons, eliminating the need to buy seeds each year. Loofah grows best in tropical and subtropical climates with lots of sun and water. In the United States, it can be grown easily in the southernmost parts of the country, where the appearance of frost is rare or unlikely. It has even been grown in parts of the Northeast and Midwest, though growing loofah in regions where the growing season is shorter than 160 days is a gamble. In all, loofah is a versatile and tasty plant.

Loofah Soup

Ingredients

1 tbsp vegetable oil

1 medium red onion, diced

2 cloves of garlic, minced or crushed with a mortar and pestle

1 tsp grated ginger

Dried spices (optional)

2 cloves, 2 cardamom seeds, 2 star anise

½ lb. shrimp, cut into small pieces

2 cups water

1 young luffa (also called sponge gourd, vegetable sponge, or Chinese okra), peeled and cut into ½-inch pieces

Salt and pepper to taste

1. Heat oil in a skillet. Add spices and heat for 1 minute.
2. Add in onion, garlic, and ginger, sautéing lightly until onions are clear.
3. Add in shrimp. Once shrimp begin to turn pink, add 1 cup of water.
4. Bring mixture to a boil; add in luffa and enough water to cover.
5. Add salt and pepper as needed. Cook until luffa is tender.

Variations: add ¼ cup coconut milk and/or ¼ to ½ tsp of chili paste

Further Reading

Burkill, H. M. *The Useful Plants of West Tropical Africa*. Kew, UK: Royal Botanic Gardens, Kew, 2000.

Duke, J. A. *Handbook of Medicinal Herbs*. 2nd ed. New York: CRC Press, 2002.

Facciola, S. *Cornucopia, a Source Book of Edible Plants*. Vista, CA: Kampong Publications, 1998.

"Luffa." National Plant Data Center. U.S. Department of Agriculture, National Resources Conservation Service. http://plants.usda.gov/java/profile?symbol=LUFFA.

Porterfield, W. M. "Loofah: The Sponge Gourd." *Economic Botany* 9, no. 3 (July–September 1955): 211–223.

Hayley Figueroa

Lotus

In science, the edible aquatic plant of the Nelumbonaceae family is most frequently referred to as *Nelumbo nucifera*. Vernacular names include lotus, Indian lotus, sacred lotus, and Indian bean.

The lotus originates in Asia, and naturally grows in subtropical fresh water lakes, canals, and ponds. Since antiquity, wild and cultivated varieties have been widely distributed in Asia (e.g., India, China, Vietnam, Japan), northeastern Africa, northeastern Australia, Europe, and America. Great cultural significance had been attributed to the lotus plant since ancient times. In India, the lotus is an integral part of life. The sacred national flower symbolizes the ultimate in purity, divinity, beauty, and fertility, and is given due prominence in architecture, poetry, and the arts. The lotus became an important religious symbol in ancient Egypt, Hinduism, and Buddhism. Gods, goddesses, and sacred beings such as Buddha are portrayed sitting or standing on a lotus, or holding the flower in their hands.

The young leaves, seeds, rhizomes, and flower are all edible, and various parts of the lotus are used for medical and cosmetic purposes.

The peltate, green, and waxy lotus leaves rise above the water on long slender stalks (or stems). The flowers have all sorts of shades of white or pink (but also deep red), with a diameter of 4 to 10 inches, and many different shapes and sizes. From the center of the flower grows a cone-shaped fruit (or seed-head) that contains seeds or nutlets. Lotus rhizomes are thin, white to light brown, and slightly fibrous, 2½ to 3½ inches in diameter, with long inner sections of 4 to 11 inches. The rhizomes grow deep in muddy waters and can become 30 feet long, are pierced with 10 air tunnels, and resemble sausages on a string.

Especially in Asian cuisines every part of the lotus is used. The flowers are soluble and soaked in wine, or dried and smoked for the preparation of fragrant teas. Flowers are also used for the decoration of salads and desserts.

Indians eat the young leaves, leaf stalks, and flowers as vegetables. The young leaves, with a chestnut flavor, are also eaten raw in Thailand where they are dipped in a savory sauce. Because of their delicate flavor, the mature leaves are frequently used to wrap food in, and steam or cook the parcels. A famous Chinese restaurant dish is Beggar's Chicken, with a stuffing of dried mushrooms, soy and wine, the chicken is wrapped in lotus leaves, and cooked in pond mud or clay.

Since ancient times, the fruit (or seedhead) is dried, ground into meal, and used to make bread. In Burma, fresh seeds are boiled and consumed as a snack. In China, these are sugarcoated, and among the sweet offering of Chinese New Year, cooked into a soup, and boiled and mashed into filling for Chinese moon cakes. The roasted seed of the lotus is a known coffee substitute.

The starchy rhizomes that can be consumed both raw and cooked are most often eaten. In Asian cuisines rhizomes are roasted, pickled, candied, or sliced and fried as chips. In Thailand, the young rhizomes are peeled and used in salads. The Chinese and Japanese stir-fry, deep-fry, stuff, and simmer peeled mature roots commonly in savory dishes. The subtle flavor and pattern of the *renkon* appeals to Japanese chefs that use it for bento (lunch) boxes and *nimono* (stews or boiled materials). In Indian cuisine, balls of cooked and mashed rhizomes are simmered in spicy sauces. The ground powder (or flour) of mature lotus rhizomes is used as a thickening agent for soups and desserts.

In Chinese and Indian stores, lotus rhizomes and seeds can be purchased canned, sliced, frozen, dried, in brine, or syrups. Fresh rhizomes are mostly vacuum-packed and sold at Asian grocery stores. Teas and infuses from lotus flowers are widely available.

Stir-Fried Lotus Root

Ingredients

1 lb. lotus rhizomes
2 tbsp peanut oil
1 tbsp sesame oil
½ tbsp soy sauce
Salt and pepper to taste

1. Peel the rhizomes; slice crosswise and thinly.
2. Heat peanut oil in a wok, over medium high heat; stir-fry the slices constantly for 10 to 15 minutes.
3. Add sesame oil, soy sauce, a dash of salt, and sugar; stir quickly to coat the slices evenly. Serve immediately.

Further Reading

Flach, M., and F. Rumawas, eds. *Plant Resources of South-East Asia 9: Plants yielding Non-Seed Carbohydrates.* Netherlands, Leiden: Backhuys Publishers, 1996.

Solomon, Charmaine. *Encyclopedia of Asian Food: The Complete Cookbook with Ingredients, Techniques, and Over 500 Recipes.* Berkeley, CA: Periplus Editions, 1998.

Karin Vaneker

Lutefisk

In Minnesota and Wisconsin, a Norwegian traditional dish known as lutefisk polarizes the residents. During the holiday season, lutefisk, literally "lye fish" is available in restaurants and even grocery stores across the American Midwest and Pacific Northwest. Notorious for its pungent, fishy odor, lutefisk is a processed fish dish that likely originated in Norway hundreds of years ago.

To make lutefisk, a whitefish, usually a variety of cod, is dried or salted to produce stockfish. Cod (*Gadus morhua*) is found in the deep, cold waters near the Nordic countries and weigh 18 pounds on average. The stockfish is then alternately soaked in water, a lye solution, and water again. When it is soaked with lye, the protein in the fish reduces, and the texture of the fish changes, losing its firmness and taking on a jelly-like consistency. (Fish soaked in lye for too long results in fish soap.) The lye used to process lutefisk in Finland often comes from birch ash.

After being processed, lutefisk still needs to be cooked before consumption. Though it was traditional to boil lutefisk, over-boiling causes the fish to break apart, so baking or steaming the fish is recommended for the non-expert cook. Despite is fishy smell, lutefisk has a mild flavor. It is most often served with a simple sauce of butter, salt, and pepper and served with peas and riced potatoes.

Many legends exist explaining the origination of lutefisk. One such story tells that a fishing village was burned to the ground. Racks of drying cod were subsequently covered in ash and debris and doused with water to extinguish the flames. A villager tried the ash-covered fish and found it edible, and thus lutefisk was born.

Whatever its origin, soaking fish with lye was an inexpensive way to preserve fish, making food available to poor Norwegians throughout the winter months when fishing for fresh catch was impossible. Although today lutefisk is a food for special occasions, originally lutefisk was an everyday food. Lutefisk is not necessarily linked with any religious rituals, but Norwegian churches in the Midwest typically host Lutefisk dinners during the early winter months.

Because lutefisk is a food so intimately linked with a Nordic heritage, consuming it or refusing to consume it is a marker of identity and a matter of contention. In the United States, lutefisk consumption seems to be becoming less popular as older people who enjoyed it do not successfully pass on the tradition to their descendants.

Traditional Norwegian Lutefisk Recipe

Ingredients

Lutefisk
Salt and pepper to taste

1. Purchase the lutefisk in advance and soak in water for a day before preparing.
2. Preheat oven to 375°F.
3. Drain the lutefisk and season it with salt and pepper. Place it in a dish and bake uninterrupted for 25 to 30 minutes. The fish will not brown.

Note: Never serve or cook lutefisk with sterling silver: the lye in the fish can stain clothing and ruin metal finishes.

Further Reading

Harden, Blaine. "Forget Eggnog; Bring the Lye-Cured Cod." *New York Times*, December 25, 2002.

Legwold, Gary. *The Last Word on Lutefisk: True Tales of Cod and Tradition*. Minneapolis, MN: Conrad Henry, 1996.

Riddervold, Astri. *Lutefisk, Rakefisk and Herring in Norwegian Tradition*. United Kingdom: Novus Press, 1990.

Ansley Watson

M

Mannish Water (Goat Head Soup, Ram Goat Soup)

A spicy, savory soup, made from the head and feet of the goat, mannish water is so-named because the mannish parts of the male or ram goat (penis and testes) are sometimes included in the dish and are believed to be a powerful aphrodisiac. In addition to the head, feet, and, sometimes, the scrotum of the goat, hard food or root tubers, vegetables, herbs, and spices go into the pot along with flour dumplings, called spinners. Thyme, an herb found in most Jamaican cooking, and pimiento or allspice, an aromatic berry also common in Jamaican cuisine, comprise the key flavors of this soup. Jamaican white rum or rum-based drinks, like rum punch are the usual accompaniment. It is unusual to find mannish water on the menu at a restaurant, as it's typically a dish made by home cooks or found at roadside stands.

A Jamaican specialty, this is a celebratory dish that is usually made in very large quantities, to be served at large social gatherings, especially weddings. Traditionally, a groom is given a cup of this soup at the wedding reception to make his back strong and put lead in the pencil (ensure virility) in preparation for the wedding night. Aside from its use as an aphrodisiac, mannish water is used to promote good health and fortify the body.

Wherever in the world goat meat is eaten, one will likely find a recipe for goat head soup to which specific healing properties have been ascribed. For example, in Iraq, a similar soup from goat head has served as a cure for hangovers. Perhaps it was this particular property that appealed to the Rolling Stones, who, when they visited the island of Jamaica in 1972 to work on their next album, became so enamored of this dish that it inspired them to name the album *Goat's Head Soup*. Mannish water has been the inspiration for reggae and calypso artists and is made mention of in countless songs, the most famous of which is *Ram Goat Liver,* recorded by Pluto Shervington in the early 1970s.

The dish is believed to have originated with the Maroons, runaway slaves who had escaped the island plantations and settled in Jamaica's mountainous regions. The Maroons were slaves brought to the Caribbean from West Africa, so it's no surprise that similar stews and soups can be found throughout that region. Isi-ewu, as it is called in Nigeria, is probably the closest in composition to Jamaican mannish water. In fact, some variation of this soup can be found in countries throughout the African continent. In East Africa, the dish tends to be more of a soup than a stew, whereas cooks from West and South Africa prefer a heartier preparation.

Mannish Water

Ingredients

5 lb. cut up goat's head and feet (tripe, scrotum, optional)

5 gal. of water

2 lb. each of the following vegetables:

Carrot

Potato

Yautia (coco)

Chayotes (cho cho, christophine, mirliton)

Ñame (pronounced, nya-may, also called white yam)

1 doz. green bananas, peeled and cut in half, crosswise.

½ lb. scallion, chopped

8 pimiento seeds (whole allspice)

6 cloves of garlic, crushed

5 sprigs fresh thyme

5 lemons, cut in half

3 to 4 Scotch bonnet or habañero peppers, cut in half, remove seeds and membranes

Salt to taste

Dumplings (spinners recipe below)

1. Set water to boil.
2. Use lemons to clean goat's head and feet, rubbing lemon halves over the meat.
3. Cut goat into 3- to 4-inch pieces.
4. Place meat in boiling water and simmer until meat is tender, approximately 3½ hours.
5. Cut remaining vegetables into 2-inch pieces. Once meat is tender, add vegetables and seasonings to the pot and cook for another hour or until vegetables are fork tender.
6. While the meat and vegetables are cooking, prepare the dumplings (see recipe below).
7. Add dumplings to pot. Let cook for another 15 to 20 minutes.
8. Remove Scotch bonnet peppers (optional, peppers may remain if diners are accustomed to extremely hot food)
9. Adjust seasoning and amount of water if needed.

Dumplings (Spinners)

Ingredients

2 cups flour

1 cup water

2 tsp baking powder

½ tsp salt

1. Place all dry ingredients in a bowl and blend with a fork.
2. Slowly add enough water to knead into a stiff ball of dough.
3. Divide into smaller balls of dough, no more than 2-inches in diameter.
4. With palms facing each other, roll one of the 2-inch pieces of dough between them until it is cylindrical shape, then form the dough so that the middle is wide and the ends are pointed. The length of the spinner should be no more than 4 inches long.
5. Repeat this process for all the pieces.
6. Add to boiling soup or stew and continue cooking for 15 to 20 minutes.

Further Reading

"Goats Worldwide: Meat, Milk, and Mohair." Fork, Fingers and Chopsticks. http://www.accessmylibrary.com/article-1G1-83582127/goats-worldwide-meat-milk.html.

Thomas, Polly, and Adam Vaitilingam. *The Rough Guide to Jamaica.* London: Penguin Group, 2000.

Hayley Figueroa

Mopane Worms

The mopane worm, or *Gonimbrasia belina*, is the edible larva of the Saturnid moth *Imbrasis belina*. It is known variously as *mashonzha, masonja,* or *amasonja.* Although known as a worm, it is in fact a caterpillar, which is indigenous to the mopane woodland in southern Zimbabwe, Botswana, and parts of South Africa. It is the backbone of a multi-million rand edible insect trade within Africa, and is considered to be one of the Big 12 insects within the continent.

Traditionally harvested by women and children for household consumption, the mopane worm is now harvested for use in bartering and trading, as well as home use. The caterpillars are available seasonally—the major peak in abundance is found between November and January, although they can also be harvested from March through May. Since the mopane worm is not domesticated, the harvest varies from year to year, with drought being a major factor in harvest size and quality.

Typically, the insects are caught in the wild by hand and are gutted before they are prepared for storage. Gutting is generally done by hand, with the harvester wearing gloves or hand protection to help guard their fingers against the spines found on the caterpillar's body. In some cases, rollers are used, however, they are viewed as less efficient in some areas. Where water is available, mopane worms are washed after being gutted.

There are two primary preparation techniques for the caterpillars. The first is boiling them in salt water, followed by sun drying. The second is dry roasting them on fire embers before sun drying. The availability of water and firewood affects the method used. In some cases, the caterpillars are then cleaned in a rotary drum. This process rids the bodies of their brittle spines, as well as dust and leaves.

The mopane worm is highly nutritious, containing 60 percent protein and notable amounts of phosphorus, iron, and calcium. Their yellow flesh is said to taste of cardboard or timber. At times partially digested leaves will still be attached to their bodies. These are said to taste slightly similar to tea leaves. The caterpillars can be eaten raw, and that is done on occasion as a snack. In Botswana, it is customary not to eat the head if the insect is raw.

If they are to be cooked, soaking is often done to rehydrate the mopane worm. They can then be fried until crisp with available vegetables, such as onions and tomatoes. They are also often served with some type of sauce. Canned versions are available in grocery stores; these are packaged with tomato or chili sauce.

Further Reading

Thagwana, M., and R. Toms. "On the Trail of the Missing Mopane Worms." *Science in Africa.* http://www.scienceinafrica.co.za/2005/january/mopane.htm.

Alexandra Turnbull

N

Natto

Natto is a paste of cooked, mashed, fermented soybeans. Bacterial fermentation yields its strong earthy aroma, often compared to ripe cheese, rotten mushrooms, or body odor, and mucilaginous texture (*neba-neba* in Japanese), the combination of which make natto an acquired taste for many. Natto is a traditional food in Japan where it is eaten for breakfast, over rice, often mixed with flavorful ingredients such as mustard, scallion, and soy sauce as well as raw egg. Stirring further develops the stringy texture. Sometimes natto is used as a spread on toast.

While the exact origins of natto are unknown, it is likely an ancient food that may have co-developed in multiple locations since it is a simple food made from a ubiquitous ingredient in China, Korea, and Japan. Natto was probably made by natural (wild) fermentation originally, helped along by bacteria found in rice straw used intentionally to encourage fermentation. Now, industrially, a specific natto starter culture, *Bacillus subtilis natto*, is used.

Natto is made by soaking and cooking soybeans until soft and then introducing the bacterial starter culture. The beans are fermented for about 24 hours, and then aged up to one week before packaging. Natto is sold in small plastic tubs (approximately 50-gram single-serving portions), usually together with small packets of sauce and mustard for mixing.

An excellent source of protein, especially when combined with rice, wheat, or egg, natto is also high in vitamin K, beneficial for bone health. *Nattokinase*, an enzyme found in natto, is said to prevent blood clots and so, in addition to encouraging natto consumption for health purposes, nattokinase pills are also commercially available.

Natto's strong odor and status as an everyday breakfast food in some parts of Japan give it important iconic status. For foreigners living in or visiting Japan, enjoying natto is considered a sign of Japanese acculturation, of having made the transition from visitor to resident. Natto is widely available in Japan and in some Asian markets worldwide.

Natto Spaghetti

Natto is traditionally served for breakfast over white rice but natto spaghetti is a popular variation.

Ingredients

⅓ lb. spaghetti, cooked and drained, reserving 2 tbsp of pasta water

2 2-oz. (50-g.) containers natto with included sauce and mustard packets

1 tbsp soy sauce

3 scallions, sliced thin

2 poached eggs (optional)

1. In a medium bowl, combine pasta water, natto, included sauce and mustard packets, additional soy sauce, and scallions. Mix well for about one minute to develop natto texture.
2. Divide hot spaghetti between two warm plates. Top with natto mixture and a poached egg.
3. To eat, break egg yolk and stir all ingredients together on plate.

Further Reading

Parry, Richard Lloyd, "It's Smelly, Slimy and Japan Can't Get Enough." *Times* (London), January 20, 2007. http://www.timesonline. co.uk/tol/news/world/asia/article1294675.ece.

"Welcome to Natto Land." Natto Land. http:// www.ynest.com. English version, http://www. ynest.com/nattoeng.htm.

Jonathan Deutsch

Nettles

Urtica dioica, also referred to as stinging nettles or big sting nettles, is a perennial, flowering plant that is native to Europe and Asia. It was brought to America where it now grows wild. It grows three-to-seven feet tall, with small brown flowers. The plant is edible, but poisonous unless properly handled and cooked. The leaves and steams are covered with both stinging and non-stinging hairs. The tips of the stinging hairs contain irritants including formic acid and histamine. The hairs do fall off when touched, but it is essential to boil, at least partially, the leaves to make them safe for human consumption.

In addition to medicinal uses, stinging nettles have many culinary applications. Once cooked, leaves and young shoots taste similar to spinach, and are often used in soup, but can also be consumed in salads. If not properly handled, the stinging hairs will inject the chemicals into the skin causing pain, itching, burning, and rash—similar to poison ivy—that can last for a few minutes to several days. Thick gloves are used when harvesting the plant to protect the hands. This special sting has given the nettle the nicknames of burn nettle, burn weed, and burn hazel.

Even though there is some risk in harvesting and preparing nettles, there is a long tradition of consuming the plant throughout Europe and Asia. There is a folk story that the Tibetan poet Milaraspa lived solely on a nettle soup, known as *satuk*, for many years until his skin turned green.

In some parts of Europe, nettles are used in the production of nettle and ginger beer, as well as herbed pudding known as dock pudding. The pudding is most commonly associated with the Caldar Valley of West Yorkshire in England. It is a mixture of oatmeal, nettles, onions, and spices and is traditionally fried with bacon.

The Scottish dish nettle kail is a seasonal dish that combines barley or oatmeal with a boiling fowl that is stuffed with oatmeal, onions, wild garlic, and combined with stinging nettles. The plant is typically first harvested at the beginning of spring and this dish is served on Strove Tuesday, the celebration of the arrival of spring.

Cheeses have been made with stinging nettles, recorded as far back as the mid-18th century in England. Several versions of present day Yarg and Gouda contain finely chopped nettles that both color and flavor the final product. Other cheeses are made in the traditional manner and wrapped in stinging nettle leaves; after they have been cleaned and de-haired.

There is a long tradition of medicinal uses of stinging nettle for humans, cattle, and horses. Stinging nettles have astringent, expectorant, milk producing, anti-inflammatory, hemostatic, and diuretic properties. They have been used to treat benign prostatic hyperplasia (BPH), urinary tract infections, hay fever, coughs, eczema, and some inflammatory diseases.

In addition to preparing fresh nettles, stinging nettle is available in some health food stores, sold as a dried tea or as a liquid supplement.

Further Reading

Coyle, L. Patrick. "Big Sting." *The World Encyclopedia of Food*, 76. New York: Facts on File, 1982.

Davidson, Alan. "Nettles." *The Penguin Companion to Food*, 637. New York: Penguin, 2002.

Kristina Nies

Ortolan

In 1996, the former president of France, François Mitterrand, dying of cancer, drafted the menu for his last meal, which he consumed eight days before his death. He dined on oysters, foie gras, capons, and finally, *L'Ortolan*, a legendary French delicacy regarded the height of culinary bliss, but now banned in its native land.

An ortolan is a small, yellow-green songbird—a particular kind of bunting, indigenous to most of Europe and parts of Asia and Africa. The bird approaches the size of a thumb or a big toe.

The procedure for preparation and serving is quite simple. After netting one of the buntings (or several), the gourmand-now-turned-poacher places the bird in a darkened or artificially lit room; alternatively, he will gouge its eyes out—both are strategies for disrupting its feeding schedule.

Then, for a month, the ortolan is fed figs, millets, and oats in order to fatten it up quite severely. Once it has grown to four times its normal size, the bird is drowned in brandy—ideally Armagnac—before it is plucked clean, seasoned with salt and black pepper, and placed in a cassole, an earthenware dish. It is then baked in the high heat of an oven for six to eight minutes. It is served straightaway, while still piping hot.

The diner places the whole ortolan in his mouth, tail first, so that the bird's head protrudes from his mouth. He then bites in, perhaps discarding the head, or at least the beak.

The ortolan rests on his tongue to cool for a moment, while the fat runs from it. He savors this still-sizzling-hot fat, and then begins to crunch away on the sea salty bones. As he continues to chew, he tastes the bitterness of the internal organs rupturing, followed by the sweetness of the Armagnac that has asphyxiated it.

Essentially, the ortolan tastes of hazelnuts, packed in a hot, fatty vessel of crunchy, salty/sweet juxtapositions.

Traditionally, the diner consumes it with a white linen napkin draped over his head, for three reasons:

1. Feasting on L'Ortolan is a sloppy affair, for the consumer and the onlooker alike.
2. To steam in the aroma of the roasted songbird.
3. To hide the cruel, decadent ritual from the eyes of God, it is said.

Eating a single ortolan will last at least 2 minutes, or as many as 15 minutes.

Currently one cannot find L'Ortolan on menus in France, for the state has banned their sale. The hunting ban has been in effect since 1998, though it was not strictly enforced until 2007.

While the ortolan population has declined, the bird does not qualify as an endangered species—since as many as 32 million remain worldwide. The French government claims the ban serves not to deprive people of the dish, but rather to preserve the species so that it might be reinstated on menus and enjoyed at a future date.

A single bird can garner at least $200 on the black market, though penalties for poaching include fines of almost $13,000, and up to six months of jail time.

Certain chefs—maintaining that L'Ortolan is a national rite enjoyed since the Roman occupation—will still serve it, discreetly, to friends or high bidders. Otherwise, enthusiasts must prepare it clandestinely at home.

Further Reading

Allen, Stewart Lee. *In The Devil's Garden: A Sinful History of Forbidden Food*. New York: Ballantine Books, 2003.

Thomas Crowley

P

Penis

Penis, the external male sex organ of a variety of animal species, is eaten across many cultures. As medicine, as novelty, and, most simply, as sustenance, penis, for many hungry eaters, is a viable source of lean protein. Bull, ox, yak, and buffalo penis are some of the most commonly eaten varieties, though potentially any male animal with a member is up for selection.

Penis is most commonly eaten throughout Asia with China as the most prevalent consumer. In Beijing, there is even a restaurant, Guolizhuang, dedicated to serving dozens of different kinds of penises from donkey to dog, and from seal to snake. The size, texture, and taste depend entirely on the type of animal they come from, but most are much longer than they are wide. Most penises of the mammalian sect, excluding humans, marsupials, and equids, contain bone.

When prepared, penis is cleaned thoroughly and usually skinned before cooking. The bones, if there are any, can be left in, like the urethra, or removed depending on the cook's preference. Naturally, penis tends to be tough and sinewy. Its texture can be gelatinous to the point of crunchy, rubbery, spongy, or stringy and does well with extended braising and slow cooking. Whether tea-smoked or chili-braised, penis tends to be a blank canvas for the flavors it is cooked or served with. The naked flavor of the meat is generally mild and inoffensive but can be gamey if taken from certain animals like seal or dog. Served in stews, hot pots, sliced thinly, or skewered, penis can be found in almost any preparation. In some preparations, the penis will be cut into one-inch segments and then nicked all around the circumference with a knife, so it blooms into a flower-like shape when simmered. Since the meat leans toward bland, penis is often served with accoutrements such as vinegars, mustards, chili sauces, or soy-based sauces for dipping.

Nutritionally, penis, sometimes labeled as pizzle or pizzler, is a lean meat, a good source of protein, iron, and zinc; however, it is more often eaten for its assumed medicinal purposes. Asian cultures believe that eating penis enhances virility, fertility, and sexual prowess and should be eaten to improve these attributes. Men have more to gain than women by eating male genitals because it is believed to enhance the ability of their own parts. Eating penis for medicinal benefits has come under public scrutiny in recent years, as tigers and other endangered animals have been poached for their parts, penises included. Dried tiger penis, though currently banned in China, is still believed by some to be a strong aphrodisiac, a sort of natural Viagra.

In Jamaica, cow cod soup is a thin stew containing hunks of cow penis, plantains, and potatoes and is seasoned with Scotch bonnet peppers. Spicy and invigorating, the soup is considered to be an aphrodisiac strong enough to make a dead penis rise. The testicles and white rum are also sometimes included, and it is served on special occasions, usually to men.

In contemporary Western culture, penis is mostly consumed on a dare. Adventurous foodies seek out unconventional animal parts, like penis, as novelty experiences with bragging rights. Nevertheless, as the snout-to-tail movement gains popularity, eating penis is perhaps on the rise. Penis is not widely available, though some, usually bull, can be found in ethnic markets and the occasional restaurant.

Penis Stew

Ingredients

1 penis, ram's or bull's
1 bunch of thyme
2 crushed garlic cloves
2 dried chili de arbol
1 bay leaf
3 tbsp olive oil
1 large onion, chopped
1 tsp ground coriander
1 tbsp salt
Freshly ground black pepper

1. Place penis in a saucepan and cover with cold water. Add garlic, bay leaf, thyme, and chili and bring to a boil. Simmer until tender, about 2 to 3 hours, skimming any scum that accumulates on top, and adding water as needed.
2. Remove penis and slice into rings.
3. In a cast iron skillet, heat oil and sauté onion until translucent. Add coriander and sliced penis, along with enough

cooking liquid to make a sauce. Season to taste.

Further Reading

Gates, Stefan. "China's Penis Restaurant." *Sunday Times*, March 16, 2008. http://www.timesonline.co.uk/tol/travel/holiday_type/food_and_travel/article3552377.ece.

Scarlett Lindeman

Pigeon

Pigeons, also called doves or squab, have served as food since the days of the pharaohs. Descended from the rock dove, the terms *pigeon* and *dove* are often used interchangeably, and there is no real distinction between the two, except that the former is used for larger birds and the latter for smaller ones. Among their relatives is the now extinct dodo bird, a flightless bird and the object of ridicule in many classic cartoons of the past. Pigeons are raised for food as well as for sport. People who raise pigeons for sport are called pigeon fanciers and most would be horrified at the thought of eating a pigeon, in much the same way that one might not relish the thought of eating his dog or his goldfish.

Whether domesticated or wild, pigeon can be found on menus across the globe. Enjoyed by royalty and the elite, squab is often sold at four or five times the price of other poultry. This bird is more commonly eaten in countries other than the United States, where it is often seen as something exotic or strange. Egypt, Argentina, France, and China are just some of the countries where one is likely to find this delicacy. Many Americans exhibit an aversion to pigeon meat that is likely attributable to the fact that the birds are regarded as near vermin by city dwellers. Their bad reputation was not helped by Woody Allen's 1980 play, *Stardust Memories,* in which he characterized one as a rat with wings. The name stuck, making it unlikely that pigeon will ever be welcomed into the average American kitchen. Pigeons found in city parks are considered feral and should never be eaten.

Pigeons used for culinary purposes are classified as utility pigeons, along with sporting and fancy pigeons, raised for competition and show purposes, respectively. Pigeons bred for consumption are generally raised on farms or in regulated dovecotes, specially constructed pigeon dwellings that facilitate the trapping of birds. The culinary term for pigeon is *squab.* The term first appeared in the mid-1600s, and is most likely of Scandinavian origin. *Skvabb,* the Swedish word for flabby skin, eventually evolved into *squab* and refers specifically to the meat of domesticated, young pigeons, and young they are. Pigeons are killed approximately one month after being hatched. Why so young? The birds are killed as soon as they have reached adult size, but before they've had the opportunity to fly, keeping their muscles from fully developing and thereby keeping their meat tender. From a purely practical perspective, it would seem an easier feat to catch a flightless bird than one who has discovered that it can fly the coop, so to speak. Wild pigeons, often less desired than their domesticated counterparts, are considered game, much like duck, pheasant, or quail, and they tend to have tougher meat because they have

developed their breast muscles through flight. Although edible, these birds are not generally sought after and serve more as sustenance rather than delicacy.

Properly prepared, squab is described as moist and rich in flavor and is prized for its silken texture. Pigeon can be prepared much like any other form of poultry, roasted, stewed, fried, or broiled. There is little meat on the small bird's frame; therefore, a typical serving may be composed of two or more birds. From a nutritional perspective, one might consider squab an indulgence with more than three times the saturated fat of turkey and nearly twice that of chicken. Calorically, squab is very dense; this, combined with its high fat content, may account for its richness. As with other poultry, removing the skin can substantially reduce fat and calories.

In Egypt, the small birds are often served stuffed with seasoned rice and grains such as bulgur. Occasionally, the head is mixed into the stuffing as a sort of prize to be found and eaten. Argentineans typically grill or roast their squab over an open fire. Like most poultry, it is versatile and well suited to a variety of preparations.

In the Middle Ages, squab was considered first a cure and then the cause of headaches. It was believed that squab supported blood production, while the meat of older birds was considered potentially unhealthy. The association of squab with healthy blood is not far fetched at all, given its rich iron content, having twice the iron found in turkey and five times that found in chicken. In fact, in a number of cultures, pigeon is recommended for women's reproductive health, particularly following miscarriage and for the avoidance of specific gynecological maladies. Pigeon is also associated with males and virility. In the Middle East, the bird is believed to have aphrodisiac properties and is served to grooms on the night before the wedding.

In some cultures, feeding pigeons carries cultural significance, while in others it's the eating of the birds that is symbolic. Many Eastern cultures and faiths believe that the souls of the departed return or take the form of birds, commonly pigeons. It's not uncommon to find large flocks of pigeons gathered around Hindu temples in India, where they are guaranteed a meal. Conversely, pigeons are served in large numbers during Chinese New Year celebrations, where they are served deep-fried.

Roasted Pigeon with Baby Bella Mushroom Gravy

Ingredients

6 1-lb. squabs
15 garlic cloves, peeled
1½ tablespoons rubbed sage
5 tbsp extra virgin olive oil, divided
6 large sprigs fresh thyme, rosemary, or tarragon
1lb. baby bella mushrooms, sliced
12 oz. chicken broth
1½ tsp of flour

1. Combine 10 cloves of the minced garlic, sage, and 2 tablespoon of the olive oil, creating a garlic-sage paste. Rub the skin of each of the birds with the paste and gently lift the skin of the breast without tearing it from the bird, creating a pocket on either side of the breast. Rub a small amount of the paste directly on the breast meat,

beneath the skin. Finally, rub the inside of the cavity with the paste. Cover and place in the refrigerator overnight.
2. Preheat oven to 450°F
3. Heat 2 tablespoons of olive oil in a skillet. Brown each of the birds, turning after about 5 minutes. Set aside skillet.
4. Transfer to a 9x13 inch roasting pan coated with 2 tablespoons of oil. Insert a sprig of fresh herb into each bird's cavity before cooking. Cook at 450°F for 15–20 minutes, until birds are browned and a meat thermometer inserted in the thigh (without touching the bone) reads 155°F.
5. Remove from oven and let rest for 5 to 10 minutes. Cut birds in half, through breastbone, and serve atop a bed of brown rice. Top with mushroom gravy.

Baby Bella Gravy

1. Heat the skillet in which the squabs were browned.
2. Mince and add the remaining garlic cloves. Sauté the garlic, being careful not to burn it.
3. Add mushrooms to the skillet and continue to sauté over moderately high heat, stirring occasionally, for approximately 5 minutes. Increase heat for 1 minute, then add chicken broth. Deglaze the pan, scraping the bottom of the pan while stirring.
4. Spoon flour into a small bowl, adding enough liquid from the skillet to dissolve. Once thoroughly mixed, add the flour mixture into the skillet and stir continuously for 3 minutes, allowing

the gravy to thicken. Reduce heat and allow to simmer for an additional 5 minutes. Add salt and pepper to taste and remove from heat.

Further Reading

Allen, B. *Pigeon.* London: Reaktion Books, 2009.

Hayley Figueroa

Pig's Snout and Tail

The pig's snout and tail—considered humble by many and delicacies by some—are to be found prepared and eaten in many ways around the world. Snouts and tails fall into the category of offal, or variety meats, that is, those parts of the animal that are cut out or cut off when preparing the carcass for eating. A pig's snout may be sold as just the snout, or it may include skin and some of the meat of the face. There are no bones in the snout, only cartilage. A pig's tail does have bones, as it comprises the end of the spine, and its meat is quite fatty and rich.

Snouts and tails are eaten all over the world: seasoned, grilled, and spiced, snouts are folded into soft corn tortillas in Mexico and stewed with black beans in Brazilian *feijoada*. Chopped, stewed, and spiced, and formed into loaves, they are the basis of Pennsylvania Dutch scrapple and North Carolina livermush. In the Philippines, snouts and tails are grilled, chopped, and fried with onions, hot chilies, and lime to make *sisig*. Pickled tails—along with ears and trotters—are served with sauerkraut and split pea purée in German *Sulperkno-chen*. Grilled snouts and tails are sold on skewers by street vendors in China, Japan, Vietnam, and other Asian countries.

Celebrated for their savor in literature and music over many centuries, snouts and tails appear in the Greek literature recorded by Athenaeus in *The Deipnoso-phists* in the 3rd century. In 19th-century Wisconsin, Laura Ingalls Wilder eagerly anticipated roasting and eating the pig's tail at the annual slaughter of the family pig in *Little House in the Big Woods*. The raucous R&B performer Andre Williams sang the praises of St. Louis–style crispy snouts, or snoots, in 1968's "Pig Snoots."

Tails, snouts, and pork in general are culturally identified with African American and Afro-Caribbean cooking, both historically in slave cooking and in contemporary cookery. Tails, in particular, are often the seasoning in the New Year's pot of black-eyed peas—the centerpiece of a traditional African American New Year's feast. Recalling the New Year's feasts of her youth, Ntozake Shange cooked up pig's tails and included the recipe Pig's Tails by Instinct in her book *If I Can Cook, You Know God Can*. In the New Year's feasts of many cultures, pork symbolizes progress because pigs root forward, toward the future.

Pigs were first introduced to the United States by Spanish explorers in the 16th century, followed by French and English settlers in the following two centuries. From colonial times until the mid-20th century, Americans who raised pigs usually handled their own slaughtering. The preparation, cooking, and eating of snouts and tails was part and parcel of the slaughter, and the ways in which people prepared these parts was influenced by their ethnic origin. European, Mexican, and African and Afro-Caribbean slave cookery formed the basis for traditional culinary preparations still made today. Examples include souse or head cheese, a jellied and molded cold meat dish that has versions in many cultures; Pennsylvania Dutch pickled snouts; and the soul food stew of black-eyed peas and pig tails.

Preparation was also influenced by the perishable nature of offal: either it needed to be cooked and eaten right away, or it needed to be preserved. Reliable, affordable refrigeration was not widely available in the United States until the 1930s. Families who raised or hunted pigs for food slaughtered them late in the fall when the weather began to turn cold and meat could be more safely processed and stored. The traditional practice was to use every part of the animal, either for food or for household items—for example, the bristly hair of a pig could be used for toothbrushes or hairbrushes. Tails were something of a delicacy. Rich and meaty, they could be roasted over a fire right at the slaughter site, along with other offal.

As family farms dwindled, urbanization and industrialization increased, and refrigeration and commercially processed pork became commonplace, the consumption of variety meats like snouts and tails became relegated to ethnic enclaves around the United States. The general perception of these parts as foreign, weird, and even repulsive spread. Increasingly, snouts and tails from the United States were exported to countries in Europe, the Caribbean, Asia, and elsewhere for consumption.

We may turn up our noses when faced with the prospect of eating the nose or the tail of a pig. But a new interest has taken hold of the modern culinary imagination, whose icon is a pig: nose-to-tail eating.

The practice of eating and cooking nose to tail is now largely dictated by choice, rather than necessity or thrift, and reflects a desire on the part of home and restaurant cooks and diners to explore the flavors and textures of all the edible parts of the animal. One can order pig snouts as a pizza topping, or munch on crispy pig tails as a restaurant appetizer.

The trend is evident in rising prices for variety meats, formerly the most economical cuts. Also contributing to the surge in consumption in the United States is its growing Hispanic and Asian populations, who have long been consistent and creative consumers of pig's snouts and tails. As of 2007, one in three consumers of pork in the United States was Hispanic, Asian, or African-American, and according to the Census Bureau, by 2050, that ratio will increase to one in two.

Health concerns related to the high fat and cholesterol content of pork, as well as the sodium content in pickled, smoked, or otherwise processed pork, deters many people from consuming pork or pork products. Religious dietary restrictions, as in Islam and Judaism, prevent others from consuming pork of any kind.

Crispy Barbecued Snoots (St. Louis, Missouri)

Ingredients

8 pig snoots
Cold water
St. Louis–style barbecue sauce (recipe below)

1. To make snoots from snouts, you'll need to trim them of excess fat and blood vessels, and the cut off the

nostril end. Or you can ask your butcher to trim them.

2. Slice the snoots into strips 2 inches across, and score them on the fat side—scoring keeps the snout from curling up while cooking.

3. Fill a stockpot with cold water to cover the trimmed snoots. Bring to a boil and then simmer briskly for 1 hour. Simmering helps cook off excess fat. Drain and rinse the snoots.

4. Prepare a charcoal fire. When the coals are glowing, push them to one side of the grill and place the rack at the highest setting. Allow the rack to heat, then place the snoots on the cooler side of the rack, meat side down. Grill them slowly for 1 to 1½ hours, turning 2 to 3 times, until the snoots are crispy.

5. Remove the crisped snoots to a pan, and dress with warmed St. Louis–style barbecue sauce. If none is available bottled at your grocery store, try this simple recipe. Makes 1 quart:

Sauce

2 cups ketchup
1 stick butter
1 cup water
½ cup Worcestershire sauce
½ cup canned meat broth or bouillon
1½ tbsp tomato paste
1½ tbsp brown sugar
½ cup cider vinegar
1 tbsp dry mustard
1 tsp cayenne, or to taste
Juice of 1 lemon

1. Mix all ingredients together in a 2-quart saucepan.

2. Simmer until reduced to a quart.

3. Once the snoots are dressed, spoon a serving onto a hearty slice of white bread, top with a second slice, and have at it.

Further Reading

Eisnach, Dwight, and Herbert C. Covey. *What the Slaves Ate: Recollections of African American Foods and Foodways from the Slave Narratives.* Westport, CT: Greenwood Press, 2009.

Elie, Lolis Eric. *Smokestack Lightning: Adventures in the Heart of Barbecue Country.* Berkeley, CA: Ten Speed Press, 2005.

Henderson, Fergus. *The Whole Beast: Nose to Tail Eating.* London: Ecco, 2004.

Shange, Ntozake. *If I Can Cook, You Know God Can.* Boston, MA: Beacon Press, 1999.

Smith, Andrew, ed. *The Oxford Companion to American Food and Drink.* New York: Oxford University Press, 2009.

Weaver, William Woys. *Sauerkraut Yankees: Pennsylvania Dutch Food and Foodways.* Mechanicsburg, PA: Stackpole Books, 2002.

Margaret Ragland

Placenta, Human

Although placenta consumption only came under media and popular scrutiny in the 1960s, human beings—typically, the parents of new-born babies—have been eating placenta for centuries; Hungarian tradition dictates that the new mother bite the freshly expelled placenta, and the Scandinavian and German words for placenta (e.g., *moderkaka* [Swedish], *mutterkuchen*, respectively) translate as "mother cake."

The placenta holds a distinction as a female's only temporary anatomical organ, and furthermore, the only disposable one.

It begins to develop at conception, and until birth, nourishes the unborn baby with nutrients and oxygen, while also facilitating waste disposal. The mother discharges the placenta—attached to the baby via the umbilical cord—after delivering her child.

An average placenta weighs about one pound, has a crimson hue, and a tree-like network of veins and arteries surrounding its pancake-shaped, blood-filled mass of tissue.

Eating one's placenta—placentophagy or placentophagia—though rare among humans, is quite standard throughout the rest of the animal kingdom, even among primates—including herbivorous ones. The mother, having just given birth, will consume the raw placenta immediately. Some explain that the consumption serves to throw predators off the scent, though others dispute this explanation, instead citing as a motivation an instinctual recognition of nutritional value contained within.

With the exception of a few rare and minor instances of superstition regarding the benefits of placenta consumption (e.g., in parts of Eastern Europe and Indonesia, to insure subsequent fertility) human beings also tout nutrition as their primary reason for eating placenta. The organ contains high quantities of iron, lipid compounds like prostaglandin, and hormones such as estrogen, progesterone, and oxytocin.

More specifically, the practice of eating placenta by new mothers reputedly prevents or assuages postpartum depression, stops hemorrhaging, and sets about the contraction of the uterus. Evidence as to its effectiveness remain primarily anecdotal, however, with scarce scientific substantiation.

Eating placenta presents no known health risks, provided a mother eats *her own* placenta. Fathers and other family members have partaken of this delicacy as well, though anyone with aspirations ought to note that feasting on another's placenta could potentially encounter Hepatitis, HIV, and other blood-transmitted diseases.

Proper storage and refrigeration—the sort necessary to preserve any other sort of organ meat—apply to placenta as well.

Though some new mothers have consumed placenta raw, placenta is more often incorporated into pastas, sandwiches, or patés, which showcase the organ in the same manner one might sausage, beef, or lamb. Hence, one may need to employ the same sort preparation as one does for other meats (e.g., tenderizing and/or grinding).

Placenta tastes similar to other organ meats, particularly liver or kidney.

Other methods of consumption include drying it into a sort of jerky, or using it as an ingredient in a Bloody Mary–style cocktail (a recipe ran in the summer 1983 issue of *Mothering* magazine). Chinese medicine makes use of the placenta as well, typically oven-roasting it to dryness, grinding it, and dispensing the powder as an ingredient, or encapsulating it for oral consumption by new mothers.

Some who otherwise identify as animal rights-vegetarians have made exceptions and eaten placenta, rationalizing that the organ is the only one that does not arrive on the plate as a result of the slaughter of an animal.

Further Reading

Enning, Cornelia. *Placenta: The Gift of Life.* Eugene, OR: Motherbaby Press, 2007.

Thomas Crowley

Poi

In various Polynesian cultures in the Pacific region, fermented taro pastes and puddings are of great cultural and ceremonial significance. Traditionally the Polynesian puddings were served to chiefs and important guests, and an integral part of feasts.

The pastes or puddings are prepared with taro (*Colocasia esculenta*) or aroids, belonging to the Arum plant family in botany known as Araceae. Taro originates in the Indo-Malaysian Peninsula from where it was probably taken into the Pacific region. This occurred around 1600 to 1200 BCE when the invention of a new type of canoe enabled societies to experience long-distance voyaging. Around 800 to 900 CE, taro migrated from western Polynesia (Samoa and Tonga) into eastern Polynesia (the Cook, Society, and Marquesas Islands). In 1769, Captain Cook and his crew observed cultivated taro in Maori plantations, after which several eyewitness accounts start making mention of the cultivation of taro, and the fermentation of pounded taro in large pits in the ground.

In Polynesia there is no generic term for taro, which is also known as *dalo, kalo,* and *talo,* also no overlapping name exists for the fermented paste or pudding locally also known as *fakakai, fai'ai, feikai, fekei, loloi, poke, po'e, poi, popoi, roroi, sua, susua, tukituki, taufolo,* and *vaihalo*. In West Polynesia grating taro is commonly applied for the preparation of the starchy pudding, and for eastern Polynesians the prevalent practice is the pounding of taro.

In ancient Hawaii, taro, locally better known as *kalo,* was one of the most important crops. The flowers, leaves, peeled corms and leaf stems or petioles all were used as food. Still today, Hawaiians are well known for their love of *kalo,* and especially for the fermented paste or pudding locally known as poi.

In Hawaii, both the plant and poi are sacred as the greatest force of life of all foods is attributed to *kalo.* According to Hawaiian mythology, taro is linked with creation. The legend is that taro grew from the body of Hāloa-naka, the first stillborn son of Wākea (father sky) and Papa (mother earth). After the burial of Hāloa-naka from this union a second child, called Hāloa (everlasting breath) was born. Hawaiians believe to be descendants of Hāloa, the second child. According to many Hawaiians, the taro plant is superior to man, and by eating poi, not only people are brought together, but also *ohana* (family) relationships are supported and the *aumakua* (ancestors) are appreciated. Poi is served at every *luau* (Hawaiian feast).

In order to prepare poi, traditionally the taro corms are cooked in the *imu* (underground oven), after which a stone pestle and pounder are employed to pound the corms. Nowadays the corms are many times peeled and boiled in water, and pounded or mashed into a smooth paste. The desired thin or thick consistency is reached by slowly adding water. By fermenting the paste for a number of days, the desired taste is reached. Fresh poi has a sweet taste, and the longer it ferments the more sour it becomes. Hawaiians indicate the thickness of the taro paste by the number of fingers needed to eat poi, which is referred to as one-, two-, three-, or four-finger poi.

In Hawaii, numerous people and companies prepare and sell poi commercially. Poi can be purchased fresh and frozen, in plastic bags, and even in cans.

Taro corms consists of 17 to 29 percent carbohydrates, 1½ to 3 percent protein, and other valuable nutrients such as vitamin C, B complex, B1, B2, niacin, and minerals. Taro contains oxalic acid, the acidity is known to cause irritation of the skin and mouth, and the corms and other plant parts have to be heated or fermented before consumption.

How to Boil Taro

Small taro corms in their skins can be boiled in salted water. The corms are boiled when they can be pierced with a fork.

Larger corms: peel and cut the corms into chunks, and boil these for approximately 40 minutes.

To Prepare Poi

Reserve the cooking liquid. Put the slightly cooled, boiled taro in a bowl (or food processor), add a little of the reserved cooking liquid (or water), and use a potato masher to process the taro into a consistent paste that clings to a finger. Add more liquid if necessary.

Further Reading

Bown, Deni. *Aroids: Plants of the Arum Family.* 2nd ed. Portland, OR: Timber Press, 2000.

Cho, John, Roy A. Yamakawa, and James Hollyer. "Hawaiian Kalo, Past and Future." *Sustainable Agriculture* (February 2007): 1–8. http://www.ctahr.hawaii.edu/oc/freepubs/pdf/SA-1.pdf.

Flach, M., and F. Rumawas, eds. *Plant Resources of South-East Asia 9: Plants Yielding Non-Seed Carbohydrates.* Leiden: Backhuys Publishers, 1996.

Laudan, Rachel. *The Food of Paradise: Exploring Hawaii's Culinary Heritage.* Honolulu: University of Hawaii Press, 1996.

Karin Vaneker

R

Rabbit and Hare

Rabbits and hares include any species of mammal found within the family Leporidae and the order Lagomorpha. The relation ends there, with all species of hare belonging to the genus *Lepus* and all species of rabbits belonging to seven or eight different genera. Native species of rabbits and hares are found throughout Europe, America, Africa, and Asia. While all rabbits and hares have well-developed hind legs and long ears—the features that lead to common colloquial confusion—there are several features that differentiate between them. Wild rabbits make their homes within burrows, where their young are born, without hair and eyes closed during the first days of life. Hares live primarily out on open land in depressions or grassy nests or forms where their young are born with full coats of fur, eyes open, and which can also walk moments after birth. Most or all species of domestic rabbit, where in the United States they are now kept mainly as pets, originate from a European rabbit species.

During the era of the U.S. Homestead Act, as pioneers made their way westward in covered wagons, the American plains and prairies offered an abundance of wild jackrabbit. This source helped stave off starvation when food would be otherwise scarce. As food supplies, especially meat, become more secure, the use of rabbit is seen to decline. Mainstream consumption of rabbit has never taken off in the United States, though during times of warfare, especially during World War II, families were encouraged to raise rabbits as rations and scarcity saw little meat available at the markets. While there is very little in terms of large-scale processing of rabbit, it can be found in smaller and specialty markets. The meat of rabbit and hare provides a good source of protein, though is very lean and has little fat. Typically, it is prepared in stews and slow-cooked roasts where fat will be added.

During the 1600s in Ireland and Great Britain, hunters would use lurchers, a breed of dog, to hunt rabbit and hare. In preparing rabbit or hare for consumption, there are various schools of thought in regard to its processing. The French will use a sharp knife at the neck. Similar to processing chicken, the debate with rabbit also includes whether to use an electric stun knife or not. Blunt force to the head is also seen. Placing the rabbit or hare on its belly with a broomstick handle at the back of the neck to swiftly pull or yank up on its hind legs is another approach. The fur of the rabbit or hare is easily removed. When preparing the traditional dish called jugged hare, which utilizes the blood, a freshly killed rabbit or hare will be hung by its hind legs to allow the blood to settle in the chest cavity. Fryer, or young rabbit, roaster, or mature rabbit, and the giblets are used in cooking.

Because both rabbits and hares can reproduce quickly and are native in several parts of the world, they are found to be used in traditional cooking throughout Europe, Africa, the Middle East, and Asia, as well as in Australia. Both rabbits and hares provide a high quality protein, with both wild rabbit and hare providing leaner meat and little fat, compared to domesticated rabbits and hares. Neither domesticated nor wild rabbits or hares would be considered a major source of fat in the diet. For this, recipes for casseroles, stews, or roasted rabbit or hare typically call for the addition of oil or fat in its preparation.

There are many instances of rabbits and hares in folklore throughout the world. Both rabbits and hares are known to be prolific breeders, and can have several litters in a given year. Due to a process called superfetation, female rabbits can be pregnant with multiple litters at the same time. Dating back to antiquity, rabbits have been associated with fertility and are a symbol of the vernal equinox and found in the Easter tradition. Symbolic and cultural associations for rabbits and hares are also found in African, African-American, American, Bulgarian, Chinese, Korean, Japanese, Jewish, Vietnamese, and Pre-Columbian Aztec mythologies. Rabbits and hares have figured prominently and extensively in literature and in various pop cultural media, including stories such as *Peter Rabbit* and *The Velveteen Rabbit*, and characters such as the White Rabbit in *Alice in Wonderland*, Bugs Bunny, and Roger Rabbit in *Who Framed Roger Rabbit*.

A Modern Recreation of a Rustic French Rabbit Stew

Ingredients

1 whole rabbit and one half-rabbit, hind quarters preferred, give away the other half to a friend, washed and cut into pieces
4 to 5 carrots, washed and cut
8 to 9 small potatoes, washed and cut
3 to 4 little turnips, washed and cut
2 to 3 salsify, washed and cut
1 can low-fat, low-salt beef broth
1 can low-salt vegetable broth
1 small can crushed tomatoes
1 bag prunes, whole, pitted
½ bottle Beaujolais
Small bit of extra virgin olive oil
3 to 4 garlic cloves, fresh, whole
Herbes de Provence
Fresh chopped parsley, dried flakes are okay
2 to 3 bay leaves
Sea salt
Fresh coarse ground black pepper

Place all of the ingredients into a large crock pot and stir. Secure the cover and set to cook slowly for 6 hours.

Further Reading

Bailey, L. H., ed. *Cyclopedia of American Agriculture: A Popular Survey of Agricultural Conditions, Practices, and Ideals in the United States and Canada.* New York: Macmillan, 1910.

Child, Julia, and Simone Beck. *Mastering the Art of French Cooking.* Vol. 2. New York: Alfred A. Knopf, 2009.

Nelson, Edward Wilson. *The Rabbits of North America*. Washington, DC: Government Printing Office, 1909.

Severson, Kim. "Don't Tell the Kids." *New York Times,* March 3, 2010, D1.

USDA. "Rabbit From Farm to Table." *Meat Preparation Fact Sheets*. USDA Food Safety and Inspection Service. http://www.fsis.usda.gov/Factsheets/Rabbit_from_Farm_to_Table/index.asp.

Walker, Barbara M. *The Little House Cookbook*. New York: Harper Collins, 1979.

Jenny Frémont

Rat

Rats live and prosper in the wild all around the world, so it is no surprise that many cultures have long taken advantage of these efficient, abundant rodents as a protein source. In parts of West Africa, rats are bred for food, and throughout Asia and even in parts of Europe, various species of rats are trapped and eaten.

Rats eaten around the world are typically not the ones city dwellers see in the streets at night or in subways and sewers. Rats are efficient foragers; in urban areas they live on scraps from human food. In rural areas, however, rats dine on wild fruits and grains and pilfer cultivated crops from farmers. Rat meat, like the meat of other wild rodents, is generally low in fat. Because they consume large amounts of fruits and vegetables, rat meat has healthy amino acids known as omega-3s.

In Thailand and other parts of Southeast Asia, rat is an everyday food. Rice-field rats (*Rattus argentiventer*) eat the tender roots of rice plants. Rice farmers take advantage of the rats' attraction by placing bamboo traps among their crops. The rice fields produce grains for people and also serve as bait for a protein source that takes little effort to obtain. Rice-field rats are said to taste like rabbit, and weigh about half a pound on average. Popular Thai preparations for rat include whole barbequed rat, ground rat with chili paste, and grilled rat with shallots and chilies.

In China, rats are eaten in soups and said to cure baldness as well as skin and kidney ailments. Rats have been consumed in Vietnam for at least 150 years. With recent increases in the price of pork and chicken, the Vietnamese increased their rat intake as an alternative protein.

Rat is a major source of protein in West Africa. The African pouched rat (*Cricetomys gambianus*) is found throughout Africa and is commonly hunted for bushmeat. These rats are 3 to 4 pounds. The West African cane rat (*Thryonomys swinderianus*) can grow up to 20 pounds and is now being domesticated in Ghana. It is also called a grasscutter. In Ghana, it is stewed with tomatoes and peppers and served over rice. The taste of rat has been compared to pork, partridge, chicken, and rabbit and seems hard to pin down. The meat is sweet and white and the bones are delicate. As an inexpensive source of meat, rat is a common food.

During times of food shortages, rats were widely eaten in Paris and are still consumed there sometimes.

Eating rat meat in the United States and most of Europe is largely taboo. Urban legends of rat parts included in fast food meals inspire terror. The Black Death, an infectious disease that killed tens of millions of people in Europe in the 14th and 15th centuries, was closely associated with the rat.

Perhaps because of the cultural memory of rats as carriers of disease, eating rat meat seems dirty and dangerous. In reality, the fleas residing on the rat carried the bacteria that caused the plague, but nonetheless, rats in Europe and the New World, were and are viewed as vectors of disease.

Before rat is prepared, the head and feet are removed and the animal is skinned.

Ground Rat and Chili Paste

Ingredients

¼ cup vegetable oil

1½ cups of dried red chili peppers

4 long green peppers, diced

8 large bay leaves, shredded

4 garlic cloves, chopped

4 small rats, skinned and eviscerated
   (heart and liver reserved)

Basil and lime to taste

1. Mash chili peppers in a mortar in pestle with a tablespoon of water. Grill small rats lightly until partially cooked. Finely chop rats or pass meat through a grinder to achieve a smooth texture.
2. Place oil in a wok over an open flame and heat; mix in chili paste. Add meat to the chili and oil mixture in the wok along with green peppers. Season and cook for 5 minutes. Add liver, heart, and basil leaves and allow to cook for another 5 minutes. Be sure not to burn the chili paste—add a little water if necessary to keep moist but not runny.
3. Add garlic and shredded bay leaves. Stir and cover, simmering to let all the flavors mix well. Serve with white rice, basil, and lime.

Further Reading

Barnett, Anthony S. *The Story of Rats: Their Impact on Us, and Our Impact on Them.* Australia: Allen & Unwin, 2002.

Hessler, Peter. "A Rat in My Soup." *New Yorker*, July 24, 2000.

Hookway, James. "For Vietnamese, the Year of the Rat Starts with Lunch." *Wall Street Journal*, February 6, 2008.

Ryan, Orla. "Bushmeat Boom Benefits Ghana's Farmers." *BBC News*, April 3, 2006.

Schwabe, Calvin. *Unmentionable Cuisine.* Charlottesville: University of Virginia Press, 1979.

Ansley Watson

Roadkill

"Roadkill" is the name given to an animal that has been rendered dead as a result of a collision with a moving vehicle. Most often, the casualties are mammals: squirrels, badgers, opossums, deer, cats, dogs, hedgehogs, rats, and raccoons. To a lesser extent, unfortunate birds such as pheasants, ducks, and pigeons become roadkill.

Roadkill is a relatively new phenomenon, introduced to modern civilization in conjunction with the automobile. Horse-drawn wagons and carriages lacked the speed and the force to routinely riddle roadways with animal carcasses.

Roadkill consumption—observed on all continents—appears to increase and become less stigmatized in leaner years. During the Great Depression of the 1930s, for example, eating roadkill, or flat meats, as some called them, was more common, and seen as less reprehensible than in the prosperous decades that preceded or followed.

When the freshly slaughtered animal happens to be a game animal (e.g., a deer), it also serves to minimize the attached stigma. For instance, a recently slaughtered buck strapped to the top of one's Land Rover is less likely to elicit cries of "Roadkill!" than a hardened, dead-for-a-week opossum.

Devouring the flesh of animals killed on roadways can be a bit dicey. Health risks include bacterial and insect infestation, disease, and/or the presence of toxins from ruptured spleens, livers, stomachs, and intestines. These toxins can prove hazardous even when dealing with an animal that has been freshly killed. Hence, prior to ingesting, one must take into account any unpleasant smell, flies, maggots, or an unusual appearance (aside from that which comes from having been run over by four tons of heavy metal), all of which may indicate the presence of sickness or disease.

Rigor mortis, which sets in between 6 and 12 hours after death, obviously provides a good indication of how long an animal has been dead. Although rigor mortis, in and of itself, does not present a health risk, it does indicate that the animal has had more time in which to become susceptible to factors which may have compromised its quality.

As with meat from any source, the temperature at which one cooks roadkill, and the length of time over which it is cooked, remain crucial, for the high heat destroys harmful micro-organisms within.

Those on the lookout for roadkill ought to inspect roads that they themselves use for transit on a daily basis. Their familiarity with a particular road will give them a more accurate idea of how long an animal has been dead. As with all sorts of food, the fresher, the better. Newly drawn, unclotted blood on the animal or on the roadside, indicates a recent expiration. One ought to shy away from animals that have been dead more than a day, unless temperatures are quite cool, in which case freshness may last a day or two longer.

Advocates of roadkill consumption argue that the animals are an ideal source of antibiotic/hormone-free meat, at low or no cost.

Roadkill has even managed to work itself onto the cutting boards of celebrity chefs. Fergus Drennan, a U.K. culinary personality known as "Fergus the Forager" has peddled roadkill meat to London restaurants such as The Ivy. He also hosted a BBC program titled *Roadkill Café* (produced by "The Naked Chef" Jamie Oliver). On this program, he instructed viewers how to skin badgers and prepare wild squirrel stew—standard culinary know-how, but with one significant twist: Drennan claims to abstain from meat unless it comes from an animal that has been killed by another's vehicle.

Prior to removing animal carcasses from the road, one should make sure to take into account any local laws in regard to absconding with such goods. In California, for instance, collecting dead animals from the road for consumption is strictly prohibited. In Illinois, on the other hand, anyone may take a slaughtered deer (and deer only) from the road, so long as they phone the Roadkill Deer Reporting System hotline within 24 hours. In Alaska, residents are required to contact the highway patrol, who then turn the dead moose, caribou, and bears over to charity organizations such as the Anchorage Rescue Mission, where they are divided and distributed to the needy.

Further Reading

Knutson, Roger M. *Flattened Fauna, Revised: A Field Guide to Common Animals of Roads, Streets, and Highways.* Berkeley, CA: Ten Speed Press, 2006.

Peterson, Buck. *The Original Roadkill Cookbook.* Berkeley, CA: Ten Speed Press, 1987.

Thomas Crowley

Roe and milts

Roe, also known as hard roe, are fish eggs. They are eaten throughout Europe, Asia, and the United States. Roe have a strong fishy flavor that changes depending on the fish it comes from. They are best fresh, but can be refrigerated for a couple of days as well. Freezing is typically not recommended, because extreme temperature changes can hurt the flavor and texture of the delicate eggs.

Roe comes pickled, canned, jarred, or fresh. They can be eaten raw, cured, fried, baked, pickled, or fermented. If the roe begin to turn grey or become discolored, they have gone bad and should not be eaten. All forms of fish roe are high in omega fatty acids. A diet high in omega-3s can help stave off heart attacks, diabetes, and depression. Roe are also a good source of protein and iron.

Many different cultures eat roe in a variety of forms and from different fish. Throughout Europe, *botarga*, or the salt cured roe of the grey mullet. is popular. It is cured for a few weeks, then the shavings of what becomes the hardened mass are used on dishes such as pasta. In Japan, the bright orange roe of the flying fish, or *tobiko*, are popular. Americans are likely familiar with it on top of sushi. Salmon roe is also popular around the world. It is used in Japan, where it is known as *ikura*, on top of sushi and served plain with crackers or toast points in many European cultures.

Salted sturgeon roe, better known as black caviar, is one of the best-known forms of roe. It is typically found in countries surrounding the Caspian Sea, including Russia and Iran. Arguably, the most coveted form of caviar, its popularity has caused decreases in the sturgeon population and ever increasing costs to buy it. In the United States, caviar that does not come from sturgeon must include the name of the fish it comes from on the package—for example, salmon caviar.

Beluga, the largest of the sturgeon eggs, are also the most expensive. The medium sized eggs of *ostera* are somewhat less expensive, while the smallest, sevruga are the least expensive of the three. Beluga importation from the Caspian and Black Seas became illegal in 2005 because of the effects its production has on sturgeon populations. What is sold in the United States is either artificial or not fresh.

The milts, or milky sperm of the fish are also eaten. They are known as soft roe to differentiate them from hard roe. Milts have a softer, creamier taste than hard roe. The milt sacks, containing the fish sperm can be cooked, fried, pickled, or smoked whole. They are chopped up and served on toast and in salads. In Britain, herring milts are sold at local grocery stores. In Japan, cod milts, or *shirako*, are considered a delicacy that is eaten both raw and cooked.

Scrambled Eggs with Salmon Roe

Ingredients

2 large eggs
2 tbsp milk
Dash of salt
Dash of pepper
Pat of butter
1 tbsp salmon roe
½ tsp dill, chopped
1 tsp crème fraiche

1. Crack the eggs into a small bowl. Sprinkle salt and pepper over the eggs. Pour the milk into the bowl at this time as well. Whisk the egg mixture with a fork until both the yolk and white are incorporated.

2. Next, heat a pat of butter in a small skillet over medium heat, until it has melted and thoroughly coated the skillet. Place egg mixture in the skillet, allowing it to spread across the skillet. As the eggs start to set on the sides, forming curds, push the curds toward the middle of the skillet with a wooden spoon while allowing the remainder of the eggs to spread to the rest of the skillet. Continue to do this until all of the egg mixture has set. Flip mixture over in the skillet to ensure that everything is fully cooked.

3. Once the eggs are done, transport onto a plate, then top with crème fraiche, salmon caviar, and dill.

Further Reading

"Caviar and Roe." The Cook's Thesaurus. http://www.foodsubs.com/Caviar.html#flying%20fish.

"Caviar Class: A Guide to Purchasing and Cooking with the Tiny, Briny Eggs." Epicurious. http://www.epicurious.com/articlesguides/holidays/newyearseve/caviar.

Caroline Erb Medina

S

Salmiakki

Salmiakki is an anise-flavored confection, which is made with ammonium chloride, giving the candy its distinctive salty character. The popular Finnish treat's name is derived from the Latin *sal ammoniac*, meaning "salt of ammonia," and is also popular in Norway, Denmark, Sweden, and the Netherlands, where it is referred to as *salmiak*.

It is generally agreed that salmiakki is an acquired taste, as it has a very strong, salty, licorice flavor with a hint of ammonia. In Finland, salmiakki is used to flavor ice cream, chocolates, chewing gums, and alcohol, including one of the most popular Finnish vodkas called Salmiakki Kosenkorva. Also known as Salmiakkikossu, the pre-mixed vodka cocktail became very popular in the 1990s with Finnish minors, which caused it to be pulled from the shelves for several years.

Although salmiakki is naturally white, it is colored with medicinal charcoal to give the candy its traditional black or very dark brown color. The candies are most commonly diamond- or disc-shaped, often marked with a cross-hatched design on one side. Popular brands include Fazer Super Salmiakki, Tyrkisk Peber (Turkish pepper in Finnish), Tervaleijona (tar lion in Finnish), and Sisu (perseverance, determination, or tenacity in Finnish).

The Sisu brand of salmiaaki capitalizes on Finland's significant historical pride of being persistent and tenacious in the face of adversity. During what is called the Winter War of 1939–1940, Finns persevered to withstand strong attacks from the Russians without outside assistance.

> The Finns have something they call sisu. It is a compound of bravado and bravery, of ferocity and tenacity, of the ability to keep fighting after most people would have quit, and to fight with the will to win. The Finns translate sisu as "the Finnish spirit," but it is a much more gutful word than that. Last week the Finns gave the world a good example of sisu by carrying the war into Russian territory on one front while on another they withstood merciless attacks by a reinforced Russian Army. (*Time*, 1940)

In January 2009, the out-going Finnish chairperson of the Organization for Security and Cooperation in Europe reportedly gave two boxes of Sisu salmiakki to the incoming Greek chairperson to give her strength for the difficult task ahead.

Excessive amounts of salmiakki may raise blood pressure due to the glycyrrhizic acid content, which is the sweet tasting compound from the licorice root. In fact, the European Union has recommended that no one should consume more than 100 milligrams of glycyrrhizic acid per day, which is equal to approximately 50 grams of licorice candy. However, ammonium chloride is known to have expectorant properties, and is used in a popular licorice-flavored cough syrup in Finland called Kvilla.

Easy Salmiakki Ice Cream

1 small box of salmiakki sweets (for example Haganol apteekin salmiakki), dissolved in a small amount of water.
1 quart prepared vanilla ice cream, partially defrosted
Mix salmiakki and ice cream together and refreeze.

Further Reading

Aldridge, James. "Northern Theatre: Sisu." *Time* (January 8, 1940). http://www.time.com/time/magazine/article/0,9171,763161,00.html.

"Salmiakki Ice Cream—Salmiakkijäde." *Mämmi and Other Culinary Adventures into Finnish Cuisine. All Vegan, Mostly Seasonal and Often Foraged* (blog). http://mammituokkonen.blogspot.com/2009/10/salmiakki-ice-cream-salmiakkijade.html.

Lisa Doughten

Scrapple

Scrapple, sometimes called pork mush, is a spiced grain and meat dish that has roots in Germany, but has become an American dish. It is most common in Pennsylvania, but regional variations occur in New Jersey, Delaware, and Maryland. The Philadelphia or Pennsylvania scrapple combines a cereal grain, meat, and spices, which are cooked together then pressed into a loaf pan. The mixture is cooled then sliced, fried (sometimes breaded), and served with ketchup or syrup for breakfast. It is often found on diner menus throughout the region.

Scrapple was originally made in winter by farm families as a means of preserving meat scraps—the final product often has a layer of lard atop it, similar to pâté. Scrapple, also known by the Pennsylvania Dutch words: *pon haus, panhoss,* or *pannhas,* is a dish that originated in the German black puddings (*panhas*—a German term originally meaning false hare used to describe a meat loaf or black pudding). The term *panhaus* originates in the 16th-century Celtic word *panna,* meaning vessel. The term scrapple originated in the 1820s with the German *panhaskröppel* or slice of *panhas.* The Philadelphia version forgoes the inclusion of blood and is often spiced with sage, thyme, savory, and black pepper and is sometimes served with eggs.

Scrapple is made primarily with corn meal, but sometimes buckwheat, barely, wheat, or oats are used. Buckwheat is strongly associated with the inhabitants of the New Netherlands colony that was briefly in Delaware. The meat is often pork meat, organs, trotters, and head meat, but can also be made of beef or other meat leftovers. It is similar to *goetta,* a German dish popular in and around Cincinnati, which combines steel-cut or chopped oats and ground meats. Livermush is a North Carolina, South Carolina, and northern Virginia version that combines pig liver, head parts, and cornmeal—an adaptation of a dish brought to the Appalachian mountain range by German settlers from Philadelphia. Livermush is sliced, fried, and served with either grape jelly or mustard, sometimes placed between two slices of bread to form a livermush sandwich.

All versions, scrapple, goetta, and liver-mush, were traditionally made in the home; today, there are commercial versions of all these products available in restaurants, diners, and grocery stores. Companies now package and market scrapple touting it as the original brown and serve food. While others refer to it as the product that contains everything but the oink. There are even vegetarian versions of scrapple available commercially, made with soy protein or gluten instead of meat.

Scrapple has become a folk food tradition with an annual food festival dedicated to the mush. Delaware is home to the Bridgeville Apple-Scrapple Festival held annually in October. The 18-year-old tradition includes a carnival, street dance, scrapple chuckin', scrapple carvin' and an all-you-can-eat scrapple breakfast. There is a Miss and Little Miss Apple Scrapple competition—with proceeds benefiting a scholarship fund. The festival also showcases other local foodstuffs, arts, and crafts.

Further Reading

Cunningham, Marion. "Scrapple." *Fanny Farmer*. New York: Knopf, 1996.

Smith, Andrew F., ed. "Scrapple." *Oxford Companion to American Food and Drink*. New York: Oxford University Press, 2007.

Weaver, William Woys. *Country Scrapple: An American Tradition*. Mechanicsburg, PA: Stackpole Publishing, 2003.

Kristina Nies

Sea Cucumber

Phylum echinodermata, or sea cucumber, is commonly consumed in China, though one wonders how the blob-like creature harvested from coral reefs originally made its way from the sea to the soup bowl. Until the fifth century it was known as *hai-shu* (translation: sea rat), but has transformed into a delicacy over time and adopted the name *hai-shen*, meaning ginseng of the sea. It is recognized for its aphrodisiac properties and is used medicinally as a virility aid for men. Because of its popularity, the population has become depleted in fishing areas close to Asia, so in recent years, export of the product from Florida and the Puget Sound, as well as waters around Australia has increased significantly.

The marine animal gets its name from its resemblance to the oblong fruit and bears tentacles at one end. It is also commonly known as a sea slug. Referred to as *bêche-de-mer*, *trepang*, or *iriko* in the culinary

Soup with sea cucumber. (© Fang Chun Che | Dreamstime.com)

sphere, the flesh of sea cucumbers is most often boiled, dried, or smoked and is employed in soup recipes. In New Guinea, where, historically, the trade of sea cumbers has been significant, the animal is called *beach-la-mar*, in pidgin English. In Japanese, it goes by *namako,* and in the Philippines it is called *balatan.*

Sea slugs are usually sold in the markets dried and are hard as rocks. To prepare the protein for cooking, they must be soaked in water for at least 24 hours, during which time it will double in size and become gelatinous and slippery with a rubbery texture. In the pan, it readily absorbs the flavor of the ingredients added to it—usually strong seasonings like garlic, chili, and fermented bean sauces. It is often incorporated in dishes with winter melon, dried scallop, *kai-lan*, Shiitake mushroom, and Chinese cabbage. Sea cucumber is rich in iron and is noted as a good source of calcium.

Most bêches-de-mer are harvested from coral reefs in the southwestern Pacific, though exports of the product from the Puget Sound and Florida have risen significantly in recent years. The most common species consumed are *Holothuria scabra* (sandfish), *Holothuria noblis* (white teatfish), *Holothuria whitmaei* (black teatfish), and *Theolonota ananas* (prickly redfish). The largest American species is *Holothuria floridana*, which is harvested from just below the water mark on the Florida reefs. Traditionally, sea cucumbers were harvested by hand on small watercrafts—a process known as trepanging. Recently, however, many of the commercial sea cucumbers in China are farmed in artificial ponds. The ponds can be as large as 1,000 acres. Wild sea cucumbers are caught by divers, and have significantly more substantial nutritional value. They are also larger than their commercially farmed counterparts. Despite the increased production of the sea cucumber farms in China, fisheries in Alaska and the Pacific Northwest are able to compete in the Chinese market given the superior quality of the naturally grown animal. A sea cucumber fisherman in the state of Washington can sell his product to Asian markets for about $9. In Tokyo, the highest caliber of sea cucumber species go for $350 per pound.

The Chinese believe that the consumption of sea cucumber enhances one's energy and strength in addition to fueling the sexual appetite—a delicacy, indeed.

Sweet'n Stinky Bêches-de-Mer

Ingredients

8 bêches-de-mer
1 cup bamboo shoots
1 scallion stalk
1 clove garlic
1 slice fresh ginger
4 tbsp sugar
4 tbsp soy sauce
3 tbsp sherry
3 tbsp rice vinegar
½ cup vegetable stock
2 tbsp vegetable oil
2 tsp corn starch
¼ cup water

1. If they are dried, soak the bêches-de-mer in a bath of water for at least 1 day until they have taken on a gelatinous quality and are rubbery to the touch. Once they have reached this point, split each in half.

2. Slice the bamboo shoots and mince the scallion, garlic, and fresh ginger.

3. Combine the sugar, soy sauce, sherry, vinegar, and stock in a bowl, incorporating all until the sugar has dissolved.

4. Heat the oil in a wide, shallow frying pan and add the bamboo shoots, scallion, garlic, and ginger. Stir-fry for about 2 minutes.

5. Add the soaked bêches-de-mer and stir-fry for about 1 minute longer.

6. At this point, add the sugar-soy sauce mixture, stirring the entire dish until everything is coated in the sauce. Then reduce the heat, cover, and simmer for 15 minutes.

7. Mix the ¼ cup of cold water into the cornstarch until it forms a paste. After the sea cucumber mix has simmered for 15 minutes, add the cornstarch paste and stir in entirely until the dish has thickened.

Further Reading

"Beche-de-Mer Information Bulletin." Coastal Fisheries Programme. http://www.spc.int/Coastfish/News/bdm/bdm.htm.

Chee-Beng, Tan. *Food and Foodways in Asia: Resource, Tradition, and Cooking.* UK: T. and F. Books, 2009.

Doughton, Sandi. "In Puget Sound, Divers Harvest Sea Cucumbers." *Seattle Times.* August 17, 2004. http://seattletimes.nwsource.com/html/localnews/2002007298_seacukes17m.html.

Herbst, Sharon Tyler. *The Food Lover's Companion.* 2nd ed. Hauppauge, NY: Barron's Education Services, 1995.

Miller, Gloria Bley. *The Thousand Recipe Chinese Cookbook.* New York: Simon & Schuster, 1966.

Newman, Jacqueline M. "Unusual Ingredients That Some Call Precious, Others Exotic." *Flavor and Fortune,* no. 2 (Fall 1995): 11–13.

Jeanne Hodesh

Seal Flippers

Seal is the primary, and most important, food of some of the indigenous peoples of Labrador and Newfoundland. The Inuit, living on the northern shores of Labrador, make use of the many seal varieties that live in the arctic waters. Seal are hunted along the edges of the ice floes and at their breathing holes. As with all animals hunted by the Inuit, all parts of the seal are either eaten or used. The blubber, meat, liver, heart, brain, eyes, and blood of the seal are eaten raw while the intestines are either boiled or eaten raw. At times, seal blubber may be liquefied and aged, and on occasion seal meat may also be aged. The skin of the seal is used for clothing and traditionally the fat was rendered for lamp oil.

The eating of seal flippers in particular, however, is a tradition of the European Canadians of Newfoundland. Although Europeans have been hunting seals since the 1600s, the industry of sealing did not begin in Canada until the early 18th century. The tradition of eating seal flippers in all likelihood originated during the early days of the sealing industry. The seal hunt traditionally took place between mid-March and early May, during the northern migration of the harp seals along the Labrador and Newfoundland coasts. The seal hunt provided off-season employment for Newfoundland fishermen, and, as a result, the majority of the by products of the seal were sold for economic gain. The skins of the seals were sold to merchants to be made into leather, and the pelts were sold for clothing. The seal fat was rendered into oil for lighting, for machine oil, for the softening of textiles, and for use in paints, explosives, and margarine. By the 1840s seal oil represented 84 percent of the value of the seal products sold. The seal flippers, having little economic value on the market, were saved for the seal hunters. When the sealing ships returned to port, the sealers could be seen selling seal flippers on the wharves.

During the peak of the sealing industry, Newfoundland was an isolated and poor area. Dried cod, salted beef, and salted pork were the staple winter foods. These meats were eaten with the root vegetables that grow readily in the sandy, rocky soil of Newfoundland, and could be stored throughout the winter in root cellars. Although the root vegetables had to last until the summer growing season, when the spring came and the sealing fleets returned from the ice, it was a great treat to have fresh seal flippers to eat.

Seal flipper meat is tender and tasty. The meat is dark, oily, and gamey with a flavor similar to that of hare, but much richer and denser in texture. The classic and most favored recipe for cooking seal flippers is seal flipper pie. Also called simply flipper pie, all recipes call for the meat to be dipped in flour and pan-fried and then roasted with onions, carrots, turnips, potatoes and parsnips. Newfoundland cooks flavor flipper pie with salt and pepper, and sometimes with Worcestershire sauce as well. A pastry cover is placed over the pan once the meat and vegetables are cooked.

Because the seal hunt takes place in the spring, flipper pie was eaten most often during the Easter season. In fact, flipper pie was the first choice of many Newfoundlanders for Good Friday supper. Conveniently, church law considered seal meat to be in the same category as fish, therefore no church laws would be broken if flipper pie, instead of cod, was eaten on Good Friday.

While seal flipper pie may have had its advent during the days of the sealing industry, it continues to be considered a treat among Newfoundlanders. The original seal flipper pie recipe calls for fresh seal flippers, but canned seal can also be used. Recipes for using canned seal meat in flipper pie can be found on the Internet. While flipper pie continues to be considered a home cooked delicacy, it can also be bought pre-made at the grocery store. And, although flipper pie is still a traditional Good Friday meal, some Newfoundlanders say that it makes a nice Sunday dinner throughout the year. Readers of Annie Proulx's novel of Newfoundland

---

Seal is not only an important cultural food for some Arctic people, it was an important subsistence food for early Antarctic explorers. High in fat, protein, and vitamin A, a diet consisting mostly of seal allowed many explorers to survive after provisions ran out, though often at a cost. Hypervitaminosis A, coupled with scurvy from a lack of vitamin C resulted in liver damage, vision problems, and hair loss.

The Shipping News will have read of flipper pie, and it is said that whenever and wherever Newfoundlanders gather, their nostalgia for their home country finds expression in thoughts of flipper pie.

Further Reading

Bélanger, Claude. "Sealing and Whaling in Newfoundland (to 1949)." *Newfoundland History*. Montreal: Marianopolis College, 2004. http://faculty.marianopolis.edu/.belanger//.htm.

Harlow, Taylor. "Personal View." *British Medical Journal* 2, no. 5859 (1973): 173.

Hiller, J. K. "The Newfoundland Seal Fishery." *Heritage Newfoundland*. St. John's: Memorial University of Newfoundland, 2001. http://www.heritage.nf.ca//.html.

Jembeth. "Flipper Pie." *Everything 2: The Everything Development Company* (blog). March 20, 2002. http://everything2.com/title/Flipper+Pie.

Jesperson, Ivan F. *Fat Back and Molasses: A Collection of Favorite Old Recipes from Newfoundland and Labrador*. St. John's: Jesperson Publishing, 1973.

Martin, Sharon. "April in Newfoundland and Labrador: Thoughts and Memories." NL Interactive. April 2008. http://www.nfinteractive.com//.php.

"Sealing History." The Seal Fishery. http://www.thesealfishery.com/seal_hunt_history1.php.

Laura P. Appell-Warren

Seitan

Seitan is the Japanese word for cooked wheat gluten. It is a food that is generally referred to as wheat meat, due to the fact that it is often used as a vegetarian substitute for meat. It very easily imitates not only the texture, but also the taste of meat.

It typically has a chewy texture and a beige color. Seitan is very high in protein and low in fat, which makes it a very nutritious addition to any meal. It is made by cooking wheat gluten until all of the starch has dissipated. It is similar to tofu in that it soaks up the flavors of whatever it is cooked with. However, it differentiates from tofu because it is not soybean-based. Tofu is not the only substance used in store-bought products. Seitan is also used in a wide assortment of products available in most grocery stores. Morningstar Farms, LightLife, and Gardein are just a few of the names that use seitan in their products.

Seitan is used most commonly in Asian cuisine and is a very popular option for vegetarian and vegan cooking. The Chinese name for seitan is *miàn jīn*. Seitan is also a staple in macrobiotic cuisine. This is a diet where grains are eaten as the fundamental base, along with vegetables and legumes, and where processed and refined foods are not eaten. However, seitan is now also eaten in the majority of East Asian countries and also in the United States.

It can be made one of two ways. The first is by kneading gluten flour with water and seasonings. This creates a dough-like substance, which can then be cooked in numerous ways. Or, seitan can be made by kneading regular wheat flour with water, and then rinsing the starch away. This leaves behind only the stringy gluten protein (Sherman, 2006). Seitan can also be found in the refrigerated section of most health food stores. It comes prepackaged in a number of ways, all of which are very convenient for the consumer. Seitan can be found in blocks,

A healthy vegan snack: a roll of seitan on a cutting board with slices of rye bread. (© Michele Cornelius | Dreamstime.com)

strips, and in pre-shaped forms (such as patties). When found prepackaged, Seitan is often infused with an assortment of flavors, all complementing the product, such as mushrooms, coriander, onion, barbeque, and even teriyaki.

Seitan was originally developed in the Japanese and Chinese cuisines. It has been an important food for Buddhists for hundreds of years, since Buddhists are vegetarians. It continues to be sold in Asian restaurants as an option for Buddhists or any non-meat eaters. Seitan was introduced to Western nations in the 1950s, and since then has become increasingly popular, not only in Asian cuisine, but for vegetarians and vegans as well.

Seitan can be used in a wide array of dishes, including stews and stir-fries. But most commonly, it is cooked in vegetable-based broth. It can be a great substitute for meat in really any recipe, even in classics, such as pot-pie.

Since seitan is lean and high in protein, it is a very healthy substitution for many meats, and even for tofu. In one 3-ounce portion, tofu contains 117 calories, 12.8 grams of protein, and 7.1 grams of fat. Seitan, however, contains 18 grams of protein, 90 calories, and only 1 gram of fat. And although the same portion of roast chicken has more protein (26 grams), it also has more calories (138) and more fat (3 grams) ("Calories," 2009).

This stir-fry recipe is a great place to start for those who have never tried seitan. It is an easy, healthy meal that is packed full of flavor.

Quick and Easy Seitan Stir-Fry

Ingredients

½ cup rice wine

½ cup water

2 tbsp brown sugar

2 tbsp hoisin sauce

1 tbsp black bean sauce

2 tsp cornstarch

¼ tsp salt

1 tbsp vegetable oil

1 tbsp sesame oil

1 lb. water-packed seitan, medium diced

½ cup peanuts, chopped

1½ tsp fresh ginger, minced

3 carrots, julienned

2 bell peppers, julienned

1 small onion, julienned

¼ cup scallions, thinly sliced

1. Mix together in a small bowl rice wine, water, sugar, hoisin, black bean sauce, salt, and cornstarch.
2. In a large nonstick sauté pan, heat 1 tablespoon vegetable oil over medium-high heat. Add the seitan and sauté until crispy, stirring occasionally, about 5 minutes.
3. Stir in the rest of the vegetable oil, the peanuts, and the ginger. Cook about 1 minute, or until fragrant, stirring frequently.
4. Add in the carrots, bell peppers, onions, and sesame oil, stirring constantly, for about 1 minute.
5. Add the rice wine sauce to the pan and stir. Reduce heat to medium, cover, and cook until the sauce has thickened, about 4 minutes. Top the stir-fry with the scallions.

Further Reading

"Calories in Seitan Traditional." Calorie Count. The New York Times Company. September 13, 2009. http://caloriecount. about.com/calories-white-wave-seitan-traditional-i85067.

Rolland, Jacques L., and Carol Sherman. "Seitan." *The Food Encyclopedia: Over 8,000 Ingredients, Tools, Techniques, and People*, 586. Toronto: Robert Rose, 2006.

"Seitan." Tofutown.net. http://tofutown.net/index.php?id=93.

Laura Mathews

Sheep's Eyeballs

No record has been found of the first time someone ate a sheep's eyeball. Was it the desperate act of someone who had nothing else to eat? Or was it merely part of a culture that believed in using all parts of a slaughtered animal? At any rate, many cultures, especially in the Middle East, view the sheep's eyeball as a delicacy. They serve it to honored guests, and it is extremely impolite for guests to refuse it. One wonders if there is a bit of cruelty, or at least humor, behind this custom, almost like an initiation rite.

In modern history, the most famous description of being served a sheep's eyeball comes from the autobiography of United States General Norman Schwartzkopf. As a teenager, he attended a feast in Iran with his father, an American advisor. To

Schwartzkopf's horror, a tribal chief gave him a sheep's eyeball:

> With all the roasting and basting, it didn't look like a staring eye—more like a brown fig. But it was still an eyeball as far as I was concerned. I said to my father, "I'm not going to eat that." He said out of the corner of his mouth, "You *will* eat it." . . . Holding my breath, I spooned the eyeball up and swallowed it whole, and everyone applauded. Afterward, Pop said he was glad I'd done as I was told. "They were paying you a great tribute, and if you hadn't eaten the eye, you'd have insulted them," he said. "But instead you ate it, and by doing that you made a contribution to American-Iranian relations. I'm proud of you." (Schwartzkopf, 1992, 36)

Many other travelers tell stories of being nonplused (or aghast!) when offered this treat. Eating sheep eyeballs was a challenge on a 2003 episode of the television show *Fear Factor*.

In the 1970s, scientists questioned whether the high incidence of Creutzfeldt-Jacob disease (CJD) in Libyan Jews might be linked to their habit of eating sheep's eyeballs (which might transmit the prions that cause scrapie in sheep to humans). However, because people around them were eating sheep's eyeballs and not getting CJD, and the sheep in the area showed no signs of illness, scientists later determined that these people had a genetic mutation that made them more liable to develop CJD (Cox, 2002).

Sheep's eyeballs are eaten mainly in the Middle East and North Africa. Several Internet sites suggest that a Mongolian hangover cure involves drinking two pickled sheep's eyeballs in tomato juice, but this seems unlikely. Tomato juice is not a typical Mongolian food, and getting the two eyeballs requires killing a whole sheep. Mongolia is far away and exotic, and there are few Mongolians elsewhere to refute this concept. It is likely that this prescription and its name are someone's idea of a joke.

The eyeball is roasted in the sheep's head, and removed immediately before serving it to the guest. To add to the effect, the host may scoop it out of the skull with a dagger, and present it to the guest on the dagger's tip.

After cooking, the eyeball is still intact, with the vitreous fluid inside. "The overall sensation has been described as somewhere between a meaty oyster and a rotten grape" (Weil, 2006). The cooked lens is hard, so if it hasn't been removed, this adds the impression of eating a hard plastic contact lens. Several food writers suggest that a person who receives this tidbit, which looks something like a prune, should treat it like an oyster and swallow it whole. One person who ate half a sheep's eye described it as having the consistency of gristle.

No one has established nutritional values for sheep's eyeballs, as they are eaten infrequently and make a negligible contribution to diet.

Further Reading

Cox, Peter. *You Don't Need Meat*. New York: St. Martin's Press, 2002.

Schwarzkopf, H. Norman. *It Doesn't Take a Hero: General H. Norman Schwarzkopf, the Autobiography*. New York: Bantam Books, 1992.

Weil, Christa. *Fierce Food: The Intrepid Diner's Guide to the Unusual, Exotic, and Downright Bizarre*. New York: Penguin Group, 2006.

Christine Crawford-Oppenheimer

Shellac

Shellac is the only commercial resin derived from an animal. It is made from the secretion of the *Laccifer lacca*, or lac beetle. It tends to be used as a barrier, coating, or binding agent on foodstuffs around the world. When listed as an ingredient, it can sometimes also be found under the names confectioners glaze or edible film.

Shellac is the end result of the female lac beetle's parasitic relationship with trees in India and Thailand including the palas, ber, ficus, and kusum. Once they have settled onto a tree, they suck out the sap, then form a protective barrier by releasing both a hard, dark red, chitinous scale, and a yellow-to-reddish resin, known as lac. After the lac hardens, the subsequent flakes are removed, washed, and sold. To be approved for use on food by the FDA, shellac flakes have to be dissolved in pure ethanol.

It is nearly impossible to avoid consuming shellac. It is a highly desirable ingredient, because it provides a high-gloss shine to food, protects the quality, and keeps it fresher longer. It can be found on chocolates, marzipan, jelly beans, and the wax coating on fruits and vegetables. Shellac is also used on pharmaceutical drugs to make them easier to swallow and to help delay the absorption of time-release drugs into the body. Besides being used for edible goods, lac is also utilized for everything from atomics to furniture finish.

Further Reading

"Eco Friendly Natural Resin." Shellac. http://www.shellac.in.

Spano, Marie. "Yummy: Bugs in Nutrition Bars." Atlanta Sports Nutrition. http://atlantasportsnutrition.com/2009/04/05/yummy-bugs-in-nutrition-bars/.

Thexyz Network. "The Story of Shellac and the *Laccifer lacca* (lac bettle)." Associated Content. http://www.associatedcontent.com/article/553651/the_story_of_shellac_and_the_laccifer.html.

Caroline Erb Medina

Silkworm

As the story goes, the Chinese empress Xi Ling-Shi was sipping tea beneath a mulberry tree when a silk cocoon dropped into her teacup. She fished it out, pulling a thread from the capsule and wrapped it around her finger, marveling at its warmth. When she had unraveled the entire strand, she discovered a small larva inside which she immediately realized was the source of the silk. She shared this finding with her people, and so began China's production of silk—a monopoly which they fiercely (and successfully) guarded for some time. It is rumored that foreign visitors tried to sneak across the border with silkworm eggs hidden in their hair. Eventually these smuggling techniques proved positive, and silk began to be produced in neighboring countries. Today, silkworms, along with bees, are of the few widely domesticated insects. *Bombyx mori* is the most common species. The silkworm's cocoon is made from a single strand, stretching from 1,000 to 3,000 feet in length. By some estimates, about 70 million pounds of raw silk are produced annually.

There may be as many variations on its tale of origin as there are uses for the material, not the least of which is the employ of silk worm larva as a protein-rich snack. In Korea, where the cost of meat can be prohibitive, silkworm larvae, known as *beondegi* (which literally translates as chrysalis), are seasoned and boiled, then served up in a piping hot heap as a cheap and satisfying alternative. Snackers pop them into their mouths one at a time, crunching through the shell to suck out the pupa (larva) inside. Sometimes the pupae are accompanied by a dipping sauce of sesame and ginger, but more often than not, they are served plain in a paper cone. Steaming cauldrons of beondegi can be spotted alongside roads in cities and villages and in outdoor markets all over South Korea, their odorous scent is immediately recognizable and not unlike their bitter flavor. Restaurants and drinking establishments serve beondegi as well, treating it as a side dish or a bar snack. Supermarkets stock cans of the larvae, selling them to the masses as commonly as Americans stock up on tuna fish.

In Japan, silkworms are an ingredient in many dishes, including some types of sushi. In southern China, where the majority of silkworms are produced, they are served with ground pork or cucumbers. In northern China, where they are considered a delicacy, the pupae are roasted or sometimes baked with satay sauces and rice. In northern Vietnam, they are simply fried in cooking oil with fish sauce and scallions, and are a popular street food. Because they are cooked once, and the precious silk thread has already been extracted, one could argue that the pinkie-length pupae protected by their exterior brown shells, are also an environmentally conscious snack, binging new meaning to the eating of leftovers.

Two Southern Chinese Recipes for Silkworm Pupae

Courtesy of *Flavor and Fortune*, a Chinese food magazine, www.flavorandfortune.com. Used by permission.

Silkworm Pupae with Ground Pork

Ingredients

6 to 8 oz. silkworm pupae
6 oz. pork butt, ground
2 tbsp cornstarch
1 tsp sesame oil
1 tbsp soy sauce
1 tbsp oyster sauce
1 tsp sugar
1 clove garlic, minced
1 scallion, minced
1 tbsp fresh cilantro, chopped
½ tsp ground ginger
1 tbsp rice wine
1 tsp solid shortening

1. Clean and chop the silkworm pupae. Mix them with all the other ingredients except the solid shortening, and add ½ cup water to this mixture. Only stir in 1 direction when mixing them.
2. Rub solid shortening on a baking dish, and pour the mixture into it. The size of the dish should be such that the contents are about 1 inch deep.
3. Steam for 10 minutes, and then serve immediately.

Silkworm Pupae with Cucumber

Ingredients

½ lb. silkworm pupae

2 medium-sized cucumbers

2 Chinese celery stalks, cut into 1-inch
lengths

2 tbsp corn oil

2 slices fresh ginger

1 clove garlic, mashed

1 scallion, cut into 1-inch lengths

Salt and pepper, to taste

1 tbsp Chinese rice wine

1. Clean the silkworm pupae, rinse them
   several times, drain, and set aside.
2. Peel the cucumbers lengthwise, leaving alternate strips of skin on them,
   then cut them lengthwise into 4 parts,
   remove and discard the seeds. Cut
   the cucumber pieces diagonally into
   1-inch lengths and set aside.
3. In a skillet, heat the oil, then add the
   ginger, scallions, and garlic, and stir-
   fry until the garlic turns golden. Then
   quickly add the celery and fry 2 minutes, then add the cucumber strips and
   fry another minute.
4. Add the silkworm pupae, salt and pepper, and the wine, and toss quickly,
   then serve.

Further Reading

Donahue, Suzanne. "Korean Silkworm Larvae:
From the Food X-Files." Associated Content.
http://www.associatedcontent.com/article/
308322/korean_silkworm_larvae_from_
the_food.html?cat=22.

Hudson, Gavin. "Silkworms: an Environmentally Friendly Delicacy?" EcoLocalizer.
http://ecolocalizer.com/2008/11/14/
silkworms-an-environmentally-friendly-
delicacy/.

Jeanne Hodesh

Snake

The revulsion with which westerners view
snakes is both unusual globally and, from
a gastronomic perspective, unwarranted.
Despite their venomous or otherwise ne-
farious reputation, snakes are more than
merely palatable, but downright delicious.
In fact, it is often precisely in their menacing demeanor, poison-laden fangs or bone-
crushing muscles that one finds a frisson
of gustatory delight, a therapeutic tonic for
virility, or merely a simple meal from an
outlandishly freakish beast that does actually taste like chicken.

The snake's infamy as a slithering killer
probably predates not only the Judeo-
Christian depiction of Satanic tempter in
the Garden of Eden, but likely the advent
of humans as a species. Our distant primate
relatives still instinctively fear writhing,
limbless bodies rustling through the grass.
Many ancient cultures feared and revered
snakes: whether the Cretan serpent bearing
priestess, the ouroboros, a symbol of eter-
nal creation and destruction (a coiled snake
consuming its own tail), or the Asclepian
healers who loosed wriggling snakes over
patients' bodies in their temple precincts—
supposedly the origin of the caduceus. But
as food, the ancients would have none of it.

Like a sideshow freak, the snake as snack
has typically been relegated to disgust-in-
ducing displays, further cementing its far-
from-appetizing reputation. Christian Bale
landed his role in Werner Herzog's *Rescue*

Dawn partly because he was one of few actors willing to eat a live snake raw. Saudi Arabian performer Jalal al-Gharbi made a sensational living chewing the heads off live snakes, then removing the skin from the still-writhing creatures with his hands and teeth—only animal rights activists were able to end his reptilian run.

But in Asia, if you were battling a bad case of the sniffles, needing to detoxify the system, or wanting to gear up for an evening with the ladies, that cold-hearted, beady-eyed, scaly scalawag can save your life or at least, bring much needed relief (as long as you tell them to hold the venom). Although snakes are eaten in many Asian cultures, the practice originated in China, where cities such as Shanghai, Foshan, and Yangshuo are famous for snake restaurants serving dishes both traditional and new-fangled. Typically eaten in the colder months, snake meat is believed to be a panacea that brings heat and restorative values to the body, whether at a restaurant or night food market, the process of ordering a snake dish is similar: you select from a display of pit vipers, cobras, fresh- and sea-water snakes, and pythons (the latter three being the most popular), and the chef expertly kills and skins the snake in front of your very eyes as part of the culinary experience. Up to 4,000 tons of snake meat is served each year in China, and it is so revered that the delicacy is listed as dragon meat on menus. Consider the following offerings: snake breast meat stuffed with shrimp, stir-fried colorful shredded snake, braised snake slices with chicken liver, deep-fried with salt and pepper, hot pot and fricasseed snake meat with cat. Warding off the ague, chills, and ills of the common cold with a scrumptious spread may be just what the doctor ordered.

Most snakes served in Chinese restaurants come from the snake repository in Wuzhou, where more than 1 million snakes are raised for consumption each year. At the Flying Snake Farm in Shenzhen, make it a memorable day out with rejuvenating baths featuring hundreds of snakes and a *snakatorium* presenting snake diet therapies, before finishing with snake skin with peppers, baked cobra, and snake semen liqueur.

On Hong Kong's Temple Street, it's hard to wiggle your way out of gawking at the array of snake delicacies on display, including munchies such as dried snake and deep-fried snake. One could start at Snake King Yan, a wine shop specializing in wine made from every part of the reptile, where each potent potion will likely leave you reeling with its kick. The famous snake queen Chau Ka-Ling has been brewing every part of a snake, including entrails, into herbal remedies at her Shia Wong Hip restaurant, and guarantees a complete recovery from any skin problem after two weeks of drinking her potion, for just $30 H.K. $4 U.S.) a bowl. An entire snake can also be had for $140 H.K. ($18 U.S.), inclusive of snuff show. Taipei's Snake Alley is a similar set-up, except that you might need the stomach to watch snakes induced into a dance of death by charmers before meeting their maker.

Because Asian food cultures don't believe in letting any part of an animal go to waste, it can only be a good thing that a snake's blood and bile are considered to be male aphrodisiacs. Also believed to be

Pit Viper Ice Cream

While American taste buds salivate over soft serve vanilla cones and containers of Chunky Monkey ice cream, the Japanese palate yawns. The home of sashimi and kobe beef also happens to be home to some of the most bizarre ice cream flavors known to man. The strangest among them? Snake ice cream.

An actual industrialized product, the Japanese did not just emulsify the average, run of the mill, garden snake. The snake selected to impart the best flavor was the pit viper, coincidentally one of the deadliest known to mankind.

It has been said to taste like vomit, with a sweetness. But flavor may not be everything. When the Japanese do reach for pit viper ice cream, what they are buying into is the snake's history as a healing aphrodisiac. Snake venom in particular is reported to help balance nerves and thin blood, reducing the chance for blood clots and heart attacks.

Currently in Tokyo, pit viper, also known as *mamushi*, is not only served in ice cream, but is available live to be drained of its blood, served in a tumbler, garnished with the gall bladder and the entire libation is served immediately to the guest. The blood and gall bladder are the most sought after parts, as they are thought to have the most healing power. Upon request, the body may be served as well, first pummeled with a hammer to crush the bones, then cooked whole.

Occasionally pit vipers can be found whole, submerged in a liter of sake. The protein-based venom is denatured by ethanol, however, imbibers are not recommended to take more than one glass, as nose bleeds may occur.

Erica Hope

good for the eyesight, lower spine, and a relief for fatigue, stag parties have been to known to get up their mojo at restaurants serving snake meat and wine before a night on the town. The ritual consists of beheading the snake and the blood flowing into shot glasses, topped off with bile, and drunk bottoms up—the trace of a possibility that some lethal venom might be lingering gets some thrill-seekers going. One lucky member of the party will get to chase the shot with a swallow of the still-beating heart—provided he can even taste it after his tongue has been numbed by the firewater sensation of the concoction.

To take the edge off, local rice wine in China, Laos, Myanmar, Cambodia, and Vietnam, where it originated, brewed with snakes are a much milder tipple, although it's more of a medicinal antidote for common maladies. Recycled whiskey and gin bottles line the shelves of dispensaries and street stands, featuring a coiled snake steeped in clear, white liquid tinged with a rosy hue from serpentine blood. At $20 a bottle, even if it doesn't seem to help with ailments such as hangovers, it's a popular souvenir toted home by Western tourists.

Closer to home, rattlesnakes are the preferred serpentine tidbit, which *Houston Chronicle* food critic Alison Cook has described as, "a sort of macho West Texas thing," prevalent at cookouts and civic festivals. Although rattlesnakes are a part of Wild West cowboy lore, standing in for protein rich filling meat on those long wagon rides across the plains, today it is a proud stamp of Texan pride, its status in the pantheons of kitsch solidified by indulgent machismo savoring of rattlesnake fajitas, chili, barbeque, and deep-fried nuggets. The annual Rattlesnake Roundup in Sweetwater, Texas, launched its popularity in the 1950s, with 250,000 pounds of meat harvested since then. You can safely procure canned rattlesnake in the aisles of southwestern grocery stores, next to the turkducken, and reputable steakhouses in Arizona and Colorado also feature it on their menus.

Snake Fry Recipe

Ingredients

1 large rattle snake
Salt and pepper to taste
1 egg
Breadcrumbs
2 tbsp butter
1 lemon, cut into wedges

1. First make sure your snake is quite dead. Cut off the head and do not go near it, as it can still bite even when detached from the body. Skin the snake with a sharp boning knife by cutting a straight line down the bottom of the snake's body, peeling back and removing the skin and discarding the internal organs.
2. Cut the flesh into 2-inch segments. Season with salt and pepper.
3. Dip into the beaten egg and then into the breadcrumbs to coat. Fry these in butter in a cast-iron skillet over an open flame until golden brown.
4. If your snake is young, you will be able to munch through the small rib bones, if not, carefully remove them as you eat your snake. Serve with wedged of lemon.

Further Reading

Ernst, Carl, and Evelyn Ernst. *Snakes of the United States and Canada.* Washington, DC: Smithsonian Books, 2003.

Mattison, Chris. *The New Encyclopedia of Snakes.* Princeton, NJ: Princeton University Press, 2007.

Desiree Koh and Ken Albala

Stinky Cheese

Most of the pungent odor from strong cheeses comes from their rinds. Until it is cut, cheese is a combination of living organisms: bacteria and molds that ferment the curds into cheese. The rind is the outer, protective coating that forms on the surface of the cheese.

Cheese is made by coagulating milk (from cows, goats, sheep, buffaloes, camels, yaks, and reindeer). Milk can be coagulated by adding starter cultures of bacteria or acid to the milk. The process can be sped up with the addition of heat. The coagulated gel is then cut; separating the curds from the liquid part or whey. The curds are then pressed together, often times into a shape or mold. The cheeses can then be eaten young or aged. Aged cheeses are often coated or brined to help the formation of the rind, or the outer edge of the cheese. The rind functions as a barrier to prevent undesirable things from entering the cheese (like harmful molds, bacteria, and insects) as well as a means of keeping good or beneficial elements within the cheese (including preventing the cheese from drying out too quickly).

Many of the strong smelling, or stinky, cheeses are wash rind or surface smeared cheeses. Époisse, a wash rind cheese made in Burgundy is a soft cow's milk cheese, whose orange rind is formed from the wine or marc that the cheese is washed in. Its intense, pungent, ammonia smell is almost exclusive to the rind—the interior of the cheese is salty, creamy, and very mild in comparison to its pungent, but completely edible, rind.

In 2004, Vieux Boulogne, a beer-washed cheese from northern France was named the world's smelliest cheese, beating out other washed rind cheeses including Époisse, Pont l'Eveque, and Limburger. Wash rind cheeses smell so strongly because of the enzyme reactions that occur when the cheese is bathed or brushed with a liquid, most often a beer or wine.

While many washed rind cheeses are strong in smell, they are not the only intensely aromatic cheeses. Camembert de Normandy, Brie de Meaux, and Brie de Melun are examples of bloomy, rind cheeses. Bloomy refers to the white and grey mold or bloom that forms on the exterior of these cheeses. They are rubbed with *Penicillium candidum*, a mold that ripens the cheese from the outside in. Younger cheeses will be much firmer than more aged cheeses, which become creamier and runny as the mold breaks down the cheese over time.

Unlike the bright white rinds found on wheels of Camembert and Brie available in many U.S. grocery stores, true or natural Camembert de Normandy and Brie de Meaux are made with unpasteurized milk. The use of raw or unpasteurized milk changes the flavor of the finished cheeses; the natural cultures are still present and not killed by the heating process. These cheeses also have a different look. Unpasteurized Camembert de Normandy will begin to develop brown markings on the rind; Brie de Meaux will form small tinges of orange and red. Most pasteurized Camembert and Brie cheeses are sprayed with extra mold to maintain their bright white and fluffy exterior, a technique that does not hurt the cheese, and is completely edible, but it does not add any flavor either.

These natural cheeses have much stronger smells than their pasteurized counterparts, but like washed rind cheeses, their interiors taste different than their pungent rinds lead your nose to believe. Camembert de Normandy has a high butterfat content, with a rich, creamy interior that oozes once cut. It is slightly salty, a bit acidic, and has an earthy flavor and aroma of mushrooms. With 45 percent butterfat content, Brie de Meaux is rich, nutty, and has creamy and milky flavors that are often described as having an acidic, hazelnut, and a fruity taste.

Stilton is one of the strongest blue cheeses. It is a cow's milk cheese that is purposefully needled with mold to promote cheese aging from both the outside and inside. After the cheese is formed, thin metal rods or needles are pressed into the sides of the cheese. This process allows oxygen into the cheese and for the mold *Penicillium roqueforti*, which was added to the milk, to grow. Over time, the mold grows, and develops the distinctive blue/green veining throughout the cheese. In addition to having a pungent aroma, Stilton, like other blue cheeses, has a very sharp and strong flavor, with a piquant or spicy finish.

Strong or stinky cheeses are not the best to use in cooking. These bold flavors will break down or become unpleasant. Its best to serve these cheeses at room temperature, at the beginning or end of a meal, or as a snack paired with dried fruits, nuts, honey, or a preserve. When pairing with alcohol, beers often stand up to these bold flavors much better than most wines, but as a general rule, its hard to go wrong if you pair these cheeses with other foods and beverages from the same region they were produced in.

Always store cheese or leftovers in parchment or butcher's paper that is loosely wrapped around the cheese, this allows the cheese to breath—until you cut it, it is actually a living organism and you need to allow space for moisture and air to pass in and out of the cheese. Do not store it in the back of your refrigerator, because it might freeze and kill the good bacteria and molds.

Further Reading

Davidson, Alan. "Cheese." *The Penguin Companion to Food*, 191–193. New York: Penguin, 2002.

Jenkins, Steve. *Cheese Primer*. New York: Workman, 1996.

Kindstedt, Paul. *American Farmstead Cheese: The Complete Guide to Making and Selling Artisan Cheeses*. White River Junction, VT: Chelsea Green, 2005.

"World's Smelliest Cheese Named." *BBC News*. http://news.bbc.co.uk/2/hi/4044703.stm.

Kristina Nies

Stinky Tofu

Tofu, otherwise known as bean curd, is a mild-tasting, cheese-like food item made from soymilk, which in turn is obtained by soaking dry soybeans and grinding them with water, essentially creating a soybean puree. Tofu has been consumed in Asia for centuries. Most histories describe tofu production beginning in China sometime during the Han dynasty 2,000 years ago. There are many different kinds of tofu, with the spectrum of textures ranging from extra-firm blocks that can withstand vigorous tossing action in a wok, to the silkiest, most fragile, that could rival custard in texture. Tofu is produced by adding a coagulant to heated soymilk. Excess liquid is then expressed from the resulting curds in amounts depending on what firmness is desired of the final product, and the formed tofu is then flavored, smoked, cured, dried, molded, or fermented to create variations on the basic item. The latter variation is often likened to Western mold-ripened cheeses. In fact, the old name for tofu in French was *fromage de pois* (pea cheese), and one of the earliest European descriptions of bean curd, from Friar Domingo Navarrette, recounts,

They drew the milk out of the kidney [sic] beans, and turning it, make great cakes of it like cheeses, as big as a large sieve, and five or six fingers thick. All the mass is as white as the very snow, to look at nothing can be finer. . . . Alone it is insipid, but very good dressed as I say and excellent fried in butter. (McGee, 2004, 495)

The traditional, most common curdling agent is calcium sulfate, with Japanese and coastal Chinese regions using a mixture of magnesium and calcium salts that remain after table salt is crystallized from seawater. As a result, like milk-based cheeses, tofu can be an excellent vegan/vegetarian source of calcium.

Stinky tofu is made by fermenting bean curd in a brine solution of salt and water. It has an extremely strong smell that many find highly objectionable at first pass and is often likened to ripe garbage. It is a popular street snack in Hong Kong, Taiwan, China, and, to a lesser extent, in Southeast Asia, especially where there are large populations of ethnic Chinese. The stinky tofu found on the streets is usually prepared by frying, and the odor can be detected from a distance of several blocks. Connoisseurs maintain that the smell is only objectionable from a distance; once up close, it becomes fragrant and appetizing. In fact, stinky tofu is actually very mild tasting, which is why in Hong Kong it is often served, on skewers and in a little paper bag, with hoisin sauce. In Taiwan, soy sauce, black vinegar, and chili oil is the preferred mixture of condiments. When properly made, the exterior should be golden and crispy-crumbly, while the interior is silky-smooth and almost creamy. The best versions display a lace-like texture in the soft interior. There is a twice-fermented version that makes the regular stinky version seem pedestrian by comparison. Stinky tofu is usually consumed on its own as a snack or side dish, but less commonly, it is also eaten cold, steamed, or stewed with other ingredients. The Taiwanese like to add stinky tofu to a Sichuan-style spicy *mala* (combination of numbing and spicy) soup base or in hot pots, where a soup base simmers over an open flame in the middle of a table (usually a specially designed version with a square hole in the middle where the single burner resides) while diners cook their food in the communal pot from a spread of raw ingredients.

Recipes for preparing stinky tofu can vary widely both from region to region and from individual to individual, but the typical one involves soaking tofu in a brine of vegetables, and/or meat that has already been fermenting on its own. The tofu is added to this, and the mix is left to ferment for another few months. The traditional method of fermenting in an open container left the end product vulnerable to contamination, so now most manufacturers use yeast to start the brine for a more hygienic, safe, and consistent product. Some recipes for the brine include items such as dried shrimp, amaranth, mustard greens, bamboo shoots, and endless combinations of Chinese herbs. Brines can be reused indefinitely by adding new brine to old when making a new batch of stinky tofu. Like old sourdough starters, old brines are prized for their complex flavor and may be passed along from person to person.

As in any fermented product, stinky tofu is full of healthy bacteria. Research has identified more than 19 different species of bacteria in stinky tofu brines; many of these were types of lactic acid bacteria, to which category probiotic strains used in health foods also belong (Chao, et. al.). Whatever health benefits may be enjoyed from stinky tofu, however, is probably dependent on its method of preparation. Unlike Korean kimchi (fermented cabbage) or yogurt, which are eaten cold and whose health benefits are widely touted, stinky tofu is usually consumed after being fried or stewed in a soup. High heat involved in the cooking process would kill most bacteria, so if a health benefit is desired, stinky tofu should be eaten cold.

Modern recipes for stinky tofu only require the tofu to soak for 3 to 5 hours in the spring/fall and 6 to 10 hours during winter. The brine might include amaranth stem, bamboo shoot, medicago, potherb mustard, ginger, licorice, and Sichuan pepper. These would be cleaned, chopped, and placed into lightly salted water that has been boiled and cooled. The mixture then ferments on its own for 8 to 10 months before it is ready to be used in preparing stinky tofu. Prior to immersion in the brine, the tofu must first soak in a solution of iron sulphate (FeSO4) for two hours. Once this is done, the tofu is drained thoroughly before it is added to the brine and fermented as described above.

Stinky Tofu with Hot Sauce

Ingredients

2 tbsp sesame oil
2 tbsp red chili pepper
Pinch of salt
2 tbsp soy sauce
Chicken stock, to taste
Stinky tofu, cubed
Canola, grapeseed, or peanut oil, for frying

For the Dipping Sauce

Heat the sesame oil, then pour into a pan with chili pepper, salt, and soy sauce, then add broth to taste.

To Fry the Tofu

Thoroughly pat dry the tofu. Heat oil to a temperature of 350°F to 375°F and fry until the cubes are golden and slightly puffed, turning once. Drain briefly on paper towels and serve with spicy dipping sauce.

Note: The inside of the tofu is usually very moist so be mindful of splattering oil. A frying screen would be helpful.

Further Reading

Chao S. H., Y. Tomii, K. Watanabe, and Y. C. Tsai. "Diversity of Lactic Acid Bacteria in Fermented Brines Used to Make Stinky Tofu." *Int J Food Microbiol* 123, no. 1 and 2 (March 31, 2008): 134–141.

McGee, Harold. *On Food and Cooking*. New York: Simon and Schuster, 2004.

Karen Taylor

Sweetbreads

The term *sweetbreads* generally refers to the heart, thymus, and pancreas of young animals, specifically lamb, calves, and piglets. The first mention of sweetbreads has been traced to a mid-16th-century reference to the pancreas. It might seem strange that sweetbreads are so named when they are actually savory rather than sweet, and they are in no way related to baked goods. The name, which is derived from the Old English *swete* or pleasing to the senses and *bræd* or flesh or meat, quite literally means, flesh or meat that is pleasing to the senses. Their texture is described as velvety and the flavor mild. The flavor and texture of all sweetbreads is determined by a number of factors including the animal they come from, the age of the animal and its diet. Most sought after (and most expensive) among these is the sweetbreads of calves or veal, and among these, the heart is considered the best, having the smoothest texture and best flavor. Sweetbreads deepen in color with the age of the animal, thus pale sweetbread are more desirable than those that are deep red in color. Additionally, sweetbreads from milk-fed animals are preferable to those from grain-fed animals.

Can't find sweetbreads in your local market? Try consulting your local butcher. Costly and highly perishable, sweetbreads are not readily available in supermarkets and must be special ordered. Before the advent of supermarkets during the first half of the 20th century, most people butchered their own meat or bought directly from a butcher and little was wasted in the process, making it fairly easy to find them. Packaged meat made its way into supermarkets, and sweetbreads, having to be special ordered by a butcher, became a delicacy.

From a nutritional standpoint, offal is typically high in protein and B vitamins, and sweetbreads, specifically, are a source of protein, though they tend to be high in fat and therefore are not recommend for those at risk of or living with gout. The thymus, in particular, is a good source of vitamin C and iron, which might explain why it's been associated with boosting the immune system and improving blood production. It is also believed by homeopaths that the thymus, which is part of the immune system, and the pancreas, which produces insulin and regulates blood sugar, are useful in the treatment of arthritis and diabetes, respectively.

Preparation of sweetbreads can be time consuming. Typically, they are soaked in salt water for several hours in order to remove all traces of blood, resulting in pale sweetbreads with a mild flavor. This part of the process is called *degorging* and not only affects the color and flavor of the sweetbread, but also the texture as the salted water draws some of the moisture from the sweetbread, firming the flesh. The next step in the process requires blanching or boiling for several minutes followed by an ice bath to halt the cooking. Blanching further removes impurities, loosens the membrane encasing the organs, and aids in firming the texture of the sweetbreads. Following this, the sinewy outer membrane is removed, and they're ready to be breaded and fried, sautéed, grilled, or cooked any number of ways.

Sweetbreads are versatile and can be used in salads, appetizers, or main dishes. How they are used often depends on where you find them. In South America, they are typically grilled, while in Spain, they are often stewed, and in Turkey it is not unusual to find them in a sandwich. It is interesting to note that what fetches double-digit prices in American restaurants is common café food in another part of the world.

Simple Pan-Fried Sweetbreads

Ingredients

1 lb. sweetbreads
1 pint milk
1 quart water
¼ cup white vinegar
1 tsp salt
Seasoned flour, eggs, and breadcrumbs
    for breading
½ cup shortening or lard, more as needed

1. Soak sweetbreads in milk at least 8 hours, preferably overnight.
2. Drain. In a small saucepan, cover sweetbreads with cold water, vinegar, and salt and bring to a boil. Reduce heat and simmer approximately 10 minutes.
3. Remove sweetbreads, let cool, and remove membrane. Wring in a clean towel to remove excess liquid.
4. Dredge sweetbreads in flour, egg, and then breadcrumbs to coat evenly.
5. In a medium cast iron skillet, pan fry over medium heat in about ¼ inch of hot fat until golden brown and thoroughly cooked (but not over cooked), about 3 to 4 minutes per side.

Further Reading

Henderson, Fergus. *Whole Beast: Nose to Tail Eating.* New York: HarperCollins Publishers, 2004.

Hayley Figueroa

T

Testicles

Rocky Mountain oysters, *criadillas*, lamb stones, and *animelles* are all names for the testicles of various animals such as bulls, goats, and sheep. Eating testicles is not a culturally specific phenomenon. Nearly every country that eats meat has a repertoire of recipes for animal organs, which often includes testicles, part of the male reproductive organ.

Testicles can be harvested at different times in an animal's life. The age of the animal determines the size of its genitals and, therefore, the subsequent cooking styles differ. The small, immature testicles of a young bull cut at castration are considered to be the most delicate. All testicles must be skinned out or removed from the scrotum and peeled before they can be cooked. This process also occurs when the animal is slaughtered at an older age. In this case, the testicles are larger and require different preparation.

Historically, many cultures believed that eating animal testicles would boost testosterone levels and help correct or prevent sexual dysfunctions in males. In ancient Rome, Pliny the Elder touted them as an aphrodisiac, and in India years ago Vatsyayana Maharhisi author and editor of the famous book of Kama Sutra said that drinking sugared milk boiled with goat testicles would produce sexual vigor. Even today, the idea of male potency surrounds the consumption of animal testicles.

In the United States, the young testicles are rolled in a flour-pepper mixture, deep-fried, and eaten whole. This is what is most commonly referred to as a Rocky Mountain oyster or a prairie oyster. Alternatively, older testicles are sliced in thin rounds and similarly prepared. Not surprisingly in the United States, eating animal genitalia has sparked numerous festivals especially in the western states. Generally, participants must be 21 or older to engage.

In Europe, eating testicles occurs in many countries. In Greece, testicles are a mainstay in the dish *kokoretsi*: a long kebab of internal organs including liver, lung, heart, and spleen wrapped in intestines and then baked. A bit to the west, the Spaniards sometimes dry mature testicles, or criadillas, thinly slice and sauté them with olive oil and parsley. In French, testicles are called animelles and served baked with paprika, hardboiled egg, tarragon, and melted butter. To the north in Iceland, sheep's testicles are pickled with whey and eaten with cheese.

Across Asia, the penis of various animals often accompanies testicles on the plate. Thought to aid a lethargic libido, tiger penis is widely coveted and often counterfeited. Tiger penis soup can sell for as much as $350 per bowl, yet you may find a dried tiger penis for $30 at the

While bull and ram testicles are readily available in the market place, you may question why boar (pork) testicles are not a mainstay. Boars are usually castrated as youths to produce more tender meat. Full grown boars that haven't been castrated may have a gamy off-putting flavor called boar taint. New production methods allow boars to keep their testicles without producing boar taint, so you may see boar testicles in the marketplace in the future.

market. Guangzhou, China five penis and testes wine, consisting of ox, sheep, dog, deer and snake organs, also allegedly deliver similar benefits. After one glass, you may be tempted to buy canned rooster and mouse testicles sold in a corner apothecary. Restaurants serving these food items caution, genitalia dishes must be eaten repeatedly to achieve their full potential.

Further Reading

Bowles, Tom P. "Rotting Shark to Picked Testicles? That's How the Icelanders Prefer their Food." *Daily Mail*. April 2009. http://www.dailymail.co.uk/home/moslive/article-1168484/Rotting-shark-pickled-testicles-Thats-Icelanders-prefer-food.html.

Chye, Peter L.H. "Traditional Asian Folklore Medicines in Sexual Health." *Indiana Journal of Urology* 22 (2006): 241–245. http://indianjurol.com/article.asp?issn=0970-1591;year=2006;volume=22;issue=3;spage=241;epage=245;aulast=Chye.

Earles, Jim. "Rocky Mountain Oysters: Expanding on the List of Organ Meats." Wise Traditions. Weston A. Price Foundation. http://www.westonaprice.org/splash_2.htm.

Hopkins, Jerry. *Asian Aphrodisiacs from Bangkok to Beijing—the Search for the Ultimate Turn-on*. Minneapolis: Periplus Editions, 2007.

Hopkins, Jerry, and Anthony Bourdain. *Extreme Cuisine: The Weird and Wonderful Foods That People Eat*. Minneapolis: Periplus Editions, 2004.

Morley, John E., and Horace M. Perry. "Androgen Deficiency in Aging Men." *Medical Clinics of North American* 83 (1999): 1279–1289. http://www.medical.theclinics.com/article/S0025-7125(05)70163-2/fulltext.

Rodgers, Joann Ellison. *Sex: A Natural History*. New York: Owl Books, 2003.

Schlenker, Debbie. "Harvesting of Bull Testicles." Deutschland Meats. Telephone interview. June 12, 2009.

Schwabe, Calvin W. *Unmentionable Cuisine*. Charlottesville: University of Virginia Press, 1988.

Stark, Raymond. *Book of Aphrodisiacs*. New York: Stein and Day, 1981.

Eleanor Barczak

1,000-Year Eggs and Other Chinese Preserved Eggs

Known in Cantonese Chinese as *pei dan* or in Mandarin Chinese as *pí dàn*, the thousand-year eggs are a Chinese food that is consumed throughout the Chinese diaspora and is also eaten in Thai and Vietnamese cuisine. These 1,000-year eggs, or century eggs, as they are also known, are not actually preserved for a thousand years. Instead, they are usually duck eggs cured from one to six months (depending on the season) in a mix of wood ash, lime, salt, and sometimes strong tea for flavor. The strong alkalinity of the mixture changes the pH of the egg and preserves it. A soft-yolk version of the egg is made by adding lead oxide, which blocks the shell's pores and slows the curing process. These should be avoided due to the toxicity of lead.

The modern process for curing *pei dan*, below, halves the original 30-day curing period and does not include any lead:

Boiling water
Black tea powder
Sodium chloride (NaCl)
Sodium hydroxide (NaOH)
Iron phosphate (FePO4)
Iron oxide (FeO)
Duck eggs

The eggs are first washed, dried, and placed in a large jar, still in their shells. The tea is added to the hot water and allowed to steep before the leaves are strained out. The NaCl, NaOH, FePO4, and FeO are then dissolved in the hot liquid. This solution is allowed to cool before being poured over the eggs, and the mix is allowed to rest at about 77°F/25°C for 12–16 days.

The curing process causes the egg white to transform into a dark-amber, aspic-like jelly that is relatively flavorless, while

Cold dish of sliced Chinese century egg and red tomato. (© Hanhanpeggy | Dreamstime.com)

the yolk becomes grey-green, sometimes gooey toward the center, and with a generally creamy texture. The yolk's slightly sulfuric, pungent flavor has been compared to that of bleu cheese, but it does not tend to attack the nasal passages quite as forcibly. Certainly it can be considered as much of an acquired taste as bleu cheese, though. Once cured, the eggs can be eaten straight from the shell as an appetizer or in hot dish preparations.

The origins of *pei dan* are murky, and no one is sure how such an unlikely recipe came to be, but there is an apocryphal story that there was once a tea shop owner

Homemade *Haam Dan*

To make a brine, the ratio is usually 1½ cups salt dissolved in 5 cups of water for a dozen eggs scrubbed clean, with the shell on. The eggs are then gently placed into a gallon container with the brine for one month, ideally with the eggs rotated once every four days.

who raised a large flock of ducks. The tea shop was along a well-traveled road so the owner went through large amounts of tea and burned a lot of wood boiling water for thirsty travelers. In a hurry to serve customers, he just threw the used tea leaves on top of his pile of wood ash throughout the day. The pile grew quite large before he finally got around to cleaning it up. In the meantime, his ducks, liking the warm pile, laid some of their eggs there. As the pile was constantly disturbed by additions of tea and ash, the ducks lost track of some eggs. When the tea shop owner finally got around to cleaning up his garbage, he noticed the buried eggs. He cracked one open, was curious enough to hazard a sample, decided it tasted pretty good, and *pei dan* was invented.

The curing process was undoubtedly used to preserve surplus eggs for later use, an important option in the days before refrigeration and when other sources of protein were considered luxuries by most of the population. Chinese cuisine is characterized by a huge variety of preserved foods—meats, seafood, fruits, vegetables, grains, and eggs are preserved by smoking, salting, sugaring, steeping, picking, drying, and soaking in soy sauce. It should not be surprising then that the Chinese have more than one way—or reason—to preserve an egg. Eggs cured in one's own urine for seven days and consumed for a course of three months were considered to be a cure for chronic asthma, but this remedy is no longer common and was never the only prescription available to asthma sufferers. During the Tang and Sung dynasties (618–907 CE and 960–1279 CE, respectively), juice extracted from the

bark of a chestnut-like tree from southern China was mixed into brine to preserve duck eggs, which would turn dark brown in the process. A type of fermented egg is made by gently cracking the shell and placing the eggs into a fermenting mass of cooked rice mixed with salt. The similarity to alcoholic beverage production is reflected in the name of this type of egg: *zao dan*, or wine eggs. The product has a predictably boozy quality and can be eaten as is or cooked first. Preservation by salt is the other main example.

With salted eggs, again, duck eggs are those most commonly salted, but chicken and even quail eggs can also be used. Duck eggs tend to spoil faster than chicken eggs, which may explain why they are more often the subject of preservation. Ducks are also more geographically restricted than chickens as the former need to be close to a body of water, posing more hurdles to the transportation of fresh eggs. Salt-eggs are known as *haam dan* in Cantonese or *xián dàn* in Mandarin. The process for salting the eggs is much more straightforward than that of *pei dan*—the eggs are soaked in a brine for 30 days, or are packed in damp salted charcoal—and therefore it is quite common for people to make their own at home using the brine method. The resulting *haam dan* are not nearly as exotic-looking as *pei dan*. The white remains white but becomes firm, while the yolk turns a bright orange-yellow. The yolk is usually dry and crumbly, but home-cooked versions, which are generally fresher, can remain moist and creamy. Salt-eggs are steamed or boiled before consumption.

The most common and simplest way to prepare *pei dan* is simply sliced into wedges (this is most easily done with a piece of string or a wire) and seasoned with soy sauce, sesame oil, minced fresh or pickled ginger, and occasionally a dash of chili oil. A common hot preparation for the eggs, beloved of many Chinese and considered comfort food, is by mixing chunks into a bowl of hot steaming *congee,* a Chinese rice porridge commonly eaten for breakfast or as a light meal, with thinly sliced pork. In Taiwan, *pei dan* are often eaten diced over rice as a condiment or in a cold side dish where they are sprinkled over cold silken tofu with spring onions, soy sauce, and a drop of sesame oil. At a formal banquet, *pei dan* may appear sliced as one of the first courses, *lahng poon* (cold platter), which is composed of various cold meats (pork, beef, and chicken) and tomatoes with a sprinkle of sugar on them. *Pei dan* even makes the occasional appearance in bakeries, where they are encased in pastry with sweet lotus-seed paste.

Haam dan's simplest preparation is steamed over rice and eaten plain. The saltiness of the egg makes it the perfect counterpoint for plain white rice, which can be sweet when eaten alone. They are also used in congee, but unlike *pei dan*, *ham dan* are commonly found in Chinese pastries. The best-known example of this would be moon cakes, which are lotus seed paste-filled cakes eaten during the Autumn Moon Festival. Traditionally, a salted egg yolk is placed in the middle of each cake to symbolize the full moon, although versions without the yolk are available for those who like their sweets to stay sweet. The same lotus-seed paste and salted egg yolk combination also makes an appearance in Chinese bride cakes, this time encased in a flaky yellow pastry. The cakes are traditionally purchased by the groom's family and given to the bride's family. Her family then distributes the cakes to friends and family as a means of announcing the upcoming nuptials. *Haam dan* also occur in the more everyday form of stuffed rice dumplings, similar to Mexican tamales. The dumplings (about the size of a fist, but can be larger) are made of glutinous rice stuffed with pork, mung beans, Chinese sausage, and *haam dan*. Wrapped in lotus leaves, tied with string, and steamed, these dumplings are a meal unto themselves.

In Chinese markets, *pei dan* can often be found with the clay and straw still packed around each egg, and they are often stored in the urns where they were cured. In the United States, the clay shell is removed before the eggs are packed into cardboard or Styrofoam cartons of four, where they may be found on the shelf with other dry goods. *Haam dan* in China can be found resting in their brine in barrels, like pickles, and in the United States are similarly packaged in cartons of four. Both types of eggs are sometimes individually vacuum-packed in plastic before being placed inside the carton.

1,000-Year Egg Congee with Pork

Ingredients

1 cup rice (long grain varieties work best), rinsed
4 quarts water
1 tbsp salt
1 tbsp vegetable oil
1 lb. boneless pork loin
Chicken, pork, or beef bones (optional, for flavor)

4 1,000-year eggs
Fresh ginger
Scallions
Salt and white pepper to taste

1. Marinate the washed rice in the salt and oil for at least 10 minutes and up to 30 minutes.
2. Set the 4 quarts of water to boil in a large stockpot.
3. Set another, smaller pot of water to boil and par-boil the pork loin and bones, if using. Skim off the scum that rises to the surface of the pot as you simmer the meat. When no more scum collects, drain off the water and set the meat aside.
4. Peel the ginger and slice into fine matchsticks. Wash and trim the ends off the scallions; chop into pinky finger-length segments. Crack open the eggs, remove the shells, and slice into chunks with a piece of string or wire. Set ginger, scallions, and eggs aside.
5. Once the water in the stockpot comes to a boil, add the rice. Bring the pot back to a boil and add the pork loin and bones. Reduce the heat to a simmer.
6. Cook the pork for approximately 20 minutes until it is cooked through, stirring the congee occasionally. Remove the pork from the pot but leave the bones. Allow pork loin to cool before cutting into thin slices or chunks, depending on your preference, and set aside.
7. Continue simmering the congee for another 1½ to 2 hours, stirring occasionally to keep the bottom from burning, until the rice blooms and the individual grains become less distinct.

Add more water if the congee looks like it's running out of water before the rice has fully bloomed. Toward the end of the cooking process, water can be added to adjust the consistency. Like oatmeal, some people prefer thick, while others like a thin gruel.

8. About 10 minutes before serving, remove the bones. Add the pork loin, ginger, and chunks of egg. Add salt and white pepper to taste.
9. Serve immediately with scallions as garnish.

Further Reading

Bladholm, L. *The Asian Grocery Store Demystified.* Los Angeles: Renaissance Books, 1999.

Chang, K., and E. N. Anderson. *Food in Chinese Culture: Anthropological and Historical Perspectives.* New Haven, CT: Yale University Press, 1977.

McGee, H. *On Food and Cooking: The Science and Lore of the Kitchen.* Rev. ed. New York: Scribner, 2004.

Zhao, Z., and G. Ellis. *The Healing Cuisine of China: 300 Recipes for Vibrant Health and Longevity.* Rochester, VT: Healing Arts Press, 1998.

Karen Taylor

Tripe

Tripe, the stomach lining of a cow, is a form of offal. Animal innards have come to be considered delicacies, but at one time, they were an important part of the human diet. It is likely that innards or offal came to be valuable because they are nutritionally and calorically dense, making them vitally important for survival in harsh conditions or where food sources were inconsistent or insecure. From an evolutionary standpoint, it makes sense that these would become prized morsels over the course of human development. Tripe, specifically, would have provided the biggest bang for a caveman's buck since the stomach lining of a cow is voluminous and the tripe of a single cow can provide sustenance for a large number of people. People's reactions to tripe usually fall into one of two camps, either you love it or you detest it. Interestingly, the word tripe in the modern vernacular has become synonymous with something worthless, nonsense, or rubbish, particularly in British slang.

Tripe used for culinary purposes usually comes from cows, although the tripe of sheep, goats, deer, and pigs can be used this way as well. Cow stomachs are comprised of four separate chambers; beef tripe is usually made from the first three chambers, the rumen, the reticulum, and the omasum. The rumen or inner lining of the first stomach is considered bland in flavor and is rarely used as a main ingredient, rather, it is used in strongly flavored dishes like haggis and head cheese, where its bland flavor is less likely to compete with the much stronger flavors of the key ingredients. Honeycomb tripe, made from the reticulum and so named because of its honeycombed appearance, is considered a delicacy and is the tripe most often used in cooking. Green tripe, made from the omasum, isn't actually green. Grey in color, it is called green because of its very high chlorophyll content. This type of tripe is used primarily for feeding animals, especially dogs. Dog breeders praise green tripe for its ability to nourish the skin, improve coat luster and color, support dental health, and increase vigor. This tripe is considered unfit for human consumption as its odor tends to be offensive to humans, but dogs love it.

Tripe isn't just good for canine health; honeycomb tripe provides solid nutrition as it is reported to be rich in potassium, calcium, and trace minerals, all of which are essential for heart and muscle function, and bone health. Tripe is also an excellent source of high-quality protein, necessary for the building of muscle. In terms of calories and fat content, it is comparable to pork and beef, though it is somewhat lower in saturated fat. It's also noted for its aphrodisiac properties. This is a popular selling point with tripe vendors in Europe, who claim that good tripe can lead to a fourfold increase in sex drive.

A tripe and onion dish in China. (© Wxin | Dreamstime.com)

Food doesn't just sustain people, it's also symbolic in many ways. In certain tribes in the Niger region of Africa, marriage customs dictate that the tripe and intestines of the wedding feast animal are given to the bride to promote fertility. In some Native American cultures, tripe soup figures prominently in religious ceremonies as a sacred food. We can even find mention of tripe in ancient writings such as Homer's *Odyssey*, where tripe was served to the guests of an important banquet.

Among its other properties, tripe is lauded in Mexico as a hangover remedy. Prepared as a hearty stew, *menudo* provides a hefty dose of the protein and fat necessary to make a speedy recovery from a night of excess. Beware, though, tripe and *tripas* are two entirely different things, and one is often mistaken for the other by tourists. Tripas are the small intestines of various animals, something akin to the chitterlings popular in the southern United States.

Tripe is enjoyed in most of the countries of the world, from Europe to Asia to Africa, and everyone seems to have their own way of preparing it. It is such a popular dish in Porto, Portugal, that the residents thereof are referred to as *tripeiros*. Common to all cultures is the preparation required in preparing tripe for culinary use. Before it reaches the marketplace, the stomach is boiled in order to separate it from the lining. The lining is then bleached in order to make it more appealing, as it is an unappetizing brownish-green in its natural state. Bleaching improves appearance, but takes away from the flavor of the tripe. After the bleaching is done, it's off to the market and that's where you'll find it in the meat case

of your local supermarket. Tripe is easily found in supermarkets of ethnic neighborhoods. It can also be found in butcher shops and specialty stores.

At home, the tripe must be thoroughly washed so that the rinse water runs clear and all grittiness is removed before cooking. In whatever manner the tripe is to be prepared, it must be cooked for 2 to 3 hours in order to tenderize it. Because of the need to cook it for long periods of time, this is not your average dinner selection. Oftentimes, tripe is reserved for large family functions or special occasions. Also due to the long cooking time, it is typically prepared in soups or stews, though it can also be battered and fried, sautéed, or made into sausage. In fact, most breakfast sausages sold in the United States use tripe as a filler. Tripe has earned a terrible reputation for being slimy and chewy. Nothing could be further from the truth. Properly cooked, tripe is tender, with just a little resistance and its honeycombed texture makes it great for holding sauces. The recipe below is a hearty Puerto Rican stew of tripe and root vegetables in a rich tomato-based sauce.

Mondongo (Tripe Stew)

Ingredients

2 lb. pork tripe, cleaned and trimmed

6 white potatoes, quartered

4 green bell peppers, finely chopped

2 onions, finely chopped

8 to 10 cups water

½ lb. calabaza (Caribbean pumpkin), peeled and diced

½ lb. batata (sweet potato), peeled and diced

½ lb. ñame (yam), peeled and diced

½ cup green olives

3 tbsp tomato paste

2 tbsp olive oil

1 to 2 tbsp garlic, minced

1 tsp cumin

1 tsp ground oregano

2 to 3 lemons (limes may be substituted)

1. Boil the tripe in ½ gallon of salted water 2 to 3 hours or until tender.
2. Rinse with the juice of 2 to 3 lemons. Final rinse with cold water. Cut into bite-sized pieces.
3. Heat olive oil in a stew pot or Dutch oven. Add the tripe and the rest of the ingredients to heated oil. Add 8 cups of water. Cook on low heat 30 to 45 minutes or until all the ingredients are tender. Add water sparingly, as needed. Salt to taste.

Serve over a bed of white rice with sliced avocado and/or *tostones* (fried green plantains).

Further Reading

Houlihan, Marjorie. *Tripe: A Most Excellent Dish*. Devon, UK: Prospect Books, 2011.

1001 Cooks. *Brains and Brawn . . . Trotters and Tripe: Forgotten and Forbidden Foods from Old Cookbooks*. Raleigh, NC: Lulu, 2011.

Hayley Figueroa

Tulip

The tulip is a bulbous plant that flowers in spring and originates from the mountainous areas in Europe, Asia, and Africa. At present, many wild, and more than 5,000 cultivated varieties, are known. The tulip is best known as an ornamental garden plant, a potted plant, and for its fresh cut flowers. The tulip stem with its lance-shaped green leaves, mostly erect, support the flute or bell-shaped flowers that usually come in a great variety of red, yellow, orange, pink, or white colors.

The plant's scientific name, *Tulipa*, has been known since the mid-1500s, when the plant reached Western Europe via Turkey (Constantinople), and because of the resemblance, its common and scientific name directly derive from the Turkish hat, the *tuliban*. Tulips especially gained popularity because the Flemish botanist Carolus Clusius (1526–1609) introduced and spread tulip varieties among fellow botanists in Europe. In and around the 1600s, and especially in the Low Countries, this resulted in tulips rapidly gaining popularity, eventually resulting in a Dutch tulip mania where in 1637 astronomically high sums were paid for tulip bulbs. The cultivation of tulip flowers and bulbs is an important export industry in the Netherlands, where the (orange) tulip became one of the country's emblems.

All parts of tulips are on record as edible. Apart from the flowers (or petals), the leaves, stems, buds, and bulbs need to be well cooked before consumption. Prior to the 1500s, records make no mention of the preparation and consumption of tulips as food. Clusius probably was the first to research and report the tulip's edibility. He, among others, describes how, in 1570, a merchant tried eating sugarcoated tulip bulbs.

It wasn't until the 20th century that tulip bulbs probably were first used as a food extensively. During World War II (1940–1945), the Dutch government announced that due to the starch content, tulip bulbs were nutritious and suited as famine food, and even started to provide tulip bulb recipes. During the *Hongerwinter* (the hunger winter of 1944/1945) many Dutch people are said to have survived by preparing and eating typical Dutch soups, hotchpotches, and pancakes with the still available tulip bulbs. Postwar, the tulip bulb became the symbol of the Hongerwinter.

The American poet Ezra Pound is on record as having eaten a table's floral centerpiece, one tulip after the other. The taste of tulip petals, and probably also those Pound ate in 1931, is many times described as having a fresh pea, bean, or cucumber-like flavor. The consumption of raw tulip petals is most probably a British invention. Most commonly, the petals are used as a decoration in salads or sandwiches, and the tulip flowers are stuffed with a filling of shrimp, chicken, egg, or potato salads. Nowadays, recipes for tulip petal vinegar can be found. For all recipes, the use of organically grown tulips is advisable, as flowers from the flower shop are not intended for consumption.

Dutch **Hongerwinter** *Tulip Bulb Pancakes*

Ingredients

5 tulip bulbs
1 tbsp flour
1 small onion
Salt and pepper to taste
2 tbsp vegetable oil (for pan-frying)

1. Remove the outer skins of the tulip bulbs, and shred the white parts with a grater.
2. Clean the onion and chop it very small.
3. Mix the onion, grated bulbs, flour, salt, and pepper in a bowl.
4. Heat the oil in a flat pan. Use a spoon to dollop out 3 heaps of batter in the pan. Flatten the heaps with a fork, and bake the little pancakes for 3 to 4 minutes on each side until golden brown.

Tulip Flowers with Egg-Stuffing

Ingredients

4 red tulip flowers
4 eggs
2 tbsp melted butter
1 tbsp (whipping) cream
Salt and pepper to taste

1. Preheat the oven to 325°F.
2. Rub 4 small ramekins or espresso coffee cups with 1 tbsp of melted butter.
3. Carefully remove the pollen and stigmas from the base of the flowers. In a large bowl, beat the eggs, butter, and cream. Season with salt and pepper.
4. Divide the mixture in the ramekins. Bake in the preheated oven, until the egg-mixture has set, approximately 12 to 15 minutes. Remove from the oven, allow 2 to 3 minutes to set, and carefully slide the set eggs into the flowers. Serve cold or lukewarm.

Further Reading

Creasy, Rosalind. *The Edible Flower Garden.* Berkeley, CA: Periplus Editions. 1999.

Missel, Liesbeth. *Sources on the Dutch Tulip History.* The Netherlands, Wageningen UR Library. http://library.wur.nl/desktop/tulp/history.html.

Karin Vaneker

Turtle

The term *turtle* refers to three types of reptiles: sea turtles (that live at sea, coming ashore only to lay eggs); terrapins (that live in fresh or brackish water near sea coasts); and tortoises (land or freshwater species, such as snapping turtles).

People eat turtles on every continent except Antarctica. Early European settlers in North America noted the abundance of turtles. Coastal Native Americans ate turtles to the point that they were called the buffaloes of the Caribbean, comparing them to the usefulness of buffalo to inland Native Americans.

Many ships carried live turtles, kept on the deck or in tanks. Turtles can go for a long time without food, so the crew could kill a turtle for fresh meat when far from land. The meat contains vitamins that kept the sailors from getting scurvy. Ships also carried salted turtle meat.

In the 1700s, ships brought live turtles from the Americas to England in wooden tanks on their decks. Because turtles were so large, restaurants or public houses were the major purchasers. Turtle meat doesn't keep well, so must be cooked as soon as the turtle is killed. To attract enough people to eat the turtle, they published newspaper notices saying they would be cooking one.

In North America, also, taverns were major purchasers of turtles. They put on popular entertainments known as turtle barbecues, turtle frolics, or turtle feasts, where people spent the day eating turtle and indulging in leisure pastimes such as drinking tea or fishing. Ships carrying turtles from the West Indies brought other ingredients for the feast, especially rum and limes for making punch. At a time when domesticated meat was not readily available, turtle meat added variety to the diet.

For a long time, Europeans considered turtles an English dish, and both France and Spain eschewed turtle meat because of their political disagreements with the British. It was not until the early 1900s that they appeared on menus of luxury restaurants on the continent.

People considered turtle soup healthful and easy to digest. It was served as invalid food, and also as the first course at banquets, to prepare the stomach for a heavy meal. It is usually highly spiced (for example, with sherry, capsicums, ginger, cloves, and nutmeg). Opinions varied about the best recipe: should one use only turtle meat for broth, or use beef as well? Should one add sherry during cooking, after cooking, or not at all? Some connoisseurs feel that sherry overpowers the turtle's musky taste (which, to others, might be a good thing) and use wine instead.

Baltimore and Philadelphia competed over the merits of their recipes for terrapin soup. The Baltimore style contained salt, pepper, and Madeira, while the Philadelphia version used butter and cream. In 1893, "an impartial jury" decided in favor of Baltimore's recipe.

Canned turtle meat became available in middle 1800s, and canned turtle soup by 1882. By the mid-1900s, exporters sent refrigerated turtle meat from the Americas to Europe.

For approximately 200 years, the Lord Mayor of London's annual banquet included turtle soup. In 1971, environmentalists convinced then Lord Mayor Sir

Edward Howard to stop serving it. An earlier description of the banquet stated, "eighty tureens of clear and half again as many of thick turtle soup comprise perhaps the most characteristic of the *plats du jour*" (Black and White Budget, 1901).

Turtle was considered an upper-class food in the early 1900s, becoming one of the most expensive foods in America by 1911. Currently, turtles have an interesting dichotomy: they are considered epicurean fare for sophisticated diners, but also inexpensive fare for rural people who hunt them. In some rural areas, people serve turtle soup at special occasions such as church fairs. While many participants are not enthusiastic about eating turtles, they are a link to the area's traditional foods.

Buddhists and Hindus prohibit eating turtles because they are venerated; Muslims and Jews prohibit eating turtles because they are considered unclean. On the other hand, in the 17th century, the Vatican ruled that turtles were fish, so Catholics could eat them during Lent. Food taboos in Hawaii prohibited women from eating turtles and from cooking them (perhaps fearing they would taste while cooking?) (Perl, 1965). Since turtles often live to a great age, the Chinese consider them symbolic of long life, and they serve them at birthday celebrations.

There are 300 turtle species, of which most are edible. In some cases, a species' meat is not edible, but its eggs are. Green sea turtle makes the best soup, but it is now illegal to export it.

Cooks sometimes keep turtles for several days before slaughter, feeding them grain, vegetables, and/or clean water, to cleanse their alimentary system. Howard

Micham suggests, "It's best to use live turtles, but dressing and preparing them is a diabolical and macabre business. If you're fainthearted . . . just buy some frozen or canned turtle meat at a good fish market or gourmet specialty store," advice echoed by other authors (Micham, 1978).

Many books glibly explain how to kill a snapping turtle: get the turtle to grab a stick, and use it to pull its head out of the shell enough to chop the head off. While one author suggests, "With a little practice, 5 or 10 minutes will suffice for [dressing] a 10-pound snapper" (Ashbrook and Sater, 1945, 300); another, based on her experience, disagrees. "The traditional way of killing a snapper is to allow it to snap onto a stick, then extend the head and chop it off with an axe. . . . Sounds easy, doesn't it? Our turtle would not cooperate. It had to be shot in the head" (Bashline, 1979, 57).

Lee Edwards Benning describes what an early American housewife went through to kill a 60-pound turtle, whose jaws could "crush a human arm" ("retractable heads have a tendency in strange surroundings to stay retracted"), concluding, "And I'm not sure but that women secretly welcomed the news that it was becoming more and more difficult to get sea turtles" (Benning, 1992, 117).

Another method for killing a turtle is to lay it on its back on hot ashes or coals; when it gets overheated, it sticks out its legs and head in an attempt to escape, and the head is then cut off. Other methods include boiling them to death, and shooting them.

Those who kill a turtle might be spooked by the fact that, having a primitive nervous system, the turtle's body almost refuses to die. Its jaws may still snap; the heart may still beat; if on its feet, it may still walk. Freshly butchered turtle meat in a skillet may twitch because the nerves still react to heat.

A cook who has killed a turtle and drained its blood must then butcher it. This involves sawing off the bottom shell, skinning the legs and neck, and removing the gallbladder (next to the liver), and any part of the liver the gall bladder has touched. As turtle meat is very perishable, one must freeze any meat one doesn't plan to use immediately, but without the fat, as it gives the meat a gamy taste.

Turtle meat is chewy and fibrous, like well-cooked pulled pork (Weil, 2006). Female turtles' meat tastes better than that of males, and is considered best at the time when they lay their eggs. Therefore, turtle steaks are from females; meat from males goes into soup. People have compared turtle meat to veal or chicken. Many sea turtles (but not the green turtle) have a somewhat unpleasant fishy taste.

Turtles have both white and dark meat. Gourmets especially prize the neck's white meat, the flipper meat, and two white fillets that rest against the upper shell. Various sources state that there are seven (or nine) types of meat (or muscle) within a turtle, each having a specific taste. In a simpler classification, cooks can substitute white meat in recipes for veal; red meat for beef; and the flippers for chicken. Many authors consider the calipash and calipee the best parts. Calipash is a green fatty jelly inside the turtle's upper shell; calipee is a yellow fatty jelly inside the lower shell. Cooks add cubes of these delicacies to turtle soups and stews.

There are thousands of recipes for turtle meat. Cooks can boil, bake, roast, sauté, fry, deep fry, steam, grill, bread, cream, curry, or fricassee it. They can make steaks, stew, soup, stroganoff, meatloaf, or vindaloo from it. A selection of soup recipes gives an idea of the variety: Brandywine Snapper Soup, Cajun Swamp Turtle Soup, Camp Town Turtle Soup, Chinese Turtle Soup, Colonial Virginia Turtle Soup, Creole Turtle Soup, English Turtle Consommé, Green Turtle Soup au Sherry, Key West Turtle Soup, Lady Curzon Soup, Maryland Diamondback Terrapin Soup, Mermaid Soup, Mexican Turtle Soup, Philadelphia Snapper Soup, Swamp Turtle Soup au Rhum, Tennessee Turtle Soup, Turtle Soup Gulf Coast, Turtle Soup Louisiana, and Turtle Soup New Orleans.

Turtle herbs, a mixture of basil, chervil, fennel, marjoram, and savory (with some variations), give the characteristic flavor to turtle soup, and also to turtle sauce, used to give turtle flavor to calf's head and beef tongue.

Female turtles sometimes contain eggs. The eggs have a membrane rather than a shell and have almost no white. Anything one can do with a chicken egg, one can do with a turtle egg: hard boil it, fry it, and make it into an omelet. A Brazilian recipe prescribes creaming the eggs to the consistency of butter and spreading them on toast.

Turtles are good sources of protein. The diamondback terrapin is 18.6 percent protein and green turtles are 19.8 percent protein (Schwabe, 1979). The meat is low in fat and cholesterol, and low calorie compared with beef.

Beware of information about availability and use of turtles dating from before

1973, when the Endangered Species Act classified most sea turtles as either threatened or endangered. Overfishing in the 1800s and early 1900s drove them almost to extinction. Despite efforts to bring up their numbers, ocean pollution and building on their nesting areas still cause problems for them. Turtles also die from eating garbage (e.g., plastic bags) in the ocean. In 2010, a massive oil spill in the Gulf of Mexico destroyed sea turtle nesting areas and killed many turtles. In response to their endangered status, some areas have changed their definition of turtles from food to tourist attraction, and use turtles as part of an ecotourism movement.

Most turtles people eat in the United States are snapping turtles. Being nocturnal, they are hard to catch, and it is illegal to catch them in some states. Their strong bite makes them dangerous; sources invariably describe their reputed ability to bite a broom handle in half.

In the United States, one can purchase meat of farm-raised snapping turtles and alligator snapping turtles (wild alligator snappers may weigh over 100 pounds, but farm-raised ones are harvested at 10 to 12 pounds). Look for turtle meat in supermarkets, gourmet stores, and Chinese markets. It is available frozen or canned. Snapping turtle soup is a specialty of the famous Bookbinder's Restaurant in Philadelphia; those who don't live nearby can purchase Bookbinder's Restaurant-Style Snapper Soup via the Internet.

Turtles have supplied other products besides food. In the time of oil lamps, turtle oil was used for lighting; it is still used in food and cosmetics. Turtle shell, especially from the hawksbill, which has a mottled appearance, is used to make hair ornaments and decorative boxes. The shell can also be made into cooking pots; Native Americans made shells into drums and rattles. Turtle skins are tanned into leather. Chinese medicine uses turtle jelly, made from the shell, as a cure for cancer and as a tonic. In some areas, people consider turtle eggs and the turtle's penis to be aphrodisiacs.

Mock Turtle Soup

A discussion of turtles would be incomplete without mentioning Mock Turtle Soup. Because turtles were so large and expensive, soon after turtle soup became popular, recipes for mock turtle soup appeared. These use a calf's head, as the brains are similar to turtle meat, plus the calf's liver and heart. The cook boils the head and other meat, then removes them from the broth, and spices and thickens it. Before serving, chopped meat and brains are returned to the broth. In *American Cookery*, Amelia Simmons gives a recipe for a turtle casserole (see below) and follows it with a recipe "To dress a Calve's [*sic*] Head Turtle fashion."

Although calf's brains substitute for turtle meat in mock turtle soup, most people who are squeamish about eating turtle are probably also squeamish about eating brains. Mock turtle soup is cheaper to make than turtle soup, but it is a long process, and it is difficult to find a calf's head. Beef can also stand in for turtle meat in soup and stew recipes. The taste is popular enough that there are even vegetarian versions. *Vegetarian Times* published a recipe for

"No-Turtle Soup," which substitutes tofu and textured vegetable protein for meat.

Recipe

Amelia Simmons, in *American Cookery*, gives detailed instructions for dressing a turtle, specifying how to separate and prepare its various inner parts, and then gives a recipe for casseroles. As was typical in recipes of the time, she gives only general directions, and does not include specific amounts of ingredients (spelling regularized):

"The meat being thus prepared and laid separate for seasoning; mix two parts of salt or rather more, and one third part of cayenne pepper, black pepper, and a nutmeg and mace pounded fine and mixed all together; the quantity to be proportioned to the size of the turtle, so that in each dish there may be about three spoonfuls of seasoning to every twelve pounds of meat; your meat being thus seasoned, get some sweet herbs, such as thyme, savory, etc., let them be dried and rubbed fine, and having provided some deep dishes to bake it in, which should be of the common brown ware, put in the coarsest part of the meat, put a quarter pound of butter at the bottom of each dish, and then put some of each of the several parcels of meat, so that the dishes may be all alike and have equal portions of the different parts of the turtle, and between each laying of meat strew a little of the mixture of sweet herbs, fill your dishes within an inch and a half or two inches of the top; boil the blood of the turtle, and put into it, then lay on forcemeat balls of veal, highly seasoned with the same seasoning as the turtle; put in each dish a gill [five fluid ounces] of Madeira wine, and as much water as it will conveniently hold, then break over it five or six eggs to keep the meat from scorching at the top, and over that shake a handful of shredded parsley, to make it look green, when done put your dishes into an oven made hot enough to bake bread, and in an hour and a half, or two hours (according to the size of the dishes) it will be sufficiently done."

Further Reading

Ashbrook, Frank G., and Edna N. Sater. *Cooking Wild Game: Meat from Forest, Field and Stream and How to Prepare It for the Table—432 Recipes.* New York: Orange Judd, 1945.

Bashline, Sylvia G. *The Bounty of the Earth Cookbook: How to Cook Fish, Game and Other Wild Things.* New York: Winchester Press, 1979.

Benning, Lee Edwards. *The Cook's Tales: Origins of Famous Foods and Recipes.* Old Saybrook, CT: Globe Pequot Press, 1992

Bronner, Simon J. *Grasping Things: Folk Material Culture and Mass Society in America.* Lexington: University Press of Kentucky, 1986.

Crawford, Dez. "On the Bayou." *Vegetarian Times,* July 1991, 30–34, 36.

Hibler, Janie. *Wild About Game: 150 Recipes for Cooking Farm-Raised and Wild Game—from Alligator and Antelope to Venison and Wild Turkey.* New York: Broadway Books, 1998.

Mariani, John F. *The Dictionary of American Food & Drink.* New Haven, CT: Ticknor & Fields, 1983.

Micham, Howard. *Creole Gumbo and All That Jazz: A New Orleans Seafood Cookbook.* Reading, MA: Addison-Wesley, 1978.

Parsons, James. "Sea Turtles and Their Eggs." In *The Cambridge World History of Food*, edited by Kenneth F. Kiple and Kriemhild Coneè Ornelas, 1:567–573. New York: Cambridge University Press, 2000.

Perl, Lila. *Red-Flannel Hash and Shoo-Fly Pie: American Regional Foods and Festivals*. Cleveland: World, 1965.

Schwabe, Calvin W. *Unmentionable Cuisine*. Charlottesville: University Press of Virginia, 1979.

Simmonds, Peter Lund. *The Curiosities of Food; or, The Dainties and Delicacies of Different Nations Obtained from the Animal Kingdom*. Facsimile of the 1859 edition with an introduction by Alan Davidson. Berkeley, CA: Ten Speed Press, 2001.

Simmons, Amelia. *The First American Cookbook: A Facsimile of "American Cooking," 1796*. New York: Dover, 1984.

"Turtle Soup." *Black and White Budget* 6, no. 110 (November 16, 1901): 229.

Weil, Christa. *Fierce Food: The Intrepid Diner's Guide to the Unusual, Exotic, and Downright Bizarre*. New York: Penguin Group, 2006.

Christine Crawford-Oppenheimer

U

Urchin

From the Latin word for hedgehog *urchin*, *erizo*, and *riccio* are all names for the spiny delicacy that pops up on plates all around the world. The urchin belongs to the phylum called Echindomera, which includes sea cucumbers and starfish. The typical urchin ranges between 6 and 12 centimeters in diameter, although some can achieve breadths of up to 36 centimeters. While many species are black, urchins can come in pink, green, or even exhibit stripes. The edible portion of the urchin is found inside the shell (called the *test*) and resembles sections of a tangerine. From light yellow to deep orange, the five sections are not roe as is commonly thought, but rather the urchin's sex organs or gonads. Sea urchins are found all over the world in shallow, rocky waters but can live up to 20 meters below the surface. Their unfriendly exterior and strong grasp on tidal rocks makes the urchin difficult prey to hunt. They are generally gathered by certified scuba divers, who can earn up to $1,000 a week in the trade, but in Korea, this is traditional women's work. The *naenyo*, or sea women are trained from childhood to dive up to 50 meters without the help of equipment to gather urchin, conch, and other floor-dwelling delicacies. Women are thought to be best suited to this job because they can withstand colder water than males, the ideal temperature for premium urchins.

The harvesting season ranges from September to April, so water temperatures remain low, producing a briny and buttery urchin. In warmer temperatures, the flesh becomes bitter and slimy.

In the United States, many people know urchin from the sushi bar by its Japanese name, *uni*. Commonly, the yellow gonad rests atop rice and is wrapped in seaweed. However, in Japan, this but one way of preparing an urchin. *Uni no kanten* is a traditional dish in which the gonad is suspended in *kanten*, also known as *agar agar*, a jelly-like substance made from seaweed, flavored with sake, soy, and dashi. Urchin is also used to make a clear soup called *inchigo-ni*, which literally translated, means strawberry boil because of the berry-like appearance the uni takes on when cooked. Urchin is considered a celebratory food, eaten during the winter holidays when it is in season. The Japanese consider it disrespectful to consume urchin when faced with a national tragedy; and in the face Emperor Hirohito's death in 1989 or a violent volcanic eruption for example, the urchin industry suffers financially.

Despite the warmer climate, the Philippians and New Zealand also feature urchin on regional menus. In a special Filipino preparation, the urchin's inedible insides are removed and the test is packed with white rice. The whole package is then steamed, and when the shell is carefully broken away from the rice, the five golden strips of gonad are left on the white sphere. Just to the south, Maori New Zealanders would submerge urchin or *kina* under fresh water for three weeks before it is eaten as a spread with butter on toast. Sometimes, kina was buried underground three-to-four months then eaten or wrapped in leaves re-buried. Today, urchin is spread on bread with lemon or mixed with olive oil and hollandaise sauce to make a dressing for fish dishes.

The Maori are not the only ancient culture to develop a taste for urchin. Both the Greeks and the Romans relished the spiked creature for its taste and ability to stimulate appetites. In Italy, the urchin was stuffed with oil, garum, pepper, and wine and then roasted, while in Greece the orange gonads were mixed with vinegar, sweet wine, parsley, and mint. In modern Europe too, urchin is popular. The French beat it into eggs to make omelets or bake it in tarts with onions and garlic, and the Portuguese cook it in a fire of pine needles. In northern Spain, urchin can be simply scooped out and spread straight onto olive oiled bread.

Although the American diet doesn't include a large enough amount of urchin to make a nutritional impact, in Japanese diets, *uni* is an important source of protein, vitamins A, B1, B2, E, and zinc. It is thought to help fight fatigue, prevent illness, and promote healthy skin.

Baked Sea Urchin

Ingredients

8 sea urchins
8 eggs
1 stick butter
Country bread

1. Preheat the oven to 450°F.
2. Cut a circular opening at the top of each sea urchin.
3. Break an egg into each urchin shell and add a tablespoon of butter in each
4. Cook for 8 to 10 minutes until egg white is set. Serve with country bread.

Further Reading

Kleiman, Dena. "Scorned at Home, Maine Sea Urchin Is a Star in Japan." *New York Times*, October 3, 1990. www.nytimes.com.

Lloyd, Nick. "Edible Sea Urchin." *Iberia Nature*. www.iberianature.com.

Moskin, Julia. "Escape From the Sushi Bar." *New York Times*, May 12, 2009. www.nytimes.com.

"Suggested Dishes and Nutrition of Sea Urchin." Kiku Fisheries Ltd. http://www.kikufisheries.com/recipes.php.

Eleanor Barczak

Urine

Urophagia, or the consumption of urine, isn't as unusual as one might think. Derived from the Old English *hlant,* lant, or aged urine, was used primarily as a cleaning agent. During the Middle Ages, one could go to a tavern and order some lant-glazed pastries and wash it down with some lanted or even double-lanted ale. In addition to ales and pastries, lant-based mouthwash was used. Using urine as a mouthwash is a practice that dates back to ancient Rome.

From centuries past, up until the early 1800s, dried deer urine was used as a leavening agent before the advent of baking powder. Deer urine, along with crushed antlers and hair, was known by several names, including hartshorn and baker's ammonia. Hartshorn, which can still be found in some pharmacies, was often used in the making of traditional German holiday cookies and was best used in hard pastries, as moister pastries allowed for the strong ammonia odor of the ingredient to remain in the food.

In modern times, there have been reports of dried urine being used as an exotic form of salt and to enhance the color of low-quality saffron. Recently, a drink called cow water (*gau jal*) has been developed in India where urine, both human and animal, is considered useful in ayurvedic medicine. In certain parts of India, one can even find packaged cow urine in some dairy shops.

While urine may not be on the ingredient list of everyone's favorite dish, it can be useful in a pinch. Many a survival story includes some mention of urine being used to stave off dehydration. Survivalist and military outfits have advocated the use of filtered and, to a lesser extent, unfiltered urine to prevent dehydration. The U.S. Army has even developed a pouch that can filter urine for the purpose of rehydrating field rations.

For some, drinking urine is not a last ditch survival strategy, but part of a daily regimen to promote health. For thousands of years, humans have ascribed healing properties to urine, promoting everything from drinking it to bathing in it.

References to urine therapy can be found in records from ancient Egypt, China, and India. It has been hailed as a cure or treatment for every conceivable disease from infertility to cancer. In fact, a Tibetan cure for infertility requires couples to drink one another's urine. Kids can get in on the act too; in Chinese medicine, the first urine of an infant, particularly a male infant, was considered to be very powerful and would be mixed with various herbs to create a tonic. Typically, one drinks from the first urine of the day, catching it midstream, and consuming it straight or mixing it with any number of ingredients to improve taste or boost health benefits. Former prime minister of India, Moraji Desai, did this for years and he lived to be 99 years old.

Perhaps this isn't as strange as it all sounds, considering that all of us started out in an amniotic sac that contains fluid, comprised, in part, of fetal urine.

For those who are curious, but can't seem to bring themselves to actually drink urine straight, it also happens to be an excellent fertilizer, due its rich nitrogen, phosphorus, and potassium content. Used as a fertilizer in a vegetable garden, it renders a fantastic crop. Some reports indicate that urine-fertilized crops out perform their commercially fertilized counterparts 4:1, and an added benefit is that tomatoes fertilized in this way tend to be higher in protein.

While the thought of drinking urine may turn the stomach and the smell is certainly off-putting, it is actually relatively sterile, though it may be contaminated with bacteria from an infection or along its path out of the body. There are even examples from history of its use to clean wounds when clean water was not available.

Even still, the Koryak, a tribe of indigenous people in Siberia, engage in a cultural practice where they consume mushrooms, which allow them to have spiritual visions. Ingestion of the urine of an intoxicated Koryak has nearly the same hallucinogenic effect as the mushrooms themselves and can induce or prolong intoxication. The less affluent of the tribe, who can't afford to maintain a supply of these mushrooms, sometimes consume the urine of their more prosperous neighbors in order to partake of the ritual.

Good Morning Smoothie

Ingredients

1 cup plain nonfat Greek yogurt
½ cup fresh fruit* (Choose the fruit according to taste or health properties. Bright colors are best.)
½ cup urine (first urine of the day, cooled)
2 tbsp sugar (honey or agave syrup can be substituted for sugar)
Ice cubes

1. Chop fruit into chunks if necessary (e.g., pineapple), reserving 1 to 3 pieces of fruit for garnish.
2. Place ingredients into blender. Blend well, adding ice until desired consistency is reached. Garnish with reserved fruit and serve immediately.

Use frozen fruit if fresh is not in season or easily accessible.

Further Reading

Kosuda, Shigeru, Shinako Katagiri, Wei Jey Ka, Shinichi Tominaga, and Shoichi Kusano. "Demonstration of the Ascending Colon on Tc-99m MDP Skeletal Imaging: Pitfall in Bone Scanning by a Faith Cure of Drinking Urine." *Clinical Nuclear Medicine* 25, no. 12 (December 2000): 1040–1042.

Hayley Figueroa

V

Vegemite and Marmite

Vegemite and marmite are food products that are made using leftover yeast from beer brewing. In vegemite, there is often also extract from vegetables. Vegemite was first produced in Australia. Marmite was first produced in the United Kingdom; however, a similar, but sweeter product with the same name was later produced in New Zealand. The New Zealand version of marmite differs only in the fact that caramel and sugar is added. The French term marmite means a metal or earthenware cooking vessel with a cover. Since the original marmite was packaged and sold in earthenware pots, this is how this product got its name. Vegemite has a salty, bitter, and malty flavor, and a sticky but smooth texture. British marmite has a very savory and salty flavor, with a similar texture to that of vegemite.

Vegemite and marmite are mainly eaten in Australia, the United Kingdom, and New Zealand. Other than in these countries, it has been difficult for both vegemite and marmite to attract a consumer base. Both vegemite and marmite are produced by autolysis, which is where the enzymes of the yeast break down its own cells. The liquid that is produced from this is then concentrated and seasoned.

Vegemite was invented in 1922 when Cyril P. Callister was hired by the Fred Walker Company. He was given the task of creating a usable byproduct from brewer's yeast. After months of work, the Australian chemist developed a salty, spreadable product. It was originally named Pure Vegetable Extract. The company decided to hold a contest in order to rename the spread. Vegemite was the winning name, and in 1923, stores began selling it. Marmite, on the other hand, was first produced in 1902 by an English company by the name of The Marmite Food Extract Company. The brewer's yeast that was used for the product came from Bass Brewery, another English company. In 1919, Sanitarium Health Food Company, located in New Zealand, began producing its distinct marmite (with the addition of sugar and caramel).

Vegemite and marmite are usually eaten spread on crackers, sandwiches, or toast, often as a breakfast food. They are both eaten as regularly in Australia, New Zealand, and the United Kingdom as peanut butter is in the United States.

Both vegemite and marmite are some of the highest natural sources of B vitamins. They both contain high levels of thiamine, riboflavin, niacin, and folic acid and are low in calories.

Vegemite and marmite are not only used as spreads. They are also used in countless recipes, such as this bean dip.

Bean Dip

Ingredients

1½ cloves garlic, minced
1 small red onion, small diced

Spreading the iconic Australian spread vegemite on to a slice of fresh bread. (© Jabiru | Dreamstime. com)

1 tsp chili powder

¼ tsp paprika

½ tsp cumin

A few pinches of freshly ground pepper

1½ tsp vegemite

10 oz. cooked kidney beans, drained

6 oz. cooked black beans, drained

5 Roma tomatoes, diced

2 tbsp fresh cilantro, chopped

1. Over medium heat, pour ¾ teaspoon of oil into a medium-sized pan.
2. Add in the first six ingredients, cooking until the onion has softened, about 3 minutes.
3. Turn the heat down to medium-low, and add the vegemite, kidney and black beans, and the tomatoes.
4. Stirring every once in a while, allow this mixture to cook for another 15 minutes. Remove from heat and add in the cilantro. Serve with your favorite tortilla chip.

Further Reading

"Calories in Kraft Vegemite." The Daily Plate. http://www.thedailyplate.com/nutrition-calories/food/kraft/vegemite.

Chapman, Dave, and James Kew. "The Marmite FAQ." The Marmite FAQ. http://www.spurgeon.org/~phil/marmite.htm.

"Marmite Yeast Extract Spread." The Daily Plate. http://www.thedailyplate.com/nutrition-calories/food/marmite/yeast-extract-spread.

Rolland, Jacques L., and Carol Sherman. "Marmite." *The Food Encyclopedia: Over 8,000*

Ingredients, Tools, Techniques, and People. Toronto: Robert Rose, 2006.

Rolland, Jacques L., and Carol Sherman. "Vegemite." *The Food Encyclopedia: Over 8,000 Ingredients, Tools, Techniques, and People.* Toronto: Robert Rose, 2006.

"Vegemite." Kraft Foods Australia. http://www.vegemite.com.au/vegemite/page?PagecRef=1.

Laura Mathews

Vieux Boulogne

Vieux Boulogne, also known as Sable du Boulonnais, is a soft cheese that is made from cow's milk. This cheese is in the same family as Munster cheese. It is washed with beer, which is a process that matures the cheese. The specific type of beer that is used to wash this cheese is Saint-Leonard beer. The cheese has a firm, orange rind that is spotted with mold. It is produced in the province of Normandy, which is located in northwestern France, along the English Channel. More specifically, it is produced in the Pas de Calais department of France, in the town of Boulogne sur Mer, which is between Blanc-Nez and Gris-Nez. The cows in this region of France live in pastures where the grass is plentiful and green, and the air is filled with salt, due to the proximity of the sea. The land in this area is typically wet, which is why this cheese has the ability to develop a type of fungus that most other cheeses cannot. Vieux Boulogne is unpasteurized and unpressed. It has been named the smelliest cheese in the world. This cheese gives off a very striking scent, often reminiscent of wet terrain, mushrooms, rotting or stinking leaves, or a farmyard. However, this odor comes only from the rind. Inside, the cheese is quite the opposite. If you can get past the smell of the rind, you'll find that the cheese itself is a rich, smooth cheese with a surprisingly mellow, yet fully developed flavor. It is classically formed into a square shape. This cheese is artisanal, which means that it is made by hand and in small amounts. Since it is not widely produced, it tends to be more expensive. The methods of production with artisanal cheeses typically remain the same, generation after generation. Phillipe Olivier was the first producer of Vieux Boulogne. He first showcased this cheese in 1982. Although he is still the main producer of this cheese, there are a few other smaller producers today.

Vieux Boulogne is mainly eaten in France, but is also enjoyed in England. However, it is rarely seen or sold outside of these two countries due to regulations that forbid it from being brought across international borders.

What gives the cheese its color and smell is the process of washing it with beer. This process ripens the rind of the cheese and helps to develop the necessary bacteria. When the bacteria in the beer come in contact with the milk enzymes of the rind, micro-organisms are produced, which let off a very strong odor (Brown, 2004). The cheese is then aged for 7 to 9 weeks, on average.

Vieux Boulogne was ruled the stinkiest cheese in the world in November of 2004 by a total of 19 judges, all of whom were members of a human olfactory panel, as well as one electronic nose. This experiment was hosted by the University of Cranfield. There were 15 total cheeses in this experiment, and Vieux Boulogne beat

A piece of Vieux Boulogne cheese. (AP Photo/ Sopexa, Simon Smith)

even Camembert, Roquefort, and Epoisses (Barkham).

Vieux Boulogne can be enjoyed by itself, and is commonly accompanied by bread and beer.

Further Reading

Barkham, Patrick. "Smelliest Cheese Honour." *Guardian*, November 26, 2004. http://www.guardian.co.uk/uk/2004/nov/26/research.highereducation.

Brown, Jonathan. "Le Grand Fromage: Why Vieux Boulogne Is the World's Smelliest Cheese." *Independent* (UK). November 26, 2004.

Nordqvist, Christian. "What Is the World's Smelliest Cheese? Vieux Boulogne." *Medical News Today*. November 30, 2004. http://www.medicalnewstoday.com/articles/17043.php.

Laura Mathews

W

Walrus Flipper

The indigenous peoples of Arctic Canada, Greenland, and Alaska commonly hunt the walrus (*Odobenus rosmarus*). These indigenous peoples were once collectively referred to as Eskimo, but in 1977, the term *Inuit* replaced the term *Eskimo* in Canada and Greenland. While the indigenous peoples of Alaska prefer to be called by their autonyms, for example the Inupiaq; they do not mind being collectively referred to as Eskimo. They do, however, object to being referred to as Inuit.

Both the Inuit and Eskimo eat many sea mammals, but the walrus has properties that are particularly adaptive for these northern hunters. Walrus meat is high in calories but is digested slowly. These properties of walrus meat allow the Inuit and Eskimos to remain out on the ice hunting for long periods of time without food.

When eating walrus, the blubber and meat is aged, boiled, or eaten raw, while the liver is generally eaten raw. The outer covering of the walrus, including the skin and blubber (called *maktaaq* among the Inuit), is also eaten raw or aged. More and more often, however, walrus meat is now being cooked before being eaten because the meat may contain trichinella, a tiny parasitic roundworm. Trichinella can cause trichinosis, a gastrointestinal illness with flu-like symptoms, which, in severe cases, can cause death. Those who prefer to eat their walrus meat raw are now storing the meat until it can be tested by laboratories for the presence of trichinella.

A traditional food treat among the Inuit and Eskimo is pickled walrus flipper, referred to as *utniq* among the Inupiaq of northwestern Alaska. Aged, fermented—pickled—walrus hide gets soft, juicy, and chewy and is said to be a delicious snack. The taste of the pickled walrus flippers has been likened to the taste of pickled pigs' feet.

To prepare this delicacy, the walrus flippers are first immersed in walrus blubber. They are then wrapped in walrus skin that is turned inside out. The traditional method of fermenting the walrus flippers is to place the meat in a grass-lined hole in the ground. In modern times, people use glass jars and plastic buckets and leave the containers in a shed to ferment.

Although utniq is a favorite dish, especially among the elders, it can be a dangerous food to eat because of the possibility of botulism. This is especially true when the non-traditional methods of fermentation are used. According to Dr. Tom Hennessy, Chief, Epidemiology Branch, Arctic Investigations Program, NCID, CDC, "making fermented foods in plastic containers with tight-fitting lids makes an ideal growing situation for the botulism germs."

Between 1975 and today, Alaska has had the highest rate of botulism of any state in America, and it is believed that this is due to the use of glass jars and plastic buckets for fermenting food. The eating of traditional foods is very important to many Arctic dwellers. Those who want to continue to enjoy pickled walrus are encouraged to use the traditional methods of fermenting food, which ideally keeps the meat cool (less than 37°F) and allows the air to circulate around the food.

Fermented Walrus Flipper

Ingredients

Desired number of walrus flippers
Salt
Rendered walrus blubber

1. Rinse the walrus flippers in fresh water that has been slightly salted; then immerse the walrus flipper in rendered (liquefied) walrus blubber until the flippers are well coated.
2. Place the flippers in a hole in the ground lined with fresh grass, cover the flippers with more fresh grass, and then cover the hole. Make sure that air can circulate around the meat. (Note: never place fermenting walrus flippers in a sealed plastic container as this can cause botulism.)
3. Leave for 2 weeks, more or less depending on the air temperature. The colder the air temperature, the longer the fermentation process takes.
4. Uncover and slice the flipper meat.

Further Reading

Centers for Disease Control and Prevention (CDC) Public Health Practice Program Office, Division of Media and Training Services. "Helping Hands: Keeping Your Family Safe From Botulism?" Public Health Training Network. Center for Disease Control, 2001. April 27, 2010. http://www2.cdc.gov/phtn/botulism/default/default.asp.

Fall, James A., et al. "Walrus Hunting at Togiak, Bristol Bay, Southwest Alaska." Native Knowledge. http://www.nativeknowledge.org///.htm.

"Fatal Botulism—Fermented Walrus Flipper." *State of Alaska Epidemiology Bulletin*. State of Alaska Health and Social Services. http://www.epi.alaska.gov///_01.htm.

Garner, Dwight. "Growing Up and Getting by in the Land of the Nine-Month Winter." *New York Times*, January 28, 2009. http://www.nytimes.com/2009/0½8/books/28garn.html.

Hensley, William L. Iggiagruk. *Fifty Miles From Tomorrow: A Memoir of Alaska and the Real People*. New York: Picador, 2009.

Schwatka, Frederick. *Nimrod in the North or Hunting and Fishing Adventures in the Arctic Regions*. New York: Cassell, 1885.

Laura P. Appell-Warren

Witchetty Grubs

Edible grubs, although considered disgusting by most Americans, are traditional foods in many cultures. Their nutritional value as sources of protein, minerals, and vitamins has been well documented. The Food and Agriculture Organization of the United Nations stated in 2004 that grubs, as well as other insects, should be considered an alternative food source as part of the efforts to increase food security in less developed countries.

Although cultures around the globe eat grubs, one of the most famous and well-publicized edible grubs is the Australian witchetty grub. Much of this popularity may come from the fact that witchetty grubs are considered *bush tucker*, foods native to Australia, and are therefore surrounded by a certain mystique. While bush tucker was seen as primitive and weird food by European Australians in the past, today this is changing as European Australians are cashing in on the mystique of bush tucker by offering eco tours during which bush tucker is prominently featured.

The name witchetty grub most commonly refers to the larvae of the large cossid moth (*Endoxyla leucomochla*), however, the name also applies to the larvae of other moths.

The witchetty grub has long been a staple in the diets of Aboriginal women and children. The witchetty grub feeds on the sap from the roots of acacia plants including the wichetty bush (*Acacia kempeana*), and are, therefore, dug up from the roots of these trees and bushes. Traditionally, witchetty grubs are eaten live and raw. In appearance, the grubs are large and white with a brown head. Their meat is rich in protein and high in calories. One large grub measuring about 4½ inches provides approximately 300 calories, 14 grams of protein, 24 grams of fat, and 3 grams of carbohydrates. Ten such grubs should provide all the nutrition an adult needs in a day. Raw witchetties have a subtle, slightly sweet almond- or peanut-like flavor and a liquid center. Witchetty grubs are often grilled over a fire. Many say they have a taste a bit like chicken or barbecued shrimp. Commercially made witchetty grub soup is available at Australian grocers.

Further Reading

Banjo, A.D., O.A. Lawal, and E.A. Songonuga. "The Nutritional Value of Fourteen Species of Edible Insects in Southwestern Nigeria." *African Journal of Biotechnology* 5, no. 3 (2006): 298–301.

Ellen, Roy. "Local Knowledge and Management of Sago Palm (*Metroxylon sagu rottboell*) Diversity in South Central Seram, Maluku, Eastern Indonesia." *Journal of Ethnobiology* 26, no. 2 (2006): 258–298.

Freeman, Catherine, and Deborah Mailman. *Going Bush: Adventures Across Indigenous Australia*. Oakland, CA: Lonely Planet, 2006.

Kruse, Maria, and Cheemin Kwon. "Edible Insects, Important Source of Protein in Central Africa: Nutritious, Income Generating, Biological Pest Control." *FAO Newsroom*. The Food and Agriculture Organization of the United Nations. http://www.fao.org/newsroom/en/news/2004/51409/index.html

Springer, Gordon. "Bush Tucker." *The Epicentre*. http://www.theepicentre.com//.html.

Laura P. Appell-Warren

Yamaimo (Mountain Yam)

Mountain yam (*Dioscorea opposita*), also known as Japanese mountain yam, Chinese or Korean yam, nagaimo, or yamaimo, is a long, beige, roughly cylindrical tuber, two to three feet in length, with scraggly roots. It is one of the few tubers that can be eaten raw, though it is usually soaked in a vinegar-water solution to neutralize the oxalic acid found in its skin before eating.

Native to southern China, mountain yam is popularly eaten in Japan, China, Korea, and some regions in Mexico. The tuber is mild in taste but mucilaginous in texture (*neba-neba* in Japanese). The most common preparation is to grate the root, which renders it slimy, viscous, and snowy white. The pale glutinous grated mass has to be slurped to consume, making it a textural challenge for those unaccustomed. Simply prepared, grated mountain yam is piled over rice or noodles like soba or udon but can also be stir-fried, incorporated into soups, and deep-fried well. A dried version is sometimes combined with buckwheat flour to make soba noodles. It is also frequently included in *okonomiyaki*, a fried Japanese pancake comprised of eggs and bits of vegetables or meat, as its gelatinous properties make it a good binder. Those who enjoy the slimy feel of okra or natto, may enjoy mountain yam's sticky texture, sometimes described akin to spittle or mucus.

Mountain yam is featured in Chinese medicine as reducing inflammation associated with menstrual cramps, stomach pains, and diarrhea. It can also aid in digestion, as its mucus-like consistency mimics fluids of the body. Supposedly, during the Edo period in Japan, mountain yam was used as a sexual lubricant.

Today, mountain yam can be found in most Asian markets, sold in manageable segments, wrapped in plastic.

Mountain Yam (Nagaimo) Pancakes

Ingredients

1 6-inch piece of mountain yam
1 tbsp dried shrimp, finely ground
½ tsp salt
3 tbsp lard
3 scallions

1. Peel and finely grate the mountain yam on a box grater. It will turn into a goopy pale mass. Mix the shrimp powder and salt into it.
2. Slice scallions for garnish.
3. Heat lard over medium-high heat in a medium skillet. Drop heaping tablespoons of the yam mixture into the hot fat, and fry until golden brown. Flip gently, and fry on the other side.
4. Drain pancakes on paper towels. Sprinkle with scallions and serve.

Further Reading

Andoh, E. *Kansha: Celebrating Japan's Vegetarian and Vegan Traditions*. New York: Random House, 2010.

Tsuji, Shizuo. *Japanese Cooking: A Simple Art*. New York: Kodansha, 2007.

Scarlett Lindeman

Selected Bibliography

Albala, K., and G. Allen. *Human Cuisine*. Seattle, WA: BookSurge, 2008.

Atkins, P., and I. Bowler. *Food in Society: Economy, Culture, Geography*. London: Arnold, 2001.

Beardsworth, A., and T. Keil. *Sociology on the Menu*. New York: Routledge, 1997.

Bell, D., and G. Valentine. *Consuming Geographies: We Are Where We Eat*. London: Routledge, 1997.

Brillat-Savarin, Jean Anthelme. *The Physiology of Taste; or, Meditations on Transcendental Gastronomy*. 1825. Berkeley, CA: Counterpoint Press, 2000.

Brown, L.K., and K. Mussell, eds. *Ethnic and Regional Foodways in the United States: The Performance of Group Identity*. Knoxville: University of Tennessee Press, 1984.

Counihan, C., and P. Van Esterik,eds. *Food and Culture: A Reader*. New York: Routledge, 2007.

Crosby, A.W. *The Columbian Exchange: Biological and Cultural Consequences of 1492*. Westport, CT: Greenwood, 1972.

Deutsch, J. *Culinary Improvisation*. Englewood Cliffs, NJ: Pearson, 2010.

Deutsch, J., and R. Saks. *Jewish American Food Culture*. Westport, CT: Greenwood, 2009.

Dietler, M., and B. Hayden. *Feasts: Archeological and Ethnographic Perspectives on Food, Politics and Power*. Washington, DC: Smithsonian, 2001.

Douglas, M. *Purity and Danger*. London: Routledge, 1952.

Gabaccia, D.R. *We Are What We Eat: Ethnic Food and the Making of Americans*. Cambridge, MA: Harvard, 1998.

Harris, M. *Good to Eat: Riddles of Food and Culture*. New York: Simon and Schuster, 1985.

Hauck-Lawson, A. "When Food Is the Voice: A Case Study of a Polish-American Woman." *Journal for the Study of Food and Society* 2, no. 1 (1998): 21–28.

Hauck-Lawson, A., and J. Deutsch, eds. *Gastropolis: Food and New York City*. New York: Columbia University Press, 2009.

Hopkins, J. *Extreme Cuisine: The Weird and Wonderful Foods that People Eat*. Berkeley, CA: Periplus, 2004.

Levi-Strauss, C. *The Origin of Table Manners: Introduction to a Science of Mythology*. New York: Harper and Row, 1968.

MacClancy, J. *Consuming Culture*. London: Chapman, 1992.

Mennell, S., A. Murcott, and A. H. van Otterloo. *The Sociology of Food: Eating, Diet and Culture*. London: Sage, 1992.

Menzel, P., and F. D'Alusio. *Man Eating Bugs: The Art and Science of Eating Insects*. New York: Material World, 2004.

Miller, J., and J. Deutsch. *Food Studies: An Introduction to Research Methods*. Oxford, UK: Berg, 2010.

Mintz, S. W. *Sweetness and Power: The Place of Sugar in Modern History*. New York: Penguin 1985.

Mintz, S. W. *Tasting Food, Tasting Freedom: Excursions into Eating, Power, and the Past*. Boston: Beacon, 1997.

Pilcher, J. M. *Food in World History*. New York: Routledge, 2005.

Pilcher, J. M. *Que Vivan los Tamales: Food and the Making of Mexican Identity*. Albuquerque: University of New Mexico Press, 1998.

Pillsbury, R. *No Foreign Food: The American Diet in Time and Place*. Boulder, CO: Westview, 1998.

Schwabe, C. *Unmentionable Cuisine*. Richmond: University of Virginia Press, 1979.

Simoons, F. *Eat Not This Flesh: Food Avoidances from Prehistory to the Present*. Madison: University of Wisconsin Press, 1994.

Index

About the Editors

Jonathan Deutsch, PhD, is a classically trained chef and Associate Professor of culinary arts at Kingsborough Community College, City University of New York and public health at the CUNY Graduate Center. He is the education editor of the journal *Food, Culture and Society* and author or editor of six books including (with Annie Hauck-Lawson) *Gastropolis: Food and New York City*, (with Sarah Billingsley and Cricket Azima) *Culinary Improvisation*, and (with Jeff Miller) *Food Studies: An Introduction to Research Methods*. A graduate of the Culinary Institute of America (AOS, Culinary Arts), Drexel University (BS, Hospitality Management), and New York University (PhD, Food Studies and Food Management), he has worked as a chef in a variety of settings including institutions, restaurants, and product development, both in the United States and abroad. When not in the kitchen, he can be found playing tuba in community bands around New York City.

Natalya Murakhver, Freelance Writer. Natalya's passion for food led her to collaborating with Jon Deutsch on this book. She earned a master's degree in Food Studies from NYU and has worked in food and wine marketing and events. She studied at the International Wine Center and the American Sommelier Association. She has done stints at several New York City restaurants and has written natural food articles for *Kiwi Magazine*. Her primary focus for the past year has been her one-year-old daughter Violet, to whom she dedicates this book. She hopes it inspires a sense of epicurean adventure in a child who is already relishing pickled tomatoes, as prepared by her Russian grandfather.

Contributors

Ken Albala
University of the Pacific

Gary Allen
Empire State College

Laura P. Appell-Warren
St. Mark's School

Eleanor Barczak
Independent writer

Emily Callaghan
Drexel University

Christine Caruso
Graduate Center, City University
of New York

Christine Crawford-Oppenheimer
Culinary Institute of America

Thomas Crowley
Wine Director, Bar Veloce

Liza Debevec
Scientific Research Centre of the
Slovenian Academy of Sciences
and Arts, Slovenia & Addis Ababa
University, Ethiopia

Lisa Doughten
Independent scholar

Marcela Duarte
Independent scholar

Sidra Durst
Independent scholar

Caroline Erb Medina
Graduate Center, City University
of New York

Hayley Figueroa
Graduate Center, City University
of New York

Sadie Flateman
Independent scholar

Nancy Freeman
Independent scholar

Jenny Frémont
Daily Prandium

Aaron Hamburger
Columbia University and New York
University

Jeanne Hodesh
Local Gourmands

Erica Hope
Freelance writer

Alexa Johnson
Independent scholar

Leah Kim
Independent scholar

Desiree Koh
Independent scholar

Scarlett Lindeman
Independent scholar

Laura Mathews
Freelance writer

Kelly Newsome
New York University

Kristina Nies
Independent scholar

Suzanne Piscopo
University of Malta, Malta

Margaret Ragland
Independent scholar

Meryl Rosofsky
New York University

Christen Sturkie
New York University

Karen Taylor
Independent scholar

Leena Trivedi-Grenier
Independent scholar

Alexandra Turnbull
Independent scholar

Karin Vaneker
Independent researcher

Gabriela Villagran Backman
Independent scholar

Ansley Watson
Peeled Snacks

Alex Yellan
Independent scholar

Malgorzata (Maggie)
   Zurowska
Kingsborough Community
   College